Learning from
the Water

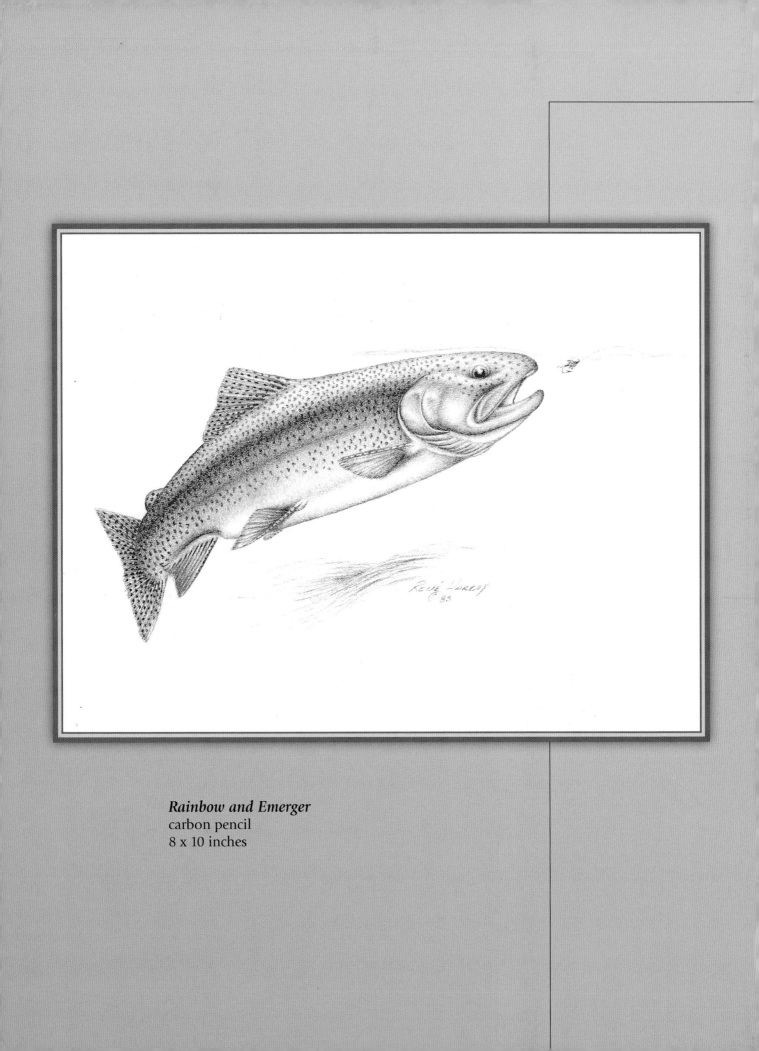

Rainbow and Emerger
carbon pencil
8 x 10 inches

Learning from
the Water

René Harrop

STACKPOLE
BOOKS

Published by
STACKPOLE BOOKS
5067 Ritter Road
Mechanicsburg, PA 17055
www.stackpolebooks.com

Illustrations by René Harrop

Printed in China

First edition

10 9 8 7 6 5 4 3 2 1

Library of Congress Cataloging-in-Publication Data

Harrop, René.
    Learning from the water / René Harrop. — 1st ed.
        p. cm.
    Includes index.
    ISBN-13: 978-0-8117-0579-0 (hardcover)
    ISBN-10: 0-8117-0579-X (hardcover)
  1. Fly fishing. 2. Nymph fishing. 3. Trout fishing. I. Title.
    SH456.H326 2010
    799.17'57—dc22
                                2009050478

To the Henry's Fork
and the knowledge it provides

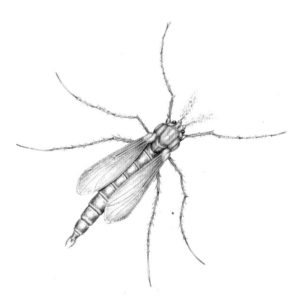

Brown Trout and Shiner
carbon pencil
8 x 10 inches

Contents

Cutthroat and Caddis
carbon pencil
14 x 18 inches

Acknowledgments

From start to finish, Judith Schnell, Jay Nichols, and Amy Lerner have provided much appreciated professionalism in producing this book.

In Japan, Masa Katsumata and Tominori Higashi have provided support beyond what could ever be expected. And it is impossible to express my gratitude to Toshi Karita for his wonderful insight and photos.

In Sweden, Thommy Gustavsson has shared far more than the lovely art that appears in these pages.

Thanks to Rich Paini and Jon Stiehl, who keep me connected to a generation of young trout hunters who drive the future of our sport.

And to Leslie and Shayne, who shouldered an extra work burden while their parents were completing this project.

Thanks also to Brady, Zach, Jake, Braxon, and Brogan, whose company on the water brings a smile to their grandfather's face.

And finally, thanks to my wife, Bonnie, whose contributions cannot be measured. Although her name does not appear as the author, this is her book as much as my own.

Tailwater Brown
pen and ink with watercolor tint
14 x 18 inches

Learning from the Water

From its beginning, fly fishing has held a special attraction to humans seeking relief from the hardness of a sophisticated world. And for most of its history, this gentle endeavor has resisted those elements that separate us from nature and its calming effects on our psyche. But a tradition once reserved for the patient and inquisitive has in large part given way to a commercially driven image of technological advantage and instant gratification. Today, literally millions of expectant participants descend upon the waters of the world with only a remnant of the original motivation for entering the sport. Many who call themselves fly fishermen will never progress beyond rudimentary skill or accomplishment. This is not to say that fly fishing can only be enjoyed by the highly proficient, but it is a sad fact that without progression few will sustain an interest for very long.

Incidental catches of immature fish might be acceptable in the beginning, but eventually that must inevitably change. Those of financial means can prevail upon the services of an experienced guide to compensate for unlearned skills or knowledge, and I do not condemn that route to success. However, there is a special sense of attainment in the ability to become personally integrated into a world understood by only a relative few and to be able to consistently locate, approach, and fool large fish. To reach this level, you must treat each day on the water as an opportunity for growth. And there is a lesson to be learned from each encounter regardless of the outcome.

The journey to fly-fishing proficiency begins with respect for the quarry and consideration of the survival requirements that dictate its behavior. As wild creatures, trout survive on instinct rather than cunning, and they endure to large size only by resisting all efforts directed at their capture. And whether man or beast, the enemies of trout are many. Few humans possess the fish-catching skill of predatory birds or animals because they do not observe or understand the prey. Although not assured to match the efficiency of wild predators, human trout hunters would do well to emulate their uncivilized competitors.

Even the most productive water is not 100 percent occupied. Trout have habitat preferences based upon either security or food. Fishing water where trout are not hiding or feeding is futile. It pays to remember where a sizable trout is located whether you catch it or not. Studying the details of the location will enable you to recognize the characteristics of preferred habitat, and, over time and many encounters, you will be able to identify the most promising water regardless of where you are fishing.

Seasoned trout have a knack for concealment, even when feeding on the surface. Looking only for serious surface disturbance is a mistake when it comes to detecting

Experienced anglers like Leslie Harrop, shown here on the Henry's Fork, understand that the water provides the solution to many of the puzzles we face in fly fishing. Watching the water can occupy more time than actual fishing.
BONNIE HARROP PHOTO

The subtle rise of a large trout to a small insect can easily be missed by those who expect to see a greater disturbance of the water. A splashy rise usually indicates a smaller fish.
MASA KATSUMATA PHOTO

the rise of a significant fish. A trout does not grow large by wasting energy, and the slightest unnatural movement of water is often an indicator of something impressive underneath. Move slowly and stop often when searching for

surface activity. Peer closely into shaded areas or near structure, where a rise can be masked by shadows or a natural disruption of the current, and store worthwhile discoveries for the future.

Working upstream is the best way to locate a fish before it sees you. And in general, the same applies to approaching a fish once the decision is made to go after it. Creeping up from behind will minimize the risk of spooking the fish and will usually reduce the length of the cast as well. However, only experience can teach you to read the complexity of the currents, which is necessary in determining the best angle of approach. This is especially true in dry-fly fishing where a natural drift of the fly is essential.

Whenever possible, wading is the most efficient way to approach a fish. Experienced anglers never make a longer cast than is needed. Instead, they are very patient and deliberate in stealthily moving to a position that is ideal for the situation. Often, the cast is only the beginning of the presentation. Mending the line to lengthen or enhance the drift can only be learned in actual conditions and is almost

With grandson Zach Wheeler, the author studies the possibilities on the Firehole in Yellowstone. From the very beginning, it is important to incorporate observation and thought into each day on the water. BONNIE HARROP PHOTO

always needed when the presentation is made from any angle other than upstream.

Sound wading technique not only helps you get closer to the fish without spooking them, but it is essential for your safety. Deep or deceptive currents must be recognized in all conditions of light and visibility if a soaking or something worse is to be avoided. Wind, rain, or heavy overcast conditions are familiar to every angler and are frequently good times to be on the water. Too often, however, these are times when the inexperienced angler becomes careless in his approach and blunders into water that holds trouble.

As a young boy, I learned the ways of water and trout through observation, and my growth as an angler continues to be based upon this fundamental of fly fishing. As a self-taught fly tier, I recognized the importance of understanding the correlation between artificial flies and the food items upon which trout subsist. Using natural organisms as models for my flies began long before I had contact with books on aquatic entomology or matching the hatch. And I have been studying what trout eat for

This big rainbow is the survivor of at least five years of harassment by anglers. Understanding its ways is the only way to overcome its resistance to an artificial fly. BONNIE HARROP PHOTO

more than fifty years. For reasons I cannot explain, some anglers do not observe what is on or in the water before selecting an artificial. And while any fly will take a trout if fished for long enough, the absence of thoughtful pattern selection seldom results in sustained success.

Patience helps prevent blunders. Watching and waiting for the perfect opportunity becomes a natural part of the thinking angler's strategy. BONNIE HARROP PHOTO

A spider's web can reveal clues about which insects are available to trout. It also pays to examine vegetation near the water's edge for similar information. BONNIE HARROP PHOTO

To understand trout, we must also understand what they eat, and it is impossible to know too much in this regard. Trout feed selectively in many of the waters where catch-and-release is a common practice, if not the law. On the famed Henry's Fork, even the world's best anglers are routinely humbled by wild rainbows of remarkable size feeding freely on a diverse menu of aquatic and terrestrial insects. Here there is no substitute for acute observation in selecting the correct fly. Often several possibilities occur simultaneously, but experience in analyzing feeding behavior will help in drawing a sound conclusion.

To some extent, I agree with the statement that fly tiers possess an advantage because they are better observers. Of course this only applies to those whose patterns are a translation of what comes from the water. Some may be inclined to install clever characteristics more attractive to the eye of the fisherman than that of a trout. Conversely, plenty of anglers rise to considerable prominence without ever touching a vise or a bobbin. Skilled at presenting the fly from all angles, they are invariably students of trout

Insects are nearly always more active during the most comfortable times of the day. Ken Muller took this Henry's Fork prize on a caddis just before dark in July. BONNIE HARROP PHOTO

behavior. And based upon observation and experience, they apply a knowledgeable and systematic approach to purchasing their flies from established and reliable suppliers.

As a civilized society, we no longer can point to survival as justification for taking wildlife, whether bird, mammal, or fish. But hunting these creatures need not be an uncivilized activity, provided that proper respect and appreciation accompany our participation. As humans, we take considerable risk in separating ourselves from nature to the point of becoming indifferent to existence outside our own species. The health of our minds and our souls is improved by reconnecting with primal instincts that rec-

ognize value in all forms of life. And while we hunt for sport rather than subsistence, it is no less rewarding to gain self-sufficiency in the outdoor world. Although fly fishing is not generally associated with the term *hunting*, it shares the elements of pursuit and capture of wild living creatures. Like any serious endeavor, fly-fishing proficiency requires study, practice, and determination. An experienced mentor can be of significant assistance, as can the sport's credible literature. However, true knowledge is a derivative of experience, and once obtained is owned forever. For the developing angler, the water is a classroom where the answers to all questions can be found. And the joy of personal discovery is the lasting benefit of any lesson.

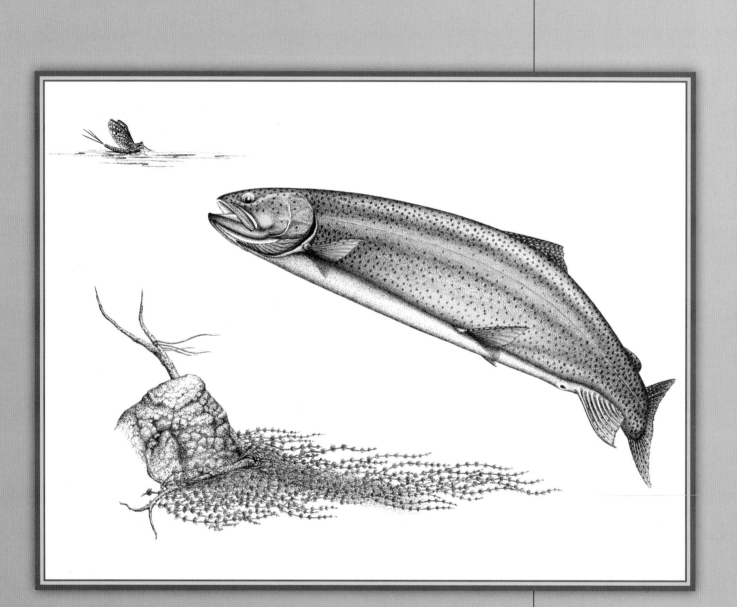

Rise to a Mayfly Dun
pen and ink with watercolor tint
14 x 16 inches

The Art of Deception

Most would agree that the Yellowstone region provides a clear window on modern trout fishing with a fly rod. In summer, one only needs to travel the roads that parallel famous rivers like the Madison, Firehole, and Gallatin to realize how popular the sport has become as dozens of well-equipped anglers ply their skills in full view of passing traffic. Most are visitors to this historically praised destination of natural wonder, and all share a common appreciation of the joys of wading clear water in pursuit of the wild and beautiful creatures that swim the sparkling currents. From a distance, one cannot easily distinguish between those of traditional influence and others who display little connection to a customary attitude and method of fishing with the long rod. A closer examination, however, reveals the predominance of a simple approach that is very easy to understand and execute.

While rather indiscriminate in its results, the popular tactic of fishing a weighted imitation beneath a brightly colored strike indicator is nevertheless enjoyable to those who choose to avoid complication in a pastime that does not employ a strict set of rules for participation. Lobbing a weighted fly at the end of twenty feet of line into likely holding water does not require hours of practice, and the eyes do not strain to follow a fluorescent indicator when it is the size of a quarter or even larger. A dozen or so beadhead nymphs in two or three sizes and colors will usually cover the needs of those who are happy to hook a fish of any size or species, and a hatch is no special enticement to be on the water. Winged insects are more an irritant than a welcome subject to be studied and then imitated as a logical attractant to trout, and an extremely light tippet need never be the reason for a lost prize. The innocence and simplicity of this type of fishing cannot be condemned as less sporting and enjoyable than another method of greater commitment and difficulty when it is responsible for bringing so many into the fold who might otherwise be excluded.

However, there are those who select a more complex and demanding path into a world that does not reveal its secrets without intense study or give up its treasures without sustained diligence and respect. These are the most obsessed anglers, and their pleasure is taken from that which more closely resembles a predator's mentality than a purely recreational attitude toward the sport. Motivated by failure rather than accomplishment, the hunter of trout is separated from the rest by a hunger for understanding that will probably never be completely satisfied. Such is the way of someone who values the grace of a perfect cast and the convincing illusion of a thoughtfully tied fly. Meshing with physical and visual aspects is the intellectual side of the pursuit of free-living creatures that exist with survival as their only purpose. Selective in his objective, the committed trout hunter is seldom satisfied with random results

An enraged rainbow reacts to being fooled. The difficulty of Henry's Fork trout makes it impossible to ever take success for granted. BONNIE HARROP PHOTO

Seasoned trout seldom succumb to flawed imitation or casting. The author engaged this Henry's Fork rainbow for more than an hour before getting everything just right. It was a memorable victory over a very admirable opponent. BONNIE HARROP PHOTO

that do not yield some sense of achievement in overcoming the defense mechanisms employed by the largest and therefore most worthy opponents.

Large trout have invariably survived multiple narrow escapes, which affect their behavior, and no predator is as calculating as the human variety in creating a perilous outcome for any mistake committed by its prey. Trout do not recognize that an angler will eventually release his catch. With self-preservation as the driving instinct, fish that experience repeated disruption to their feeding activity become more and more difficult to fool with an artificial fly when it becomes a recognizable source of discomfort.

In my opinion, extremely selective feeding behavior is generally a consequence of elevated angling attention and the tendency of fly fishers to release rather than kill their catch. A released trout may live to fight again, but any recurrence serves to reinforce the memory of a struggle it would choose to steer clear of. To avoid repeating the mistake, trout conditioned to angling pressure must find ways of obtaining nutrition that does not hold the promise of a stinging hook and several minutes of unwelcome restraint.

Short-distance accuracy with a long leader creates better opportunity for correct presentation. This is made possible by a stealthy approach that may require five minutes or more. BONNIE HARROP PHOTO

Their elevated resistance to even minute flaws in presentation or pattern is the bane of the modern angler determined to become a hunter of trout.

Hunting trout in clear water where depth and current speed are moderate is a deceitful contest reserved for the patient, observant, and determined participant. Learning the habits of trout is a product of watching; the clues revealed in observation should dictate the overall strategy of approach, fly selection, and presentation in each situation involving a special fish. By necessity, a feeding trout must be monitored from a distance, but the object of its attention is a different story. Close-up examination is the only way of gathering the information needed to make a sound decision in selecting an imitation.

Casual observation will not usually reveal the full picture of the types, volume, and position of food items available in the water. Neither can key physical characteristics of individual organisms always be accurately determined from a rod-length away. Minimizing luck in fly selection depends on a reasoned appraisal of which insect form is most likely to match the feeding behavior of an individual

Results like this come from understanding the essential ingredients of deception. Presenting an accurate representation in the correct manner is the best way to fool a big Henry's Fork rainbow. BONNIE HARROP PHOTO

Clear and shallow water heighten the need for precise pattern selection and presentation. Bonefish Flat on the Henry's Fork will test the skill and resolve of any angler. RICH PAINI PHOTO

The legendary Quill Gordon displays a method of imitating mayfly duns that originated over a century ago. Though certainly not without current value, this style has given way to patterns that more closely reflect the natural insects.

FLY TIED BY RENÉ HARROP /BONNIE HARROP PHOTO

trout. The highest number of available insects frequently represents the most efficient feeding opportunity, with superior size of individual insects being secondary. For example, in late summer trout will ignore sparse numbers of size 16 *Callibaetis* in favor of more numerous Tricos in size 22. A feeding pace more proportionate to the volume of larger insects would indicate a preference for the *Callibaetis*. Many other examples can be cited in support of watching and thinking while on the water as opposed to making careless assumptions that are often proven to be wrong.

The common tendency to frantically change from fly to fly is founded only on hope, and problems with presentation must be cured before any blame can be placed on the imitation. Drag is the primary culprit in betraying a fraudulent offering in situations where the actual food items (on and beneath the surface) are moving in unison with the current. Poor casting is a correctable barrier to progress, and success is directly proportionate to an ability to present the fly correctly. An imitation may be visually perfect, but it is worthless if fished in the wrong manner, and changing flies is not likely to change the result.

Fly fishing in the United States dates back to the late nineteenth century when eccentric individuals like Theodore Gordon established a connection between aquatic insects and rising trout. Well over a century later, the attraction of this enigmatic relationship continues to draw the interest of those who combine the activities of fly fishing and fly tying into a composite skill set that is systematically applied to the capture of trout. Anchored in substantial understanding of these humble yet complex creatures, fly tying is a method of solving problems associated with a prey far more sophisticated than could have been imagined by Gordon and other pioneers of the sport. The simple luxury of concentrating upon a limited selection of insect forms is a historical feature that has vanished along with silk lines, wicker creels, and a tendency to kill every trout that was taken. What remains is the inexhaustible challenge of convincing a wild and wary trout that a cleverly disguised hook is actually a living organism worthy of consumption. Also surviving are the elegant expressions of life as seen through the eyes of the founding fathers of our sport. While mostly antiquated in the sense of modern fly design, the patterns of the old ones continue to serve as reference for fundamental fly-tying technique, thus preserving a respectful connection to the past and those to whom so much is owed.

Today, our efforts at imitating the food on which trout feed is complicated by the necessity of imitating small flies. On some waters, a fly larger than size 16 can be a luxury during a season in which the majority of hatching insects are significantly smaller. Gaining confidence in flies size 20 and smaller is simply a matter of giving them an honest try, and a major step forward in fooling large, selective fish. Small hooks and the light tippet material they require are significantly more reliable in withstanding the rigors of playing big trout if care is taken in selecting the highest quality in both items. A smooth running reel with a large arbor provides additional confidence in what might otherwise be considered a precarious connection.

Whether floating or subsurface, a fly that is even one size larger than the available naturals will often result in failure. A trout can recognize and usually rejects an artificial that is 20 percent larger than the natural. Fish of modest size may be fooled by an oversized pattern, but they are not the usual objective. The trait of a seasoned trout to consider size when accepting or rejecting an imitation is not limited to the smaller end of the hook scale. In adequate abundance, larger insects can summon intensely isolated attention, especially when they appear over a prolonged period of time. Selectivity to characteristics including size is especially pronounced during the lengthy caddis hatches on the Madison, when a size 16 will often outproduce a size 14 two to one.

Whether buying or tying flies, it is extremely important to recognize the correct proportions of a fly pattern. Any fly can be made larger than is proper for a given hook size if the wings, tail, legs, or other imitative features exceed the equivalent body parts of the natural it is intended to imitate. Even minor familiarity with the anatomy of key insects will enable the tier to use the hook to its best effect in duplicating the actual size of the subject.

The writings of Theodore Gordon and others who laid the groundwork for matching the hatch emphasized the winged stage of the insects encountered in the northeast region of the United States. With mayflies being central to their scope of interest, most surviving fly patterns of that era display a constant profile indicating a rather simple approach to what is now a very complex aspect of the sport they helped to establish in this country. Gifted with minimal disruption from competing anglers, early participants did not have to understand multiple images associated with a single insect subject. By today's standards, trout were relatively undisturbed during feeding activity, and few survived any encounters with an artificial fly. Little variance beyond size and color existed in those days, and extremely small insects were ignored mainly because hooks of an equivalent size could not be obtained. Basically, the pursuit of rising trout with a standardized selection of dry flies ruled the attention of those predecessors who fished in blissful indifference to anything more complicated. With the exception of wilderness fisheries in remote locations, most trout waters in modern-day America do not support the simplicity of a bygone age. Today, the ability to consistently prevail over visibly feeding trout while applying the concept of specific imitation is vastly more complicated than could have ever been imagined by those who created the game.

In the beginning, most attempts at duplicating individual aquatic insects are directed toward the stages most easily observed. Of course, winged air-breathing forms offer the most convenient opportunity for examining the physical characteristics that identify the subject in its adult stage. Establishing size is the next item of business, followed by an adequate appraisal of the overall shape of the organism.

Any pattern intended to imitate a specific food form must bear the physical traits of the living model to be truly effective, and it is shape in general that determines its suitability in any selective feeding situation. A dry fly shaped like a caddis is unlikely to be of much value when mayflies are drifting on the water, even if it is of similar size and color.

Big trout observed feeding in shallow water on subsurface forms are fair game for the alert who recognize the opportunity. Differences in shape extend to immature insects that bear slight resemblance to the winged forms, but underwater stages are not as easily studied. An aquarium seine is indispensable in collecting organisms that are drifting beneath the surface. Again, shape will reveal separation between classes of aquatic invertebrates, such as mayflies and caddis, which must be applied to the respective artificial.

Interim phases known by fly pattern as "emergers" are not natural life stages, but they often must be addressed. Emergence from the nymphal or pupal stage into the winged stage is a process that varies in the time required for completion. Unless injured during metamorphosis, the shape a trout sees will change progressively as the act is completed, and no single image will last very long. Effective imitations often combine characteristics of both subsurface and air-breathing forms, and the resulting shape is significantly different from either stage. Insects completely freed from the exoskeleton but not fully capable of flight feature undeveloped wings and legs that are not yet functional. An appropriate imitation would reflect these inadequacies as compared to the shape of a fully emerged adult.

A significant percentage of aquatic insects are unsuccessful in completing the process of emergence. Known as "cripples" to the discerning angler, they are casualties of the inability to gain freedom from the exoskeleton, which acts as an anchor in preventing escape from the water. These victims are highly attractive to trout that recognize a distinct shape as an invitation to an easy meal. Floating patterns that convey this helpless form are among the most effective tools in dealing with highly resistant trout found feeding on the surface.

Trout seem to possess a high degree of color recognition, which makes it reasonable to factor this distinct characteristic into the thoughtful imitation of aquatic insects. Floating patterns viewed from beneath against a brightly lit sky may appear in silhouette, but evening and overcast conditions will make colors more easy to discern. I believe that closely matching the color of the natural produces superior imitation, whether that is the color of the specific species or the individual life-cycle stages, which can vary in color. In mayflies, for example, a rust-colored spinner can follow an olive-colored dun, and the pupa of a brown caddis adult is often mostly cream colored. While the role of color may rank behind size and shape, it is only prudent to gain familiarity with the coloration of key insect forms. I know of no instance where an artificial failed because its resemblance to the natural was too strong.

It is frequently more difficult to make an imitation behave like its natural counterpart than to simply produce an acceptable image. Much of making a pattern behave correctly is connected to presentation. Usually, one must understand the organism in order to know if a drift without drag is the appropriate method when the subject cannot be observed on the surface. Plenty of subsurface forms have the ability to move against the current, and a swimming motion or a lift must be intentionally applied with the rod tip and sometimes the line hand to duplicate the motion.

Caddis adult TOSHI KARITA PHOTO

Midge TOSHI KARITA PHOTO

Callibaetis *spinner* TOSHI KARITA PHOTO

Jake Ohs studies the water during a Henry's Fork sunset. Low light conditions complicate the angler's ability to identify the object of a trout's attention. Pattern selection should be based on up-close examination of the natural insect. BONNIE HARROP PHOTO

Trout also commonly concentrate their attention on a specific point in the water column. This is especially true when insects reach a particular point of vulnerability during the process of emergence, such as is often encountered during a hatch of PMD mayflies. It is believed by some who have been tormented by this occurrence that highly conditioned trout find those areas in the column where few anglers focus their efforts, thereby feeding in relative peace despite the presence of ill intent. Capitalizing on this behavior depends on determining the right depth and fishing the correct nymph or emerging pattern. Intended to sink, the fly must be manipulated into the target zone with deft mending and strategically applied tension on the line.

Soft materials that yield to the force of the current replicate the natural's movements. Even floating flies will appear more lifelike with the subtle flexing of natural fibers such as CDC, which is extremely buoyant as well. Used as legs and wings, CDC replicates the often fragile texture of the natural counterpart. It is reasonable to assume that trout will not accept a rigid fly with the same confidence as it will one that emulates the natural's texture.

Motion is more pronounced in subsurface insect forms, whether swimming, drifting with the current, or emerging. With no flotational requirement, soft and absorbent feathers from wild or domestic birds like Hungarian partridge or poultry hens are a valid choice for creating lively movement beneath the water.

Though trout may not use the sense of smell to identify food, smell may act as a deterrent. Fly dressings with a natural base of CDC oil or other scent-masking agent help to conceal odors that can be associated with danger by wary trout. Caution in this area of deception is not unwarranted if one applies the mentality of the efficient hunter who gives respect to the full range of senses possessed by his prey.

Trout and their food sources are inextricably linked, which means that both must be studied and understood if the angler is to consistently catch fish. The complexity of aquatic insects serves as fuel for learning, and that is what makes this approach to fly fishing truly special. No individual will ever understand it all, but many will give it their best effort. Boredom is nonexistent in an engagement where the will of both participants is tested to the fullest extent and the outcome is always in question. Enticing a large, sophisticated trout into accepting an artificial food item is an act of deception in the highest order of the art, and nothing in fly fishing is more satisfying.

Pale Morning Dun
pen and ink with watercolor tint
8 x 10 inches

A Working Fly Box

Although our tackle has changed over the years, fishing the right imitation is as important as it was at the earliest point in the history of the sport. Modern tools enable a far greater efficiency in presenting the fly and then playing the fish once it is hooked. Routinely speaking, today's practitioners are able to make much longer and more accurate casts with far less effort than those who were forced to rely on bamboo or even fiberglass rods. Precisely engineered reels of space-age alloys protect a 6X tippet as efficiently as their relatively clumsy predecessors handled 3X. But if a lesson from the old masters of the past has been lost, it is in the way they organized and protected their ammunition.

Perhaps it was as much necessity as practicality that prompted the meticulous care that our predecessors gave to their flies. Compared to the past twenty-plus years of abundance, the supply of good flies was never quite adequate. Unlike today when hundreds of thousands of flies are produced in foreign factories, a relative handful of individual resident professional fly tiers supplied the U.S. market. It was, and is, a difficult trade in which to make a living, and their production never seemed to match the demand. Even anglers who tied their own faced limitations similar to those who chose to purchase flies. In terms of the availability of high-quality fly-tying components, tiers of today

exist in a state of luxury. As one who clearly remembers a different time, I am continually amazed at the readily accessible array of premium quality hooks, hackle, thread, and other items requisite to a perfectly tied fly, as compared to what was available in 1954 when I began tying flies for myself, as well as through much of the nearly four decades that mark my time as a professional tier. Perhaps it is this history, and the memory of those old-timers whose influence helped to shape my direction, that has caused a long-standing attitude to endure: From the very beginning I have understood the beneficial nature of not only carrying the right fly but also having it quickly available when needed.

For those who fish a lot, the right fly for a given situation is usually selected from among several possibilities contained in one or more fly boxes. If you are somewhat obsessed with fishing like I am, your vest may be loaded with more than a dozen boxes representing hundreds of flies that may be useful at some point. Although admittedly excessive in this regard, I take comfort in knowing that I am well prepared for one of the few things in which I have influence while on the water. While wind, light, temperature, and water conditions are elements we cannot control, the possibilities for success are significantly improved if the pockets of our vests contain thoughtful and organized selections of flies.

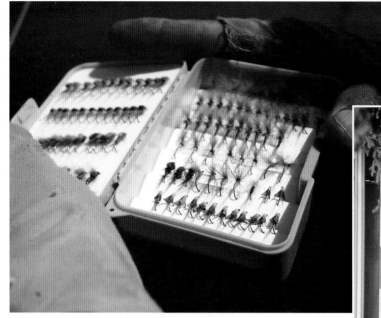

An organized fly box simplifies access to the preferred pattern. This box contains imitations for PMDs of all stages plus emerging patterns.
BONNIE HARROP PHOTO

Green, Brown, and Gray Drakes are similar in size, time of appearance, and duration. Grouping them into a single fly box makes sense. BONNIE HARROP PHOTO

Admitting to some degree of excess, the author selects a fly from one of eighteen fly boxes carried during the peak of the season. BONNIE HARROP PHOTO

Time on the water is the most precious commodity to any fly fisherman. Opportunity for a truly significant fish can be fleeting, and nothing is more frustrating than having that opportunity slip away while frantically fumbling for the right fly. Minimizing this requires an investment of thought and effort, but not during the highly pressured situation on the water when there is none to spare.

Fly organization begins with an empty box. Preferably, it is the kind that isolates each fly in an orderly row and permits quick identification and access. Flies stored randomly in compartmented fly boxes usually grow into a tangled mess that defies convenient identification. Most who have tried this method of storage have also had the horrifying experience of opening the lid only to see hundreds of dollars worth of flies swept away by an unsympathetic wind. Simple and inexpensive boxes where flies are kept in place by pressing the points into raised foam

ridges make very serviceable organizers. Even better are the fly boxes of C & F Designs. Known throughout the fly-fishing world for its clever and functional concepts, this innovative Japanese company has designed an impressive system for arranging and holding flies. Here, the flies are securely held in thin slots that do not require the flies to be pressed into the foam. Although somewhat more costly, the boxes are sturdy and come in a variety of sizes and ranges of capacity. Fly boxes featuring metal clips or coils to hold the flies do offer individual separation, but they do not protect the flies quite as well and may cause the hooks to rust.

The appropriate number of fly boxes and the degree of sophistication in their organization is an individual preference. Mostly, this is determined by the amount of time the angler spends on the water and the kind of fishing he does. For those more casual in their approach, as few as

These six fly boxes will cover the majority of patterns needed on the Henry's Fork in midsummer. Mayflies, caddis, midges, and terrestrials comprise this grouping. BONNIE HARROP PHOTO

three boxes may be needed to organize relatively simple selections of drys, nymphs, and streamers. More obsessive types, like me, who may spend more than a hundred days with fly rod in hand, will need considerably more.

Because I fish in all seasons of the year, my fly requirements are extensive. My vest is as light as it will ever be in winter, when midges account for the majority of surface activity and most effective nymph patterns are quite small. Streamers, at this time of year, are a last resort, and I carry only a handful of favorites. Four fly boxes easily contain all of the flies I could possibly need during most of December, January, and February. The number of flies I carry increases proportionally with the warming of the season and then gradually begins to fade as winter again draws near. For me, no vest was ever made with too many pockets. By June, I am laboring under the weight of a vest laden with as many as eighteen fully-loaded fly boxes and an

equal number or more waiting in reserve. Certainly, I do not attempt to justify such extremism to others, but it does indicate just how far some are willing to go in an effort to gain strategic advantage over trout.

Following the copious and varied hatches of an extraordinary trout-rich region has literally forced me to systemize my flies as a means of spending more time casting and less time searching for the appropriate fly. Some hatches are relatively short in duration or unreliable in their appearance on the water. Occasionally, only a single stage of the insect occurs in a strong enough concentration to become a specific target. Multiple patterns representing such limited insect availability are usually combined within a single box, but grouped separately into patterns that address the viable stages of a single hatch-producing insect. For my area, the big Gray, Brown, and Green Drakes are a good example. Usually, these oversize mayflies all

In a variety of sizes, shapes, and colors, terrestrial insects are important trout food. Ants, beetles, and hoppers are the most common of these land-based insects. BONNIE HARROP PHOTO

The organization of this box of caddis imitations allows quick access to any stage, size, or color that might be needed when caddis are active.
BONNIE HARROP PHOTO

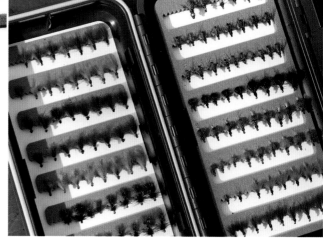

While generally quite small in physical size, midges can occupy a sizable role in the diet of trout. Though often overlooked, midge fishing can provide as much action as any of their larger aquatic cousins. BONNIE HARROP PHOTO

appear within a forty-five day time frame and frequently overlap, but none seem to last individually for more than two weeks. At size 10 and 12, drakes require greater depth in a fly box than is usual. And although the need for a great variety of patterns is not the rule, my drake box is among the largest I ever carry.

Terrestrials are important trout fare during the time when freezing temperatures do not prevent their activity. Hoppers, beetles, ants, and other land-based insects are well represented in a rather large box that holds many variations. It stays in an accessible pocket from May through September and may be restocked several times during that period.

The availability of caddisflies, to some extent, mirrors the seasonal duration of terrestrials, which in my neck of the woods is about half the year. Similar to my terrestrial

patterns, I house my caddis patterns in a single, large box. The life cycle of caddisflies features four distinct stages, each of which must be addressed, making a system for their organization more complex. Although I do not carry imitations of more than six or seven naturals, my caddis box contains nearly two hundred flies, arranged in specific representations of larva, pupa, active adult, and spent adult insects. And since I fish varied waters, it is important to carry heavier and often brightly tied subsurface patterns for the Madison's deep, rushing pools and sparsely dressed patterns for the Henry's Fork's slow, shallow flows. Additionally, the same variation in water characteristics places a different emphasis on the flotational properties of a surface imitation. Typically, flies dressed fully enough to ride the chop of the famous Montana river would be spurned by the scrutinizing inhabitants of the gentle currents of its

A close-up view showing the distinct differences between several insect types and how they are imitated. Mayflies, caddis, midges, and terrestrials all possess individual characteristics that must be addressed. BONNIE HARROP PHOTO

Idaho neighbor less than an hour away. Interim patterns known as emergers also add to an assortment intended to cover as many variables as possible. Except for the impressive size 8 October Caddis, most naturals can be imitated by size 14 flies or smaller.

One fly box that never leaves my vest is rather small, but it holds more flies than any other. Midges are year-round trout fare, and on some waters they are consumed almost daily. This is despite their typically small size, and failure to consider their role in the food chain is a sad but common mistake. Although midges are more commonly associated with cold weather, it is never a surprise to find a trout sipping midges even in July. Like caddisflies, midges are a four-stage insect, which contributes to a sizable variation of imitations. Although some lake species require patterns as large as size 12, most are much smaller. A size 20 midge would be considered large on most of the waters I fish, and a thousand bucks worth of the minute imitations would easily fit into a box that is smaller than your wallet. My midge selection is arranged according to color and stage, with emergers also included. Since extremely fast water is not their preferred habitat, I am not compelled to vary the weight or flotational characteristics to any great extent.

Due to a fondness for the kind of fishing they represent, mayflies comprise the majority of my rather vast selection of personal flies. Above all other aquatic organisms, mayflies have influenced both my fishing and tying from the start. This is reflected in both the waters that I fish and the contents of my fly boxes. The humble and seemingly helpless appearance of these delicate creatures belies a complexity of behavioral characteristics that can be perplexing to one who is attempting to sort out the many variables that a mayfly hatch can represent. Although limited to three stages in their life cycle, mayflies have inspired more pattern variations than any insect I know of. Witness to this extremity are the Pale Morning Duns, which by themselves occupy two full fly boxes that stay in my vest for at least four months of every year. Volumes could be written on this one mayfly alone, but that is a story for a different time. Fortunately, not every mayfly species is as complex, and therefore does not require such an extensive assortment of fly patterns. I do, however, carry a box dedicated exclusively to *Baetis*, which hatch nearly everywhere in all but the most viciously cold weather. Most of my mayfly boxes contain seasonal groupings of two or more hatch-matching systems. These selections imitate insects

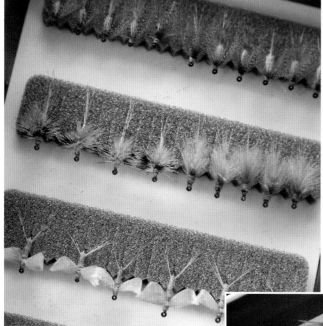

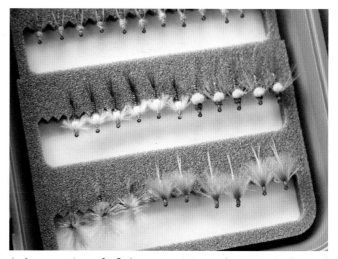

A close-up view of a fly box containing only PMD cripples and emergers. BONNIE HARROP PHOTO

Some individual hatches are so complex that they require a separate fly box. Pale Morning Duns are an extreme example. This is only one of three boxes of PMDs that I carry. BONNIE HARROP PHOTO

PMD duns and spinners can vary in size and color. These two stages represent enough diversity to warrant a separate fly box. BONNIE HARROP PHOTO

that occur during similar time frames and naturally go together. There are instances where one fly box may contain a mixture of imitations not limited to simply mayflies. Tricos, for example, may hatch for as long as three months, and therefore present the need for a sizable number of flies. At size 20 and smaller, however, it is easy to store a season's supply on one side of an average-size box. The other half of the storage is used for Damsels, Craneflies, and Little Yellow Stones, which follow a similar seasonal emergence pattern. Incidentally, the big Golden Stones and giant Salmonflies have a box of their own that only comes out a relatively few times each year.

A less specific but no less vital selection of generic nymph patterns such as beadheads and flashbacks are go-to flies that may not exactly imitate anything but produce when nothing else seems to work. Like most others, I have my favorites that are organized according to their history of success. Streamers are treated in a similar fashion, although some specifics are applied to the type of baitfish being imitated. A selection of mostly subsurface patterns such as scuds, leeches, and other organisms that typify stillwater constitute a system I rely on when fishing nearby lakes and ponds.

Experience over many years has revealed numerous minor insect possibilities that do not justify great emphasis as far as fly patterns are concerned. However, each season seems to hold the potential for appearances that deviate from normal hatch patterns. Some are mysterious creatures that defy identification, but which occasionally prompt attention from the trout. Although these insects are unpredictable in their availability, I concede that something unusual can occur on the water at almost any time.

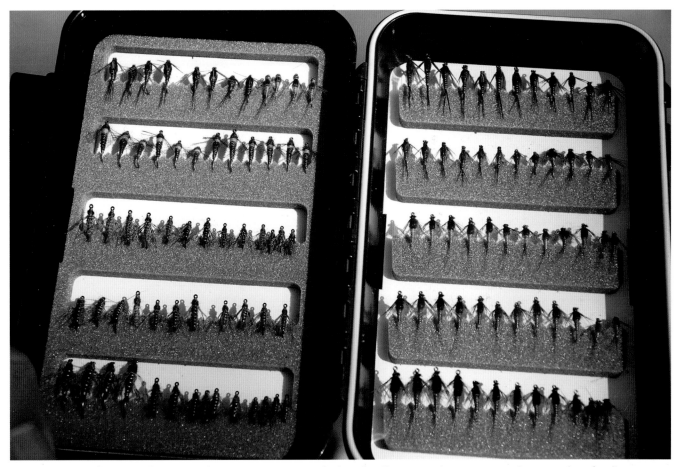

The selectivity of seasoned trout can be just as pronounced when feeding on underwater organisms as when feeding on top. Accuracy in imitation and presentation are no less important when nymphing than at any other time. BONNIE HARROP PHOTO

With this in mind, I keep a box of imitations that address incidental opportunities in the back of my vest. Many are rather strange-looking creations that make sense only to me, but I like the idea of being prepared for things that only might happen.

The systems I have devised for my own flies vary in number, complexity, and importance. In every instance, however, the patterns are easily identified and accessed. They are also well protected. For the person who fishes a lot, flies account for a far greater dollar value than any other category of fishing gear. Although realistically considered disposable, a well-tied fly is frequently capable of giving service for an extended period of time. Soaked and fish-slimed flies will become matted and disheveled if placed directly back into storage. Rinsing the fly after use and then allowing it to dry in a fleece patch pinned to the front of the vest before replacing it in the box will add to its lifespan. Rust is also the enemy, and it can spread like cancer if moisture is allowed inside a fly box.

Economy joins efficiency in a systemized fly box. Restocking in the off-season is accurately guided by the vacancies in the orderly rows of remaining patterns. Because time and money is involved, effort spent in the organization of flies is rewarded in ways other than the advantages found while on the water. For most of us, it is no less important to avoid overstocking than the reverse. This applies to those who buy their flies as well as those who tie their own.

Finally, a working fly box is like a journal. It can tell a story of success and failure and in the process preserve the memories that are the reality of fly fishing. And for those who are truly connected, these memories are all very good.

Spring Creek Emergence
pen and ink with watercolor tint
12 x 16 inches

Fishing the Clock

Although there are notable exceptions, trout streams within two hundred miles of Yellowstone National Park are large. Typically, they flow through open terrain where wind is a daily factor. Add to this the fact that these are highly popular waters that receive constant angling pressure during most of the year. The practice of catch-and-release has the inevitable effect of producing extraordinary elusiveness, which increases as the trout grow older and larger. And these are the objective of the selective trout hunter.

Handling the complexities of the Henry's Fork, Missouri, or Snake depends on numerous factors, but effective casting rises above all other requirements. As primarily a wading angler, I love to hunt the big water where the quarry carries spots and fins rather than fur or antlers. With minor shame, I confess to seeking only large fish in most circumstances, and the game begins when I locate a desirable target. There is always one best angle from which to take the shot, and although we do not always have a choice, the ability to identify the ideal casting position is a distinct and worthy skill. And a stealthy approach to that location is no less important. Depth, speed, and complexity of the current will influence the stalk, as will also the speed and direction of the wind. A wide, shallow river like the Henry's Fork often provides a variety of choices from which to present the fly. This is because you can usually wade freely to virtually any point desired. And while complexity of current, instream structure, and water depth will frequently influence how the fly is presented, wind is the most common determining factor.

Options also become limited when a trout is holding close to the bank. Unlike the wind, sunlight will not influence the actual execution of the presentation. However, nothing is more certain to alarm a trout than a shadow moving overhead. When planning your approach, always remember to factor in the direction of the sun.

"Fishing the clock" is a descriptive term for the ability to present the fly from any angle to a fish in moving water. Attaining this level of competence depends on mastering a variety of casting techniques that will allow you to effectively counter the host of obstacles that often present themselves. Of equal value is learning to determine the best position from which to present the fly and minimizing the length of the cast by wading strategically.

When given a choice, I prefer to make my approach from the side and slightly downstream from a large surface feeder, and with the current moving from right to left. A positive curve cast will place the fly in the trout's window of vision ahead of the leader while keeping the line well out of view. This method of presentation requires considerable practice and is usually limited to forty feet or less.

Brooks Montgomery demonstrates a perfectly executed negative curve cast to a Henry's Fork rainbow. BONNIE HARROP PHOTO

A backhand cast will keep the line and fly away from your body when the wind is coming in on your casting arm. The stroke is made over the opposite shoulder. BONNIE HARROP PHOTO

In most instances, the positive curve cast is executed sidearm with a tight loop and extra line speed that overpowers the cast. An abrupt stop of the stroke applied at just the right instant will kick the fly and leader to the left in a pronounced curve. With the proper control, the amount of curve can be as long as the entire leader or as short as just the tippet. This control comes from the tip of the rod, which must be fairly stiff in order to develop the line speed needed to make a perfect presentation.

An upstream wind can aid a positive curve cast, which can be delivered with less line speed but requires precise tip control for suitable accuracy. Too much flex in the tip will disrupt the aerial mend that allows the wind to induce a positive curve in the line.

A curve cast from a similar position but with the current moving from left to right requires a completely different maneuver if the angler is right-handed. Simply described, a negative curve cast is almost an underhand lob. With the rod held vertically, allow the backcast to dip slightly, and then sweep the line beneath the tip with an underpowered stroke that lifts the line upward and to the left, producing an upstream curve. Stop and drop the tip when the fly is in line but upstream of the target. This will kill the energy of the stroke and produce what is essentially an incomplete cast because the leader and part of the line are not allowed to straighten before the fly arrives on the water. Precise accuracy is not a general characteristic of the negative curve because it is often hampered by wind. However, with practice it becomes a useful tool for covering a sizable amount of water with a fly-first drift.

When the trout's location allows an approach from the side or somewhat upstream, a reach cast is a fairly easy way of obtaining a fly-first presentation. Begin this cast by starting the forward stroke toward the point on the water where you want the fly to arrive; then move the rod tip upstream.

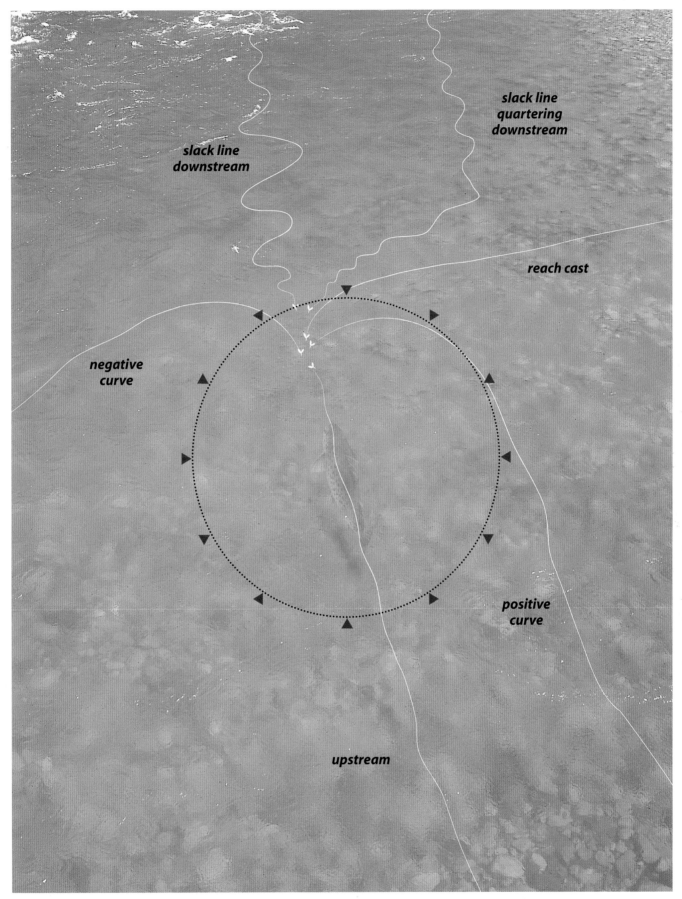

slack line
downstream

slack line
quartering
downstream

reach cast

negative
curve

positive
curve

upstream

In any fishing situation there is one best angle to present the fly. Learning to recognize the most advantageous casting position and being able to execute the appropriate cast come from experience and practice. THOMMY GUSTAVSSON ILLUSTRATION

A negative curve cast (left to right) is executed by bringing the line under the rod tip and stopping the power before the line has straightened. Drop the tip to allow the line to settle on the water in a wide curve. BONNIE HARROP PHOTO

This photo shows the proper time to drop the rod tip when executing a negative curve cast. BONNIE HARROP PHOTO

The fly will travel on its initial path while the line follows the rod tip upstream. Quick snap mends that add slack and length to the drift will enhance the effectiveness of this method of presentation. A reach cast to the right is used when the current is flowing from right to left; the left-hand reach is used when the situation is reversed. As in all casts, adjust your line speed to the wind force and the distance to the target.

Perhaps the most favored presentation among anglers of limited casting skill is made from a position nearly directly upstream from the objective. And while it can be relatively effective, two negatives can come into play when the fly is presented from upstream. It is seldom that any trout will tolerate an angler's presence within its window of vision, and it is never a good idea to allow the line to pass over the fish either in the air or on the water. This is especially true in extremely shallow water or when the angle to the target is close to being directly downstream where the line cannot be led far enough away from the drift line to avoid alarming the trout. However, I concede that there are times when a directly downstream presentation is the only option, but I usually assume it will be a one-shot deal.

A careful approach is always a key element regardless of the angle from which the cast will be made. Clumsy

A 16-foot leader and a long upstream cast are frequently required when trout move into shallow feeding areas. Keeping the line away from your opponent's view is an absolute necessity when casting upstream. BONNIE HARROP PHOTO

A long reach cast right to a Henry's Fork rainbow. A reach cast right begins by starting the stroke toward the target and then dropping the rod tip to the right. The line will follow the rod tip upstream, while the fly arrives where it was aimed. A fly-first presentation is the objective of a reach cast right or left. BONNIE HARROP PHOTO

wading practices inevitably spell defeat by sending trout warning sounds or water disturbance ahead of your advance. Each step must be taken with slow deliberation. Feel the bottom with each foot as you move forward, making certain of stability before placing your full weight on that foot. A successful stalk of fifty feet or less may take five minutes or more to complete, and it is here that many battles are lost without ever making a cast.

A downstream presentation becomes much more logical in water at least thigh deep and should not exceed a 45-degree angle unless absolutely necessary. It pays to use any obstruction such as a dense weed bed or large rock that

can shield your approach and shorten the casting range. Bending low over the water will lower your profile and allow a closer approach than were you to come in standing straight up. As a rule, you should expect the cast to be considerably longer when positioned anywhere upstream of your objective. I consider anything beyond forty feet to be a long cast when presenting the fly to a surface-feeding trout. And of course, the difficulty of proper execution increases in proportion to the length of the cast. However, a long downstream presentation can often be accomplished with a cast that is considerably shorter than the actual distance to the trout. And this is undoubtedly what makes

An upstream cast is the best way to deal with spooky trout in clear, shallow water. A close approach and a fly perfectly placed with a long leader are key in gaining success with this presentation. BONNIE HARROP PHOTO

A slack-line cast made downstream allows the fly to reach the fish before the line and leader. Approaching the fish and making the cast without being detected can make this a difficult presentation to successfully execute. BONNIE HARROP PHOTO

this approach so attractive to those of minimal experience with a fly rod.

It is not uncommon to witness some success from anglers who get by with a rather weak delivery of the fly that arrives well upstream from the target but also beyond the correct line of drift. The fly must then be pulled into the desired position by dragging it across the surface. Assuming it is still floating, the fly is allowed to proceed downstream by dropping the rod tip and feeding slack into the drift with a series of mending actions. Hopefully the trout has not been put off by all the disturbance created directly upstream. Because all slack in the leader is removed prior to the beginning of the drift, this technique is not reliable when the fly must follow the subtleties of a complex current in order to arrive at the target in a natural manner.

A much more precise and dependable way of delivering the fly from an upstream position is to use a strong casting stroke that generates more line speed than is needed to reach the target. Allow the full length of the line and leader to straighten well above the water, and then pull back sharply with the rod tip. This will cause the line to recoil back against the rod, and the leader will fall in loose curves to the surface. With some some time and a little effort spent in perfecting this technique, you will be able to efficiently place the fly where it needs to be and with enough slack to avoid drag. Using this method, it is possible to shorten the length of an otherwise long cast by depositing the fly on the water well upstream but in line with the feeding position of the fish. A series of crisp mends with the rod tip will allow extra line to be fed into the drift as described earlier. With the correct technique and the right rod action, it is not uncommon to maintain a fly-first drag-free drift for thirty feet or more. This is especially valuable in extremely shallow water where an approach to less than fifty or sixty feet will most certainly spook your objective. If the presentation is not accepted, always remember to allow the fly to drift well beyond the trout's position before leading it away from the drift line with the rod tip. Strip the now submerged fly back upstream until you are certain that the motion of lifting the line for the next cast will not disturb the fish.

It is my opinion that the shorter you cast, the better your success, and the one angle most likely to allow a close approach is from directly behind the fish. For many anglers, however, a straight-line cast made directly upstream is intimidating despite its fundamental simplicity. I think this is because this presentation is highly dependent upon accuracy and does not allow for manipulation of the fly's position after the cast or mending to improve the drift.

An upstream presentation is performed with the rod in a vertical position, and the stroke is made directly in line with the flow of the water. Aim the cast slightly to the side of the target, allowing only the leader to pass overhead.

Prevailing over a wary opponent like this handsome male rainbow is largely dependent on perfect presentation of the fly. Learning to present the fly from a variety of angles makes a favorable outcome much more likely. BONNIE HARROP PHOTO

(The fish is less likely to touch the leader if the fly is an inch or two to the right or left.) Accuracy is more important than a long drift when fishing upstream. In slow water, a distance of two feet beyond the rise is usually sufficient to allow the fish to see the fly and intercept its drift. Faster water may require as much as double that distance. However, a fish that is holding close behind a surface obstruction such as an exposed weed bed may require that you put the fly literally on its nose. A tippet longer than thirty inches will hinder this kind of accuracy, especially when wind is a factor. Allowing the leader and line to arrive on the water before the fly will induce premature drag. This can be avoided by stopping the rod during the delivery stroke at precisely the right instant to permit the entire leader to straighten just above the surface, thereby minimizing the effect that wind has on the placement of the fly. Drop the rod tip at this point to soften the impact.

An upstream cast that angles across the directional flow of the current creates a significant increase in the difficulty of creating a natural presentation of a dry fly. A fly cast straight upstream will be carried in a line that does not conflict with the direction of the flow. Conversely, a cast made even slightly across the current will encounter quick drag as the flow pushes against the leader, causing the fly to move sideways rather than following the current directly downstream. A partial cure for this malady is to make a positive curve cast with a significant upstream mend. However, this technique can only be implemented from one side of the fish and is limited to a very short drift. A more versatile alternative is to use a check cast in conjunction with a longer tippet of forty to fifty inches. A tippet of inordinate length

Bonnie Harrop prepares to make an upstream cast to a big surface feeder on the Henry's Fork. RENÉ HARROP PHOTO

always carries the potential for diminished accuracy, but there are situations when this is the best way to go. A vertical casting stroke that keeps the line as parallel to the water as possible is best applied when making a check cast. Slightly overpower the delivery, and then stop the rod sharply as the leader straightens about four or five feet above the surface. The leader will spring back toward the rod tip and then pile in loose curves on the water with more slack than is usual. Pulling back with the rod tip will exaggerate the recoil, bringing even more slack into play if desired. The result will be a considerable delay in drag-producing tension on the leader as the fly drifts downstream. The check cast can be effective anytime a difficult current is working against you.

Over time, each of us should develop a confident relationship with a specific fly rod based upon personal preference and individual casting style in addition to the conditions most frequently encountered on the water we fish. After more than fifty years, I have developed a preference for an 8½- to 9-foot rod possessing a fairly quick tip and stiff butt section. In fly-rod terminology, the action would be considered medium fast with a continuous taper. Because casting the line and presenting the fly are not necessarily synonymous, I prefer this rod design for its ability to accommodate the variety of presentation angles that must be dealt with on any given day on the water. Precise tip control is key to developing line speed without the need to double haul, and this is where I find a problem with a slower action rod. Line speed generated by a compact stroke emphasizing quick recovery of the tip is not dependent upon hauling the line or loading much if not the entire length of the rod. In short-range casting, I am looking only to load the tip of the rod and rely upon a fairly long leader of 16 to 18 feet to bring delicacy into the presentation. Flex in the rod increases in proportion to the distance to the target as will the length of the stroke. When dealing with the wind or in gaining accurate presentation at a distance, I find a slow action rod to be a handicap. The same is true when attempting a high line speed delivery that transfers enough energy through the leader such as is needed when executing a positive curve cast. Slow tip recovery impedes my ability to get the fly quickly to a feeding fish that is moving quickly out of range.

Many devotees to slower action rods rely upon a weight-forward line despite its tendency to limit control both in the air and on the water. Most weight-forward lines are 90 feet in length with a front taper of 30 feet. The remaining 60 feet is level line of a thinner diameter and is intended to make shooting the cast much easier. A problem arises when more than 30 feet of line is needed to present

Wind direction, water depth, and obstructions such as exposed weed beds can influence the position from which the cast can be made. Here, an upstream cast was the only viable option. BONNIE HARROP PHOTO

the fly in a controlled manner. Unless you are double hauling, a functional cast cannot be made when the front taper or head is outside the rod tip. In this condition, it is impossible to execute anything other than a straight line delivery with little control over how the fly arrives on the water or the amount of slack that can be induced. Mending for the purpose of anything beyond extending the drift cannot happen when only the level portion of the taper is in the guides. However, a weight-forward taper usually works adequately for any distance under 30 feet plus the length of the leader.

The belly of a double-taper line is its longest and thickest part. No one expects a double-taper to shoot with the ease of a weight-forward taper. But in contrast to its counterpart, which is specifically formulated for distance casting, a double taper is generally superior when line and loop control are the foremost requirements, and this is my choice for dry-fly fishing on moving water. A strong butt section of the rod is needed to comfortably carry enough line in the air for a long cast and is also helpful in lifting

the line from the water in preparation for the next cast. A skilled caster can easily shoot an extra 15 to 20 feet of double taper if the butt section is strong enough to really drive through the delivery stroke. A double taper also facilitates the sophisticated mending techniques often needed to manipulate the drift of the fly when it is on the water.

My personal fly rods are not the excessively rigid tools preferred by some who specialize in distance casting but instead carry the characteristics of subtle and uniform flex throughout the length of the rod. A 4-weight line covers most of the waters I frequent, and I use it at least 70 percent of the time.

These opinions are specific to my personal perception of dry-fly presentation. Others may disagree and challenge my statements, which is something I anticipate and accept. Among those things that make fly fishing so unique and appealing is that it is a sport of individuals. And because of this, we are each free to participate in our own way, satisfying only our personal preference and desire. And this is as it should be.

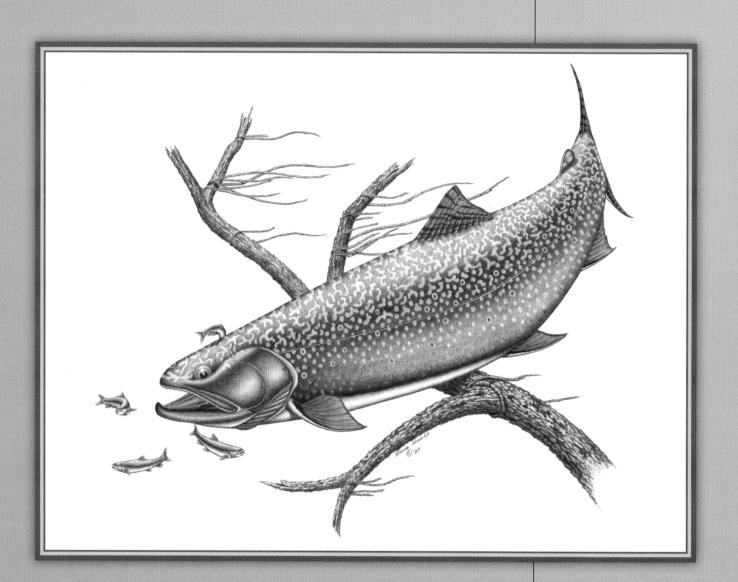

Brook Trout and Dace
pen and ink with watercolor tint
16 x 20 inches

Into the Mesh

In fly fishing, we are able to study our subject from afar with the assistance of countless volumes of instructional material from the written page or on video. Casting, the requisite skill of our sport, can be practiced to near perfection on land or water where fish do not even exist. Through these means, it is possible for a beginner to function correctly in many aspects of fly fishing without actually experiencing time in the domain of trout.

As a former guide who has spent numerous days with inexperienced clients, I can recount many days when simple rudimentary casting skill on the part of my guest made success at least a possibility even on the often brutally difficult Henry's Fork. But choosing the right fly and getting the fish to accept it is only the beginning of the complex process of actually landing the prize. Hooking, playing, and netting a trout of any size requires a separate and distinct set of skills that can only be practiced in actual fishing conditions, although mental preparation can ease the learning curve. This can be accomplished by remembering the rules of combat as applied to the fundamental goal of all fly fishers.

Cautious wading is a slow-motion dance intended to bring the angler within range of a feeding trout where closer nearly always translates to better. There is grace in the rhythmic flow of the casting stroke as it propels a thoughtfully selected fly toward its target. Perfectly executed, the drift carries the fly in unison with the current with no advance warning that it is anything but real. When it occurs, the take can vary from a quick, slashing explosion to a slow, deliberate acceptance that barely disturbs the surface. And if properly timed, the lift of the rod will seal the deal as the point of the fake offering is driven home.

On the surface, setting the hook might seem somewhat trivial in comparison to other relevant abilities such as casting, mending, or selecting the correct imitation. And while lifting the rod is indeed a very simple act, its timing must be precisely coordinated with the character of the rise and the size of the fish. Strength of the tippet plays a role in the amount of force that can be applied, as a heavy-handed set on fragile 6X can prematurely end the game with even a smallish trout.

Absolute concentration is essential as the fly drifts near the fish. This can be a problem especially during a heavy hatch when the artificial must compete with many naturals for attention. Often, several dozen attempts must be made before everything comes together perfectly and the fly is accepted. Attention can wander during such marathon sessions and can often be the cause of a mistimed hook set. Understanding that a take can come on any drift, you must avoid the distraction of other rising fish or the activity of another angler. Remember as well that a trout seldom rises in exactly the same place every time, and acceptance of the

Only complete concentration on the actions of the fish will allow the net to finally come into play. It is futile to attempt landing a big trout before it is completely subdued. RICH PAINI PHOTO

fly can occur a foot or more in any direction of the last appearance.

Fishing in the mountains of Japan in the spring of 1995, I enjoyed wonderful and surprisingly challenging fishing to the beautiful cherry trout, or yamame. Seldom more than a foot long, they were unique in their elusiveness and spirited fight. My generous hosts provided everything I needed, from help in finding the wary fish to the flies needed to match what appeared on the water. The best stream was a small, placid river where the trout fed close to a steep bank on tiny black midges. I immediately discovered that nothing short of perfection would fool these little jewels, but the presentations were not complicated by heavy weed growth or in-stream structure. What could not be provided, however, was preparedness for the lightning strike of these miniature rockets as they attacked and released the fly in what seemed like the same instant. It was nearly an hour and at least four takes before I got the timing of the hook set just right to the cheering of my gracious friends. It was an experience I will never forget, and I returned to the Henry's Fork with a newfound respect for trout of a size that would not get a second glance on my home waters.

Fishing and guiding on the fabled waters near Yellowstone do not ordinarily necessitate the pursuit of small trout, and as such, the use of an extremely quick hook set is infrequently required. This is not to say, however, that the speed and force of the set does not vary even when the trout are of adult size. Neither will the riseform remain consistent among trout of the same size when there is variation in the conditions in which they are feeding. For example, a 20-inch trout holding in slow-moving and shallow water can intercept a drifting insect by merely tilting its body upward, allowing the fly to be carried into a moderately open mouth by the flow of the current. A riseform of this type is slow and deliberate, and the response from the angler at this time should reflect the absence of urgency displayed by the fish. At normal casting range, it is wise to wait at least a count or two to allow time for the mouth to close and the nose to disappear beneath the surface before lifting the rod with only enough force to tighten the line and bury the hook. Rarely is such a take missed because the hook set was too slow. However, missing a hookup is almost always assured if the set is too quick. Maintaining the discipline required to delay the set for even a second is difficult for those accustomed to reacting to the quick take of a small trout.

Lifting the rod before the fish has closed its mouth on the fly is the most common explanation for missing a take, and the tendency to do so must be overcome if one expects to feel the weight of a heavy fish.

The delay before setting the hook is less pronounced as the distance between angler and trout increases. When you have more than 30 feet of line on the water, you probably will not set the hook too quickly, but when you have a lot more line than that out—perhaps even 50 feet—you should begin setting the instant a slow-rising fish appears to take the fly. By choice or necessity, however, most fly fishers infrequently fish a dry fly at a distance of more than 50 feet.

Timing of the hook set can also be influenced by the amount of slack line in the drift. Naturally, a quicker and stronger hook set is required when a substantial amount of slack line must be tightened before pressure can be applied to the fly. Anglers usually have a grace period of several seconds before a large trout recognizes its mistake and expels the phony insect. Still, it is prudent to use only as much slack line as is needed for a downstream presentation to avoid the need for an extremely long rod lift, which may or may not make the connection when a take occurs. The same applies to retrieving slack line as it drifts toward you during a presentation made upstream. Anglers who rely on piling an extreme length of tippet on the water with the notion that an exceptionally long drift is the best way to entice a take face the same disadvantage of being forced to move the rod tip a much greater distance to set the hook. A manageable tippet length of 36 inches or less is much more accurate and easier to control and also will not contribute to excess slack, which can complicate the hook set. In slow water, a two- to three-foot drag-free drift will usually provide adequate time to allow the feeding fish to identify and accept the offering, provided that the fly is placed in the correct alignment with the target.

Passive feeding is when a trout holds in a relatively stable position while it allows the current to deliver the meal. The rise to a floating insect is not hurried, and the surface disturbance is subdued. And while a slow and even delayed hook set is appropriate in this situation, the same cannot be said when the fish feeds more aggressively. Trout holding in deep or heavy currents are compelled to move quickly over what can be a considerable distance in order to collect a targeted food item from the surface. This becomes especially pronounced when the objective is one of the larger variety of insects, which usually do not appear in the same heavy density as the smaller types. Sizable trout will attack a big stonefly or fat hopper with a purposeful surge that can bring a startling explosion to the surface that is capable of unnerving an inattentive angler.

With jaws spread wide and gill plates flared, the trout intends to deftly capture the floating objective and then

A large bow net with deep mesh will best accommodate the bulk of a big trout. It pays to learn good netting skills for those times when an exceptional trout is the hard earned prize.
BONNIE HARROP PHOTO

A lovely native cutthroat from the South Fork of the Snake.
BONNIE HARROP PHOTO

quickly return to the depths. The jaws snap closed like those of a spring-loaded trap, but an intake of water is required before the fish can ingest its prize. And if that prize happens to be your fly, there will normally be a brief instant of perhaps a second before it is expelled as a fraud. In this instance, the reaction to the take should be a controlled but fairly rapid lift of the rod as compared to setting the hook on a fish feeding passively in a gentle shallow flow.

Although significantly more restrained, cruising trout in slow or stillwater are also considered aggressive feeders as they hunt for food floating on the surface. This is because they too are not waiting for the current to do the work but rather engulfing insects with forward movement and the mouth more than slightly open. An audible gulp is the sound of air collected during the rise being expelled through the gills when the mouth is closed and the rise

A big rainbow lifts over the surface at the end of a long run. Plenty of line backing is needed on broad water like the Henry's Fork where runs of a hundred yards or more are not uncommon. BONNIE HARROP PHOTO

The fury of this rainbow as it reacts to the hook demonstrates the power and determination of a big trout. Only complete concentration on its every move will result in victory for the angler. Small flies and fragile tippets can make the task even more difficult. But it can be done. MASA KATSUMATA PHOTO

completed. The timing of the hook set for a cruising trout can best be described as being slightly quicker than for a passive feeder but somewhat slower than is appropriate for a deep-holding fish that has just blasted to the surface. Concentration and discipline combined with an understanding of different feeding situations will advance the likelihood of a successful outcome once the fly has been accepted. Proper setting of the hook is a learned skill that should be treated as seriously as anything associated with fly fishing.

Those who are schooled only by fish of modest size in confined habitat cannot comprehend the scope of playing a large trout on the big waters of the Rocky Mountain West. Unlike the skill of casting, it is impossible to practice playing large fish on light tackle. Trout here can demand delicate and precise presentations of small imitations. Tangling

with a trout approaching two feet in length and weighing as much as six pounds is excitement enough, but add the complication of a light rod and line, a 6X tippet, and a size 18 or smaller dry fly and you really have your hands full. This is especially true when the fish has a hundred yards or more of water to use as a battlefield and the cunning to incorporate submerged weeds, rocks, logs, or other structures into its defense plan.

Those who say that the reel's only role is to store line have not experienced the searing run of a Henry's Fork rainbow that can drain the reel of all the line and much of the backing in a matter of seconds, or a heavy Missouri River brown powering across the shallows in a purposeful exit toward deep water on the far side, its determined progress punctuated periodically by a ponderous twisting leap that can shear a light tippet in a heartbeat. In these

Leading a big fish away from the heavy main current will reduce its ability to resist the pressure of the rod. Lower the rod tip and apply lateral pressure toward the shallow edge of the water. BONNIE HARROP PHOTO

and countless other examples, a sturdy case can be made that a high-performance reel is the most critical item of equipment when it comes to prevailing over a heavy trout on light tackle. And in this regard, we are in great shape, as skilled engineers and machinists who also happen to be anglers have responded to the evolving demands of modern fly fishing with smooth-running, high-precision reels that protect a light tippet and its precarious connection to a small fly. A fine reel, like a great rod, can be a virtual work of art and worth every penny.

One hundred yards of backing may seem excessive to anyone unaccustomed to big trout in big water, but I have experienced times when even that much insurance was not enough. There is no more disheartening feeling than to watch the final turns of backing disappear from the spool along with the agonizing reality that in this instance the fish has won the battle. On the Henry's Fork and other wide waters, I capitalize on the full advantage of a large arbor reel, which has the capacity to hold at least one hundred and fifty yards of backing. And it is key to use care when retrieving backing and line onto the spool to avoid tangles or jammed turns that can disrupt the free flow of line during the next battle. Large arbor reels require the backing and line to be distributed across the width of the spool in tight, even turns that must be manipulated into place with the fingers of the rod hand. This can be tricky at first, but eventually it becomes an automatic part of the retrieval process.

While a very slow or soft action rod will do the best job of protecting a fragile tippet when setting the hook or playing a large fish, it is not the best for precise casting, especially in the wind. Like many, I am charmed by the graceful flex of a slow action bamboo rod, and even a soft fiberglass or graphite rod can be a pleasure on simple currents when the wind is low and the trout are sympathetic. It becomes a different story, however, when wind, distance, and complex currents complicate the presentation, and the trout are large, seasoned competitors that can spot the slightest flaw in the offering. When the encounter is ruled by these conditions, a more assertive tool in the form of a quicker action rod will handle the most demanding aspects of getting the fly to the fish. With practice, one learns to rely on only the tip of the rod for a controlled hook set that protects the tippet, and the same applies to feeling what the trout is doing as it exercises every opportunity to break free once it is on the line. Rod strength also plays into the ability to apply pressure during the fight while withstanding heavy weight during the landing process.

Gareth Jones lifts the head of a big rainbow. This tactic reduces the trout's ability to escape at the critical point of netting.
BONNIE HARROP PHOTO

Fortunately, modern tippet material is remarkably strong for its diameter. In the higher range of quality, a 7X tippet is equal in strength to what 5X would test as recently as the 1980s. As one whose experience predates that era by twenty-five years, I can say with reasonable confidence that no advancement in fly tackle has contributed more to our ability to bring a large trout to hand than today's amazingly strong tippet material. Combined with hooks that seldom fail, we are better prepared to deal with a rampaging trout than at any point in history.

Surviving the often violent reaction to the sting of the fly is frequently a small victory for an angler who has just hooked his first big trout. In many instances, there is considerable slack line that must be dealt with before the reel can begin to do its work. Keeping the line free of tangles as the fish makes its first furious run is critical in maintaining control of the tension during the precarious period before the reel can assume this duty. Trapping the line between the forefinger of the rod hand and the cork handle will enable the slack to be fed smoothly through the guides while applying enough tension to retain connection to the fish. Remember to watch for snarls behind the rod hand and use the free hand to deal with any problem that could quickly develop into a catastrophic knot in the line.

Things become somewhat simpler when the fish can be played directly from the reel, but there is no time when complete concentration is not in order. I set the drag on the reel at a rather low resistance point and control pressure on the trout by keeping the line between the first two fingers of my rod hand. The small finger on the same hand is used to distribute line onto the wide spool when I can retrieve line.

The rod tip should be held at an angle of 45 degrees or less when the fish is running, and dropped low to the water if the fish leaps, to prevent it from falling on a tight leader and snapping the tippet. When you notice the fish's resistance weakening, you should apply pressure. The fight is shortened considerably if the trout is not allowed to rest even momentarily. Use a pumping motion with the rod to retrieve line when there is no force beyond weight to contend with. Lift the rod high to gain slack and retrieve line onto the reel as you lower the tip. Force the trout to fight the rod by holding it high and applying pressure to the line between your fingers, but remain prepared to instantly drop the tip and release line at the slightest hint that the trout might again bolt away. A lapse in concentration of even a second can spell disaster if the fish shakes its head or surges against a tight line.

To make the trout to fight the current rather than the rod, force its head laterally toward the bank. This maneuver not only depletes the fish's strength, but you also lead it to shallow water where it loses the advantage of depth and current speed. Apply pressure toward the bank only when the trout begins to show signs of tiring, but keep it constant once this maneuver begins to work. Easing downstream as you move the fish closer will reduce the amount of force needed to bring it into this position, while allowing more line to be retrieved onto the reel. Surrender is not in the makeup of any wild creature, so always be prepared to release line even when you may be convinced that you have the upper hand. Escape is never beyond the realm of possibility as long as the trout remains in the water.

At no point in the course of bringing a large trout to hand is there a time when discipline and concentration can be relaxed. And although surprising to some, any river guide will tell you that landing the fish is the most highly pressured duty he performs for a client. Even when wading, most will carry a long-handled boat net with a large bow to counteract a client's poor landing skills. With this oversize tool of the trade, many have gained the ability to deftly snatch a sizable fish while it is still holding in waist deep water and at a distance of twenty or more feet from the angler. No aspect of this technique is practical for the individual who must land his own fish without the encumbrance of a three-foot-long landing net.

Most of those with experience wading large western waters carry a deep, meshed, short-handled net with a bow at least sixteen inches in diameter. With the right landing technique, a net of this size will comfortably handle fish larger than 20 inches, and it is not so large as to be disruptive when carried between the shoulder blades until it is needed. The relatively new magnetic net attachments, which allow quick access and release, have proven to be of considerable advantage at the dramatic point when the net is put into use.

Losing an exceptional fish at the critical netting point is easily the most frustrating experience in fly fishing, and although usually avoidable, it happens far too frequently. Although sad in fact, it is almost comical to watch a well-played trout being chased around by an excited angler with net in hand but no clear plan of how to properly use it. Often, the fish is too far away to reach, and the net is submerged way too deeply to bring it effectively into play. Stabbing recklessly beneath the water with the net is almost futile, and the trout is placed in a greater state of alarm by the commotion. This undisciplined behavior nearly always results in an unintended but predictable outcome.

A defeated fish normally requires only enough pressure from the rod to keep the hook in place. At this time, you should be in position above the fish but not trying to bring it upstream toward you. Instead, reel down to a position

A tired trout should remain out of the water for no longer than one minute. Snap a quick photo and release the fish as quickly as possible. BONNIE HARROP PHOTO

about the length of your rod plus no more than 3 to 4 feet. Be extra cautious when the leader to line connection is inside the guides, as is the case when the leader is in excess of 12 feet in length. A trim needle knot coated with a durable flexible adhesive will flow through the guides without hanging up should the fish spook and pull out line. Do not even touch the net until the line is secured between the index finger and the rod handle, and then comes the tough part. Keeping minimal rod pressure on the resting fish, release the net from its magnetic clasp and shake the mesh free of any twists or tangles. Immerse the net and place it in the water directly upstream from the quarry. Lifting the fish to the surface is the most effective way of disabling its resistance. Pushing the rod tip high overhead, slip the forward bow of the net beneath the exposed head; then lift sharply upward when at least half the length has started into the mesh. The rest of the body will follow the heavier front portion, and the prize will be yours.

The pleasure and excitement of landing a great trout is not without some burden of responsibility. Consider the well-being of the fish by playing it as quickly as possible so that it can recover sufficiently to survive the ordeal. This can be accomplished by applying pressure on the fish at every opportunity during the fight and bringing it into the landing position as quickly as possible. When photographing a trophy, do so within a minute or two of removing it from the net, and remember to immerse the fish between snaps of the shutter.

Revive the fish by facing it into the current and induce water through the gills by moving it back and forth until equilibrium and strength returns. A fully revived trout will pull free from your grasp on its own, and upon its departure you can be secure in the knowledge that it will live to fight another day.

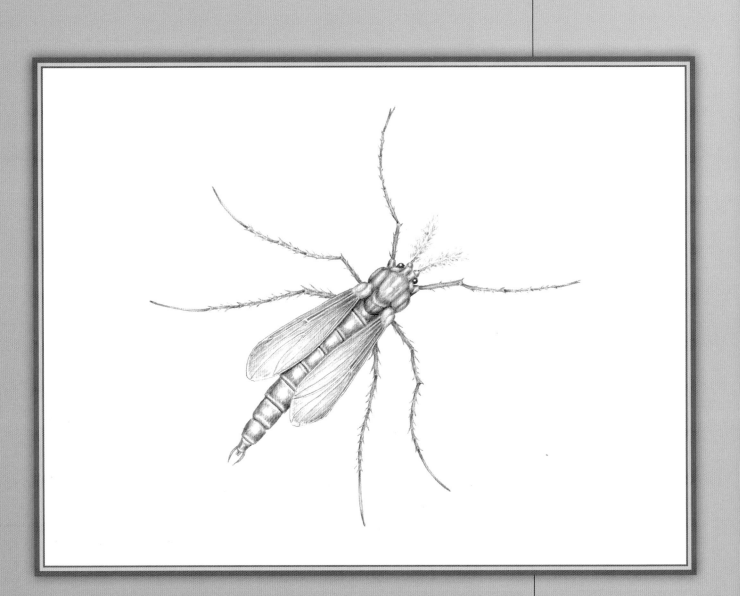

Midge Adult
carbon pencil and watercolor
8 x 10 inches

A Long Leader

In clear water less than knee deep, the big rainbow feeds nervously over clean gravel that offers little shelter. It is late morning and the autumn sun is nearly directly overhead. With no other way to conceal my presence without trying to execute an extremely long cast, I select an approach from downstream that, if properly performed, will bring me to within forty feet of the busy trout. Pausing frequently, I inch my way over the cobbled bottom in a careful stalk that requires nearly ten minutes to complete.

The fish is of a size that is seldom associated with a *Baetis* hatch, but its attention seems fully locked on the tiny olive mayflies that litter the water. Well within comfortable casting range, my fingers tremble just a bit as I clinch the size 22 emerger to the 6X tippet. While not a stationary target, the big guy feeds in a limited area of about six feet in diameter, and I feel confident that I can get the fly over him with a minimum of attempts. I could not have been more mistaken.

The fly had not touched the water on the first cast when the gently riffled surface erupted in a violent boil that terminated in a wide wake that traced a startled retreat toward the safety of deeper water. The opportunity of fishing to a truly exceptional trout had ended without a single drift of the fly, and I was left to puzzle the reason why.

This experience occurred nearly two decades ago, but it remains fresh in my memory as a moment of awakening to a different approach to presenting the fly to wary trout. And like most other points of natural learning, the explanation for my failure came as a result of logical thinking. Not every trout would be so easily spooked by the simple presence of the line overhead, but this one was unique. Its exceptional size spoke to years of survival in a hostile environment filled with peril from every direction. A moving shadow on the water warns of potential danger from overhead, and a wary trout will not consider its source before reacting. Through instinct or conditioning, fleeing from a perceived threat is a rule of nature that came into play the instant my line passed over the trout during that ill-fated engagement so long ago. Since that time I have developed a solution that has substantially reduced opportunity lost to trout-alarming line shadow.

As a beginning angler, I was not gifted with an attentive mentor who could explain the finer points of fly fishing to a young boy. What could not be gained by watching others was self-learned through trial and error, and there were many mistakes. My first leader was a 5-foot length of 8-pound level monofilament. Remarkably, I actually caught a few fish with this clumsy setup, although they were invariably quite small and unsophisticated.

Bonnie Harrop lifts the head of a hefty rainbow in preparation for netting. A 14-foot leader allowed a successful upstream presentation. RENÉ HARROP PHOTO

The advantages of a tapered leader would come into the picture several years later, but economics and poor availability kept the commercial product out of reach. Like I did for many other tackle needs, I learned to make my own tapered leaders at an early age. And while no longer restrained by financial limitations, I have never stopped making my own leaders. Time and experience taught me how to control the performance of my personal leader designs, and I learned how to adjust the taper to accommodate a variety of fishing situations. Suspecting that the reason for my foiled engagement with that memorable trout of the 1980s could be corrected in future encounters, I began to reconsider a fairly long-held preference for leaders shorter than 12 feet in overall length. I have never regretted that decision.

The main purpose of the leader in fly fishing is to separate the line from the fly. When feeding under the surface in deeper water, trout do not feel nearly as vulnerable to overhead danger as when rising to take floating food forms from a placid surface or when feeding in shallow water where the penetrating eyes and talons of an osprey or eagle bring considerable risk to this natural act of survival. While

this is not always the rule, deep-water fishing does not usually necessitate gentle presentation or a concern for the movement or shadow of the line as it passes overhead. Therefore, an especially long leader or fine tippet is not generally associated with this type of fishing. The same can be said for dry-fly fishing on fast water where a broken surface makes a trout's presence more obscure to flying predators while hiding line movement or shadow from above. In any of these instances, a 9-foot leader or a tippet of 4X or heavier will usually suffice. The game changes, however, when fishing dry flies on slow, clear currents or sight nymphing in thin water.

The largest trout become so by resisting the forces that act to eliminate them. Among these forces is the human predator whose intent may or may not be lethal. On the Henry's Fork and other notable waters in the western United States, trout receive near constant attention from anglers, most of whom release their catch. Abilities derived from experience allow surviving fish to become adept at resisting the best efforts of even the most skilled of the international fly-fishing community. Anglers come here for the unique experience of pursuing only big trout that feed

Bonnie Harrop has just completed a long, stealthy stalk that has placed her in position to make an upstream presentation.
RENÉ HARROP PHOTO

This fine rainbow was the reward for the flawless upstream presentation of a caddis emerger. RENÉ HARROP PHOTO

throughout their lifetime on a diverse menu of aquatic and terrestrial insects. Engaging these veterans on the terms of this behavior is an intellectual exercise that requires a distinct game plan for each individual trout. Fly selection must accurately depict the natural organism upon which the trout is feeding, but the challenge does not end there. Flawless presentation cannot be overemphasized for trout that can recognize the slightest amount of drag, and this is undoubtedly the most difficult problem to overcome. An extremely small tippet as light as 7X and very small flies can add to the complication of hooking and landing a trout of 20 inches or longer. Additionally, a careless approach or anything unnatural on or above the water near the trout's position is almost certain to put an early end to any possibility of success. Succeeding in fooling a wise old trout is seldom the result of a single cast. There have been numerous times when I have spent more than hour of near continuous casting without spooking the fish but also without getting it to accept my fly. While small in comparison to winning the battle, there is satisfaction in knowing that I have made more than one hundred casts without

alarming my adversary. This is not an easy accomplishment on a river like the Henry's Fork, where a trout will often flee at the most innocent casting error.

Perhaps the most underrated skill in dry-fly fishing is the ability to recognize the most advantageous position from which to present the fly, and then having the ability to effectively execute a cast from that angle. The least preferred but often most effective presentation is one that is

An upstream cast and a 14-foot leader allowed Leslie Harrop to present a PMD Emerger to a big rainbow she found feeding secretively in this riffled section of water. BONNIE HARROP PHOTO

made from directly downstream of the trout's feeding position. While fundamental in the early years of the sport, the upstream cast has given way to a downstream presentation that requires less skill and accuracy to perform. Proponents of this method cite the advantage of having the fly precede the leader on its path to a feeding trout. While undeniably effective, relying exclusively on a downstream presentation is a self-limiting approach that frequently excludes a realistic opportunity at trout that will not tolerate an approach from upstream.

Failure does not promote confidence, and this is what I experienced in early years as I worked to develop proficiency with an upstream presentation. The accuracy and control of my casting was largely dependent on a leader of $10\frac{1}{2}$ feet on the 7- to 8-foot rods I preferred at the time. With increased leader length identified as a distinct contributor to my progress, I entered a rather complicated phase of adjusting my casting style to accommodate the longer commercial tapers that were available at that time. Moving to a rod length of $8\frac{1}{2}$ to 9 feet brought some improvement, but my advancement hit a wall when I tried to extend the leader length beyond 12 feet. Truthfully speak-

ing, I had not found a commercial leader that would meet my expectation for performance in a length that would be of assistance to my effort. While I was accustomed to making my own, it would still require nearly two years of trial and error to develop a fully functional, 6X tapered leader of 14 feet in length. The leader formula is as follows:

.030/24", .025/20", .020/18", .015/16", .011/14", .010/12", .009/10", .008/9", .007/8", .006/6", .005/30"

Incorporating the smaller diameter of a 3- or 4-weight line with the longer leader contributed even more to my ability to make a gentle yet accurate upstream cast. Though far short of 100 percent, my success ratio with this angle of presentation reached a point of eliminating the dread of an upstream cast. On the Henry's Fork, a 50 percent success rate on big surface feeders is considered quite respectable for even the most accomplished of anglers, regardless of the position from which the presentation is made.

There are many different presentation angles and techniques that will be applied during any given day on the water. Successfully adopting a long leader as standard

More than 15 feet separate the fish in the foreground from the tip of the line. I made more than two dozen casts before hooking the fish with a reach cast to the left.
BONNIE HARROP PHOTO

equipment is dependent upon its ability to handle any casting situation that might be encountered. In addition to a straight line cast upstream, reach casts and curve casts both right and left are not accommodated by weak turnover, which is the greatest obstacle to overcome when trying to formulate a long leader that is fully functional for dry-fly fishing or delicate sight nymphing. The problem becomes increasingly prominent in windy conditions or when a very fine tippet is involved. And this is what prevents the suitability of increasing the length of the leader by simply adding a longer tippet.

My longstanding opinion regarding the ideal tapered leader is that it should function as an extension of the line. Accuracy and control suffer greatly if there is any interruption in the transfer of energy between the tip of the line and the fly. Of course, proper leader design is of foremost importance in this respect, but it is important to know that not all fly lines will function correctly in turning over a long leader. An extremely short or very slow action rod can be somewhat problematic for anyone who is not proficient

Looping the belly of the leader around the reel after securing the fly to a guide near the tip of the rod keeps the long leader outside the guides and ready for action. BONNIE HARROP PHOTO

with these rod types. A medium-fast 9-foot, 4-weight rod is my preference when fishing larger rivers with smaller flies. In the wind I might go to a 16-foot leader by reducing the tippet length and adjusting the taper on the lower end. I frequently call upon a leader as long as 22 feet, especially when fishing the Henry's Fork in autumn when the water is very low and the trout are extra wary. My usual leader length, however, is about 18 feet with a tippet of 30 inches. I like an 8-foot rod of similar action for smaller waters

A slack-line cast quartering downstream was the best angle for this Henry's Fork bank feeder. A well-designed, 18-foot leader handled the situation perfectly. BONNIE HARROP PHOTO

where the average casting distance is shorter and a 14-foot leader is more appropriate.

Most anglers who shy away from a longer leader have never tried a really well designed taper. Most with whom I have shared my own leader designs are amazed at the ease with which they can be handled. I recommend starting with a leader of about 14 feet and then gradually increasing the length as confidence and comfort progress. I certainly understand and accept that some will never graduate to a leader that may be double the length of the rod. But I also maintain that most who can handle a 10-foot leader with reasonable proficiency will experience little difficulty adapting to the longer length, assuming they are fishing the right taper. My wife, Bonnie, is a diminutive grandmother who also happens to be a nonswimmer. By both necessity and choice, she mainly works the shallow edges of the Henry's Fork and other larger waters we fish together. While not especially strong with her casting, Bonnie finds the majority of her very respectable success while fishing upstream using a 16-foot leader on a 5-weight line. A stealthy approach and deadly accuracy out to about 40 feet is her basic

means of compensating for physical limitation and restricted mobility while wading.

Managing a longer leader when casting is not actually taking place may be the most difficult adjustment for those unaccustomed to this setup. To avoid bringing the leader into the guides and the resulting delay in putting the rod into action, attach the fly to the guide that allows the most line to extend from the tip when the belly of the leader is looped around the reel spool. This guide may be very close to the tip when the leader is nearly double the length of the rod. In extreme cases when the leader exceeds about 18 feet, I am forced to bring as much as 4 feet of the butt section into the guides. I acknowledge that this can make things rather complicated when preparing to cast, but the advantages often outweigh this minor discomfort when a special fish comes into play.

Bringing a long leader into the guides is often unavoidable when drawing a hooked trout to within comfortable range of the net. Trimming the free ends of all knots as close as possible will help to minimize the likelihood of losing a fish due to the leader being caught in the guides. This especially applies to the leader-to-line connection and the larger knots in the butt section, which are most likely to catch in the guides. Coating each knot with Pliobond or another flexible adhesive will also contribute to a smoother flow of leader through the guides.

Tying your own leader requires a selection of leader spools ranging in diameter from .030 inch down through the smallest size you expect to be using as the tippet, which is usually 7X (.005 inch) for the fishing I do. The sample formula for a 14-foot, 6X taper provides a general description that can serve as a starting point. Extension of the butt section or tippet will provide additional length if so desired.

After years of urging, I am finally seeing some commercial knotless tapers that meet my expectation for perform-

ance in a longer leader. As is the case with all commercially produced nylon leaders, however, the tippet on these new tapers is quite fragile in the smaller sizes. This drawback can be easily corrected by replacing the original tippet with one of fresh nylon or fluorocarbon.

While there are some who will discard the notion of a long leader as unnecessary complication, I am convinced that taking this step may be the solution for unexplained failures with wary trout on pressured waters. To progress as fly fishers, we must be continuously willing to put aside comfort in exchange for improving our skills. If increasing the distance between the line and the fly improves our odds of fooling large, selective trout, then I believe that advancement to a long leader is an effort worth making.

This old veteran required four fly changes before falling for a CDC Emerger. Success came just before dark when any delay in accessing the correct fly could have produced a different outcome. BONNIE HARROP PHOTO

Caddis on Budding Willow
carbon pencil with watercolor tint
11 x 14 inches

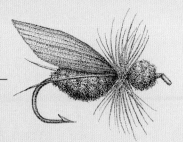

Fishing on the Edge

It was sound rather than sight that revealed the presence of a large trout tucked tightly against a moderately undercut bank, obscured by overhanging grass and other vegetation. The audible gulp was the sound of a drifting insect being inhaled from the surface; the exhaled bubble of air gave visual evidence of what lay beneath the slightest disturbance of shaded water. The sound and accompanying bubble of air were repeated approximately every thirty seconds as I cautiously guided my client into casting position about thirty-five feet out and slightly upstream from the busy fish.

It had been a long and thus far fruitless day guiding a young angler from Japan on the famed fly-only water of the Henry's Fork. Although scant in number, there had been several opportunities to fulfill the young man's dream of landing one of the great free-rising rainbows for which this river is so well known. It was obvious that he was well prepared for the challenge by the way he gracefully extended line during a few practice casts to a modest-size trout earlier that morning. It was a different story, however, when his composure was overwhelmed by the excitement of a first encounter with a truly large fish. The initial presentation was a disaster that sent the line crashing into the mirror surface, causing his target to flee in a surging wake across the shallow flat. Three more times before the spinnerfall ended, we stalked patiently into casting range of

nice fish. A mistimed mend that created excessive fly drag cancelled a very good cast to a second fish, and it simply stopped feeding at that point. Things were going better with the next player until a gaping mouth opened to accept the fly that was promptly ripped away by a premature hook set, and this fish also disappeared. Failing on the fourth candidate was not truly my guy's fault because the shadow of a trumpeter swan passing low overhead caused the trout to spook after only three or four casts.

Visible rises began to dwindle along with the number of insects remaining on the water. With the end of feeding activity looming near, we spotted a lone feeding trout that my client intercepted with an impressive fifty-foot cast. The hook set was perfectly timed, and for a few exciting seconds, he found himself connected to more trout mass than he had ever before experienced. They parted company through no failure of the angler; it was simply a case of too much fish for the 6X tippet and size 18 fly. Dejected, he retrieved the flyless line and fifty feet of backing onto the reel. The spinnerfall had ended, and the flat now lay empty of rising fish. Words intended to comfort did little to console the young man, who fought back tears of disappointment and self-blame. I'm not sure my tone was at all convincing as I assured him that he would have another chance before the day's end. It was midsummer, and although an hour short of noon, the temperature had already risen to a point

Trout of the Henry's Fork find a diverse menu of aquatic and terrestrial insects along the edges of this legendary river. Miles of open bank provide unique opportunity to stalk trout without wading more than a few feet into the current. BONNIE HARROP PHOTO

of near discomfort. Added to this was the typical midday breeze, which, combined with the heat, would hinder most insect activity until the cool and calm of evening.

For the next three hours, we worked back upstream toward our starting point more than a mile away. I searched the familiar spots that might hold a good fish. This meant wading back and forth several times across the broad and relatively shallow river beneath a sweltering August sun that sapped our strength and resolve in equal proportions. A delayed lunch break found us cooling our feet after walking a long stretch of grassy open bank. Soggy sandwiches and tepid bottled water were nonetheless welcome for two weary but still determined souls not quite ready for surrender. Lying back in the cool grass, I was close to dozing off when I heard the audible gulp of a feeding trout.

The exhaled bubbles emanated from a shady location barely twenty feet upstream from where we reclined on the downwind bank. Prodding my napping client, I leaned forward to try to determine what insect life might be gaining the attention of the secluded trout. Closer examination of the water revealed a sprinkling of small dark caddis collected by the wind into a narrow drift line tight against the overhanging vegetation.

After checking his tippet knot for strength and attaching a size 20 CDC Caddis, we carefully retreated sixty feet downstream and then eased toward midriver to begin the stalk. We were ninety feet from the bank before pushing directly upstream to a point slightly ahead of the trout's position. From there, we inched our way forward, bending low over the water to minimize our profile as we approached the unsuspecting fish. The wind that riffled the surface provided extra concealment, but it would still be a difficult proposition to get the fly into a feeding lane little more than an inch wide. From a distance of thirty-five feet, a slightly downstream presentation would have to kiss the overhead grass that shielded the trout from virtually all predatory attention.

Although there was no questioning my client's resolve, I knew that luck was as much a part of the equation as was his casting skill. For nearly an hour, he worked the same cast, and time after time he came up empty. At no time did the trout deviate from its determination to feed exclusively from the narrow drift line. Many times the cast was too long, and twice it was necessary to replace flies left hanging in the tough blades of meadow grass. More often, however, the fly was ever so slightly outside the defined path of acceptance.

A trout feeding close to the edge reveals little of itself. Generally opportunistic, bank feeders often do not display the selective feeding tendencies of trout found at midstream. A good presentation of something familiar and edible is sometimes more important than fishing an exact imitation of something more specific.
BONNIE HARROP PHOTO

Keep an eye along the edge when prowling open banks. Many opportunities for a big trout are missed by those who concentrate their attention on open water and neglect what might be lying at their feet.
BONNIE HARROP PHOTO

More than once, a dragging fly seemed to put the fish down, but each time it returned to feeding after a few minutes of disruption. As the attempts mounted to a number approaching one hundred casts, I began to wonder if this was one of those invincible trout that just would not be fooled.

However, my client's disciplined concentration would not waver. Finally, during a brief lull in the stiff breeze, the moderately overcast fly hung momentarily in the grass and then dropped gently to the surface in perfect position. And there was no surprise for either of us when a twelve-inch drift was interrupted by the subtle appearance of a dark nose that sucked the fly from view and then disappeared. A slow lift of the rod tip closed the deal, and the fight was on.

The battle was not typical of a Henry's Fork rainbow but rather a wallowing, head-shaking slugfest that involved no reel-searing runs or acrobatic leaps. Neither my client nor I felt the slightest remorse when the unspectacular event ended less than five minutes after hookup. By most standards, the ponderous old male could not be a truly beautiful representative of its species, but to my client and me he was absolutely splendid. Far past his prime but made wise by years of surviving in the wild, the beauty of the trout lay in his size and formidability as an adversary. A quick photo prior to its release preserved the memory of a dream fulfilled. A respectful bow accompanied by an admiring gaze

followed the 20-inch form as it glided slowly toward midstream. Overcome by the power of the moment, the tired angler slumped down in the grass with his face in his hands. And for the second time that day, he was overcome by tears of emotion. But the tears this time were of overwhelming joy.

It was by necessity that I learned to find trout on the edges of waters I fished as a young boy. My small size and the absence of wading gear kept me on or close to the bank, where the limitations of my crude tackle dictated a very short cast with bait or fly. Time and experience on the water taught me to recognize likely holding areas where a trout might find food and shelter within range of my restricted tackle and skill. Regardless of its size, any trout caught was appreciated because most of the larger fish were easily able to resist my clumsy offerings. But visually probing the edges for prospects became a habit that continues still, and it was the beginning of a quest of understanding the habits and behavior of trout. Early adulthood brought about a lifting of those early barriers that prohibited access to a larger percentage of the waters I frequented, but to this date no lesson from the water has been more vital to my success as an angler.

Wade deeper, cast farther, and look good doing both seems to be the formula for fly-fishing accomplishment if one listens to the message of certain segments of the industry that sell equipment matching those objectives. But while some aspects of our sport do indeed benefit from technological advancement, the vast number of beginning anglers will be better served by a more practical approach that emphasizes finely tuned skills of relatively short-range presentation and a carefully planned approach that often takes place in water of moderate depth far from the center of a stream.

The ability to find trout is perhaps the most overlooked ingredient to a fruitful day on the water, and the most desirable are amazingly adept at concealing themselves from the probing eyes of all predatory creatures, including the human variety. A surface-feeding trout finds sanctuary from overhead detection beneath undercut banks, overhanging vegetation, or exposed weed beds at streamside that deter the danger of a drifting artificial fly as well as the purposeful dive of a hunting osprey.

Safety is not the only reason that many large trout find comfort away from the main flow. A favorable wind will collect drifting insects such as mayflies and caddis tight along the bank, creating an opportunity to feed on a concentrated food source that does not exist elsewhere on the stream. In addition to the Henry's Fork, I find this to be essentially true on the Firehole River in Yellowstone, where stiff winds are a daily feature in the open meadows. Although seldom large, the rainbows and browns present a real challenge in their refusal to accept a perfect drift that is even an inch outside the established feeding lane. Although the length of the cast is often within twenty feet, it

is a real test of a 3-weight rod to achieve the kind of precision needed to fool these spirited 10- to 14-inchers.

Land-dwelling insects known as terrestrials are an available food source during the warmer months of the season. Trout become accustomed to the appearance of ants, beetles, and hoppers that thrive in the lush vegetation that fringe the edges of many waters. Fishing imitations of these familiar food forms that seem to be almost constantly falling helplessly to the water is always a good idea and becomes even better when a friendly wind accelerates the availability. From May through September, I keep a small black ant pattern on my tippet when stalking the banks between hatches. And remarkably, it is not always necessary to change flies when other competing insects are on the water.

While some trout live almost exclusively along the edge, others are temporarily drawn there at certain times. Finding trout in very shallow water can be surprising to an angler accustomed to looking for trout in deep lies or other conventional holding areas. But in reality, greater depth means greater effort for a fish that must consume literally hundreds of insects during a typical feeding session, and far more sizable trout gravitate to the shallows during prime feeding times than might ever be imagined. Many times I have observed trout in knee-deep water feeding almost indiscernibly, tipping their heads just slightly up or down or from side to side as they intercept their miniature prey. Deeper water does not necessarily translate to more aquatic insect life since it is the stream bottom not water depth that determines habitat. If the volume of available insects is essentially equal in both deep and shallow water, it only makes sense that a trout can feed more efficiently in a foot of water than if the depth is significantly greater. No creature, whether wild or otherwise, will intentionally expend more energy than is necessary.

I find many of the year's largest fish in open shallow water close to the bank. Aerial predators will not attack otherwise vulnerable trout if the plummeting dive holds the risk of a collision with the stream bottom. Large predators such as river otters can outswim even the fastest trout but only if the water depth accommodates their sizable bulk. Natural camouflage allows trout to blend in with waving aquatic vegetation, which causes considerable difficulty for probing eyes that search relentlessly for a victim. High-quality polarized eyewear is indispensable for cutting through surface glare and detecting subtle visual indications of a suitable target. Suspicious shadows beneath an invisible form or the wink of a white mouth opening briefly to accept a drifting morsel will tip off the presence of a worthy objective, but the broad pectoral fins just behind the head are the most consistently reliable indicator.

A trout feeding visibly in thin water presents a unique opportunity for both dry and submerged artificials, but either method demands flawless approach and presentation.

I found this hefty hen tucked beneath an undercut bank draped with dense meadow grass. It took several dozen casts to get the drift just right, but she inhaled a small black beetle with complete confidence. BONNIE HARROP PHOTO

Trout of surprising size and numbers can be found in small side channels away from the main flow. Rick Smith hooked this spirited brown in mere inches of water in a side channel of the Madison. BONNIE HARROP PHOTO

Keenly alert to their vulnerability in this situation, the fish go scurrying for cover at the slightest shadow or movement. And unless the fish is showing itself with a distinct riseform, it is always best to approach and present the fly from downstream. A leader of 14 feet or more will minimize the chance of spooking the fish with the shadow of the fly line. With patience and caution, it is possible to wade within 30 feet or less when making the stalk from behind. A cast from any other direction may require a cast as much as twice that far.

The shoreline of lakes and ponds is the domain of small baitfish and young trout. Fished from a boat or cast from the bank, streamers often catch large marauding trout that haunt the edges for food. Aquatic weed beds are host to a multitude of stillwater organisms such as scuds, leeches, and other attractive trout foods. *Callibaetis* and Trico mayflies are also a prominent feature of the same habitat and do not usually exist in extremely deep water far from shore. Trout in stillwater are constantly on the move, which creates a distinct contrast to the common behavior of trout feeding in moving water. Uninfluenced by current, cruising trout do not offer a consistent target as they feed without rhythm or pattern. Often, the greatest

challenge in lake fishing is to get the fly in front of a fish that is constantly changing speed and direction as it hunts down its next item of food.

Side channels that branch away from a larger main flow are in effect miniature rivers that hold their own character and identity. Intimidating size, depth, and current speed are characteristic of large burly rivers like the Madison, Yellowstone, and Snake. For the wading angler, it makes more sense to avoid battling what can be dangerous conditions by focusing attention on more manageable water where safety is a far smaller concern.

The fish-holding potential of small side channels can come as a surprise to those who visit the larger rivers of the Rockies, but trout have every reason to occupy a hospitable environment that possesses their basic needs of survival. Big rivers and float fishing are often synonymous. And therefore, it is understandable why shy trout find comfort in edge waters too narrow and shallow to accommodate a drift boat.

My days as a strong and reckless wader are far in the past, and while float fishing is certainly enjoyable, I still prefer the intimacy of fishing on my feet to casting from a moving boat. The same applies to my wife and constant

Trout feeding tightly against the bank must usually be approached from the side. A patient approach made cautiously to within casting range may take several minutes. BONNIE HARROP PHOTO

fishing companion, who is an enthusiastic but small individual with limited wading ability. Advancing in age together, Bonnie and I continue to enjoy the fruits of big waters without the burden of dragging a drift boat as we travel or struggling to deal with depth and current more suitable for the young.

Perhaps the most memorable day of the past season was spent with longtime friend Rick Smith and his wife, Minori. For nearly ten consecutive hours in mid-June, we enjoyed the constant presence of the most amazing caddis hatches I have ever witnessed. The number of trout we caught and released bordered on obscenity, with many in the 18-inch class or better. And most were the product of small side channels in water seldom more than knee deep.

Late afternoon found us far upstream from our vehicles, where I worked the outside edge of a long, narrow island. The rise nearly forty feet upstream did not trigger the thought of anything special, but as I closed to within half that distance, the shadowy form of an exceptional brown trout came into view. Finning gently in only a foot of water, the big hen sipped leisurely from the surface with only the slightest disturbance of water. She took the little caddis emerger on the third drift and then exploded at the

sting of the hook. There was no panic in her departure to the heavy flow of midstream, where she parked behind a large boulder and sulked. Putting all the force that I dared on the slender 3-weight, I was finally able to turn her head toward the bank. Enraged by this disruption of her obvious advantage, she powered in a quartering angle downstream and then lifted magnificently in a twisting leap that could easily have fractured the 5X tippet had I been unprepared for the tactic. Dropping the rod tip provided just enough slack to absorb the shock, and the battle continued. Angling away from the pressure and into the flow, she allowed the current and her considerable bulk to draw line from the reel at a slow but still alarming rate. Desperate to keep her out of the backing as her ploy took her farther and farther downstream, I followed clumsily in the rocky shallows, retrieving line gradually as I went, while continuing to apply a firm but gentle force toward my side of the river. By then, she was fighting the current as much as the rod, and the distance between us gradually began to shrink. Nearing the bottom of the island, the outside water began to thin as it began to break over a long gravel bar. Sensing the loss of deep-water advantage, my weakening opponent began a side-to-side head-shaking maneuver, wanting freedom from the relentless restraint. Separated now by only fifty feet of line and leader, I softened the pressure, allowing her to drift over the gravel bar in water that would not cover the massive form, and now the fight was only against weight and the violent thrashing of a near helpless fish that had run out of options.

But my advantage would be brief as we crossed the gravel bar together into slow but deeper water downstream. Separated by only a dozen feet, we came together as weary combatants in the gentle confluence of the side and main channels. Resting near the bottom, this brute of a brown trout would only need to be lifted about eighteen inches and the prize would be mine. Freeing my net from the magnetic clasp between my shoulders, I shook the tangle from the mesh and then dipped the bow beneath the surface to begin the final round. With two feet of leader butt inside the guides, I began the lift that would bring victory to the conflict. Slowly, the solid weight yielded to the slender rod tip, and the head of my spotted adversary rose toward the surface. But as the rod strained under the heavy load, I made a critical error that would cause a far different ending from the one that a second earlier seemed certain.

The trout was clearly defeated and there was no urgency to rush the netting process, but I did just that. Rather than bringing the toothy head above the surface and over the rim of the net, I thrust my hand downward. The trout made one desperate surge, and I heard a sickening snap as the rod tip collapsed under this final forceful move. Heartened by the effect of its action, the still defiant fish lunged away, causing the tippet to break free of the fly an instant later. Shocked by my lack of discipline and concentration, I watched in disbelief as the exposed olive back crossed the broad, shallow riffle and then disappeared into the boulder-strewn depths of the Madison.

From a hundred yards distant on the opposite side of the separating island, I heard the excited sounds of my companions as they continued to find action in the adjoining side channel. It was only early evening during the longest days of summer, but the sun had settled behind a steep ridge a short distance away, leaving our side of the river in shadow. At least three hours of fishing light still remained as I wistfully looked far downstream to where a spare rod lay waiting in a vehicle that was barely in sight. With the bright heat of midday now behind, the swarm of caddis over the water intensified as prime time approached. For a brief moment I considered making the twenty-minute hike for the backup rod and continuing to participate in the action. But this thought was cut off when I saw my wife and friends heading back my way along the streamside trail that led downstream. Relieved to some extent, I joined them on the trail with the story of the broken rod and the memory of an epic encounter with a truly special trout.

Lost in individual reflection of shared pleasure, four tired anglers walked in silence along the river's edge. Resisted but certainly not ignored, dozens of trout of varying sizes fed with undisturbed enthusiasm along the shaded length of the return trip to the parking area. Few were more than a short cast from the bank, giving firm reinforcement to an often overlooked aspect of trout behavior. It was a fine ending to an exceptional day.

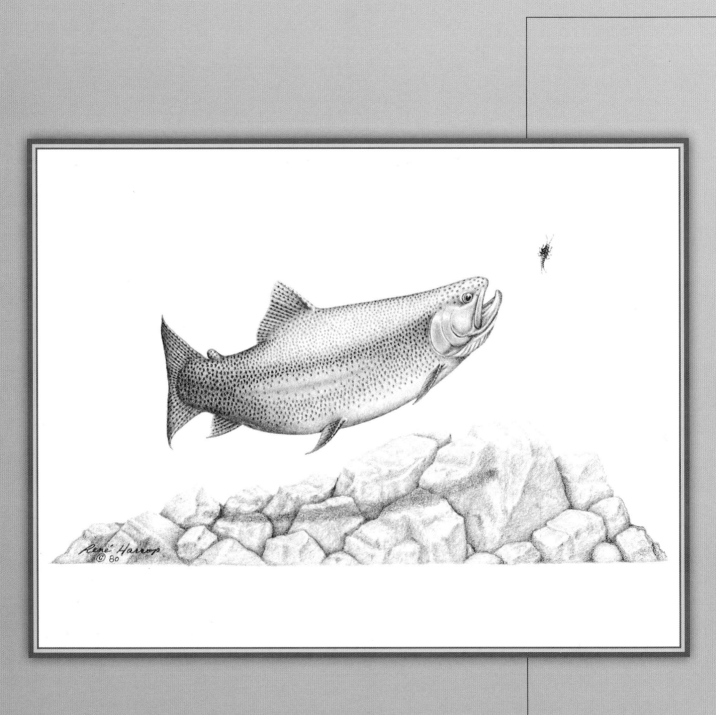

Rainbow and Stonefly Nymph
carbon pencil
9 x 11 inches

Selective Nymphing

Dry-fly fishing drives my angling consciousness. I love the idea of knowing what I am fishing to and the process involved in accomplishing a singular objective. But most of all I love the beauty and satisfaction of a perfect cast. However, the window of significant dry-fly opportunity is one of the most limited luxuries we enjoy on the water. Hatches and other on-the-water insect activity are usually of rather short duration, and their appearance does not guarantee substantial numbers of rising fish. Some of the largest trout are extremely reluctant to feed on the surface, and others never do. Therefore, even the most dedicated dry-fly advocates must diversify their approach to be able to catch fish consistently. Fortunately, you can still fish subsurface without sacrificing many of the most attractive components of dry-fly fishing.

As a descriptive term, nymphing typically involves the subsurface presentation of flies intended to imitate immature forms of aquatic insects. This is a generalization that includes caddisflies, midges, and others that are not characterized by a nymphal stage but rather by larval and pupal stages. One could also argue that egg patterns, aquatic worm imitations, and scuds also fall into the category of nymph fishing, although they do not necessarily apply to what follows. Neither does that popular practice of blind casting multiple weighted flies beneath a large strike indicator, although I acknowledge the effectiveness of this technique.

Although not for everyone, selective nymphing can provide as much challenge and visual stimulation as most anglers will ever require. Actually, finding, approaching, and fooling a large nymph-feeding trout may require more skill, patience, and discipline than any other way of fishing with a fly rod. And if success is measured in the size and significance of the trout, selective nymphing may be the most effective means of accomplishing that ambition.

Like any wild creature, a trout will exert no more energy in the process of obtaining food than is absolutely necessary. And when applied to the effort of finding and fooling fish, this simple fact of nature holds the key to much of what must be understood in order to become a truly proficient fly fisher.

Even the most prolific waters hold areas where trout will not be found and which therefore are a waste of time to fish. Conversely, some of the most favored holding areas are not easily identified by structure or other aspects associated with security. And while it is true that fish find comfort in deeper water, active feeding often takes place in shallow water as large trout maximize their opportunity to obtain food. This is especially true for insect-dependent fish that must subsist for the most part on the daily consumption of literally hundreds of drifting aquatic organisms. Thinking logically, it is easy to assume the benefit of having all subsurface food items concentrated into a shortened

Fishing a subsurface pattern in shallow water to a big brown like this can produce a level of challenge and excitement equal to that of any other type of fishing. BONNIE HARROP PHOTO

Trout feeding selectively on subsurface organisms can require precise imitation of their objectives. No less care should be taken when tying or selecting a nymph pattern than for any other insect stage. BONNIE HARROP PHOTO

Big trout often prefer subsurface feeding even when floating insects are available. Knowledge of this behavior and the associated skills it requires came together with this splendid Yellowstone cutthroat as the result. BONNIE HARROP PHOTO

water column. Effort measured in inches rather than feet translates into a high degree of feeding efficiency.

Most nymph fishermen either ignore or simply are not aware of the fish-holding potential of shallow water. And those intent upon dry-fly action usually look only above rather than beneath the surface of any water. But for the multidimensional angler who is always on the hunt for a shot at something special, peering into shallow water often reveals the most impressive target of the day. This is the habit of some of the best anglers I know, and it is not an accident that they are very good at what they do. None are satisfied with just any trout, and it is this unrelenting selectivity that sets them apart from the rest.

Finding fish during hatchless periods is a skill unto itself. In prowling shallow water, only constant stealth and observation will allow you to spot a fish before it sees you. This can only be accomplished by moving cautiously up-

stream. Frequently, streamside vegetation or other obstructions make wading a necessity when searching for thin-water trout. However, much more of the stream bottom will be revealed from an elevated bank, and the view will be expanded as your height above the water increases. Underwater visibility is best on bright days with few clouds to produce glare, and high-quality polarized sunglasses are essential for detecting a naturally camouflaged quarry.

When feeding actively beneath the surface, large trout are relatively easy to spot as they move laterally to intercept drifting insects. But it becomes a different story when they lie motionless against a cluttered background of aquatic weed, stones, or other debris. The prominent pectoral fins just behind the head will often betray an otherwise invisible fish, as will a distinct shadow beneath its body.

In adequate light conditions, you can usually see about thirty feet ahead, and this is where your attention should

I spotted this big rainbow nymphing in less than a foot of water along the edge of the Henry's Fork. Three fly changes and a perfect upstream cast were needed to fool the wary fish. BONNIE HARROP PHOTO

Natural camouflage allows a trout to blend in with its surroundings even in extremely shallow water. Nymphing subtly between tendrils of aquatic vegetation, this big rainbow was a real test of approach and presentation skills.

BONNIE HARROP PHOTO

be focused as you slowly work your way upstream. Pause often to more carefully scan any subsurface terrain that appears especially interesting. When an attractive prospect is located from the bank, it is always a good idea to move carefully back downstream before entering the water. Always remember to mentally mark the trout's position since it will likely be out of sight at this point.

Working with a partner in this type of fishing is even more effective. Keeping the fish constantly in sight, a friend on the bank can guide your approach and direct the cast when the target is out of your view. The most effective way to use this team approach is to have the angler facing directly upstream. The casting angle to the trout is treated as though it were a number on a clock, and the distance to the trout is called out in feet by the observer, e.g., "Two o'clock at twenty feet." Trout will not be alarmed by a loud human voice above the water, but tread lightly both on the bank or while wading to avoid subsurface vibrations that can signal danger.

Always bear in mind that in this situation you are presenting the fly rather than simply making a cast. Nymphing trout in shallow water are easily spooked and require no less exactness than when they are feeding on the surface. Well-lighted water may make it easier to see the fish, but it also increases the potential for warning motion, shadows, or disturbance that can instantly end the contest. It pays to use the longest leader you can handle in order to keep the line as far from the fish as possible. Delicacy and accuracy describe a perfect cast, and a well-designed leader will promote both necessities.

In most instances, I use the same leader for selective nymphing as for precise dry-fly fishing. The quick taper turns over well, even though it is longer than twelve feet. Advanced technology in tippet material provides an

Casting from an elevated bank allows you to keep a nymphing trout in view. An upstream cast is the only way to present the fly in this situation without being spotted by the fish. BONNIE HARROP PHOTO

Teaming up with a partner to spot the fish and direct the cast allows the wading angler to be successful when a nymphing trout is out of view. BONNIE HARROP PHOTO

amazing strength-to-diameter ratio. In my opinion, the great advantage of a fine tippet is not that it is better hidden from a fish, but that it obeys the nuances of current that complicate a natural drift. A small-diameter tippet is also less likely to impede the sink rate of the fly.

Trout that are not aggressively feeding present a less complex situation in terms of correctly selecting and presenting the fly. Resting but also alert for something edible, such a trout is likely to impulsively accept a nondescript artificial such as a Pheasant Tail Nymph or Gold-Ribbed Hare's Ear. Although not exclusively exempt from this type of fishing, beadhead flies and other flashy sinking patterns are perhaps better reserved for deeper and faster water where such features are more likely to trigger a response. Although exact imitation is not always required during periods of sparse insect availability, it is reasonable to assume that a trout will respond more favorably to a familiar food item. For instance, a *Baetis* nymph makes perfect sense in October when that mayfly represents the dominant hatch.

An artificial nymph drifting with little or no competition for attention will often be taken even when the cast misses its mark to the right or left. When at least four good presentations have gone unrewarded, try changing the depth of the drift before changing the imitation. Of course, on occasion a trout simply will not be interested in anything, but keep in mind that it very well might be found in the same place and in a more receptive mood on another day.

Fish feeding intensely on a heavy and diverse subsurface drift of aquatic invertebrates raise the level of both opportunity and complexity. Even a wild creature is comparatively easy to approach when deeply preoccupied with feeding, although you still must be cautious. The sight of numerous large trout ravenously consuming insects can be more than slightly unnerving, and you must exercise discipline. Like the shotgunner who must learn to pick a specific individual from a flock of quail, it is imperative that a single trout be the exclusive recipient of your attention. Random casting to more than one target places a higher dependency on luck rather than skill and seldom produces a favorable result.

Remarkably and with rare exception, trout target and consume each organism individually regardless of its size or the density of its numbers. Efficient feeding is a process of recognizing a moving prey with enough time allowed to intercept its drift. Economy of energy is paramount during an intense feeding session that may last several hours.

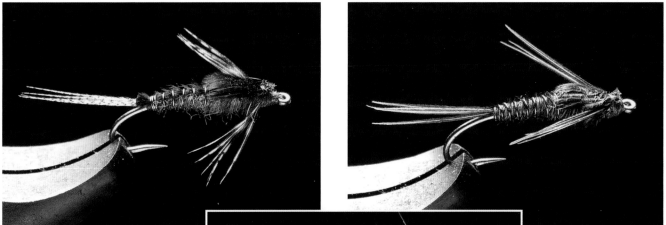

The fundamental design for a mayfly nymph is demonstrated by this *Baetis* pattern. Simple size and color adjustments are often all that is needed to imitate a variety of different mayflies in the nymphal stage. BONNIE HARROP PHOTO

There are many variations of this international favorite, but my version of the Pheasant Tail Nymph is tied to reflect the basic image of a mayfly nymph.
BONNIE HARROP PHOTO

The Gold-Ribbed Hare's Ear is a generalized nymph pattern that can work for several aquatic organisms, including mayflies and caddis. BONNIE HARROP PHOTO

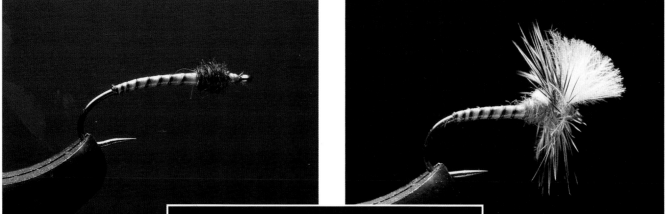

Midge larvae are abundant in most trout waters worldwide. Despite their often tiny size, they can be the target of surprisingly large fish. BONNIE HARROP PHOTO

Possessing good flotation and visibility, the CDC Hanging Midge imitates a midge in the process of emergence. It can be fished independently or as a very suitable indicator fly for a subsurface midge pattern. BONNIE HARROP PHOTO

Caddis pupae rising to the surface during emergence are a strong enticement to hungry trout. The Ascending Caddis is a lively duplication. BONNIE HARROP PHOTO

Minimized movement reduces the amount of exertion, but this is not to say that insects occurring in superior numbers will always be the prime objective when a choice is available. It is not uncommon to see a trout move a foot or more to intercept larger individual forms. This is often despite the fact that several lesser insects could be secured with less effort. The point here is that trout feeding subsurface can be no less demanding of correct fly selection than when they are feeding on top. Nymph-fishing experts leave nothing to chance in this regard. Seining beneath the water with an aquarium net will reveal the menu at hand, and the behavior of a feeding fish can aid in selecting the right pattern from multiple possibilities.

An exceptionally busy trout showing little range or lateral movement is likely to be concentrating on the form that represents the highest volume of drifting food. Comparing this observation to what is captured in the mesh would lead to selecting an imitation of the most dominant insect in terms of numbers. A slower feeding pace marked by aggressive movement to the left or right might indicate a larger but more sparsely distributed objective. Again, check the mesh of the collection net for an indication of what the trout might be taking, and select your pattern accordingly. Acute subsurface selectivity is not constant, but it is far more common than some might expect. This especially applies to large seasoned fish in waters of concentrated angler activity.

Fertile spring creeks and tailwaters are known for possessing the qualities necessary for selective nymphing. Most notable are a high volume of aquatic insects and clear, shallow water where subsurface trout can be easily observed. These often well known and highly productive streams are also noted for the requirements they place on accuracy as it applies to artificials. And while it is common to place strong emphasis on close depiction of winged and emerging forms, it appears that only a comparative handful of serious players follow similar guidelines in imitating subsurface stages. The time-honored rule of size, shape, and color used in identifying the structural priorities of imitative fly tying applies equally to both wet and dry patterns.

A trout's view beneath the surface is considerably superior to what it sees on top. But most effective nymph patterns are far less complicated in construction and design than their floating counterparts. Most are easy to tie, though tiers frequently overlook simple but important details. Although seldom elegant, a credible subsurface pattern is a neatly tied definition of the essential components of the natural it is intended to imitate, and since additional materials aren't required to help it float, there is no justification for overdressing a sinking pattern.

Presenting a sunken artificial to a visibly feeding fish almost always requires an upstream cast. And although this may seem simple enough, it is surprising how few can execute this basic skill with the delicate accuracy needed to be successful in shallow water. Perhaps this can be explained by a growing tendency among dry-fly anglers to present the fly from above rather than below the fish, which reduces the need for accuracy because the fly can be manipulated into position after it is on the water. It is a deadly maneuver but also one that carries risk for those who become exclusively dependent upon it. To me, the upstream presentation is fly casting in its most pure form, and I appreciate its aesthetics nearly as much as its practicality.

Typically, trout holding in two feet of water or less do not require a heavily weighted fly. Specially designed nymph hooks contribute both weight and functional shape to the finished fly, and attention should be given to their selection. Soft, absorbent materials provide built-in movement while contributing to a quicker sink rate as well. In my experience, a tight double wrapping of gold or copper wire in the thorax area (often just a continuation of the abdomen ribbing) is usually enough added weight to help the fly penetrate the surface while maintaining the slim profile of the natural. The depth of the drift is determined by the distance from where the fly arrives on the water to the location of the fish. This will vary according to current speed, but seldom is it necessary to deposit the fly more than three or four feet ahead of the target. Deeper water or excessively quick current may require that you add a small split shot to the tippet. These I carry in assorted sizes in an empty floatant container with the dropper tip removed. This is more convenient than the usually cumbersome dispensers in which they are purchased.

With a gentle delivery, place the fly slightly to the side rather than directly over the fish. This will minimize tippet interference with the take and also is less likely to spook your objective. As with dry-fly fishing, you are trying to produce a natural drift. And likewise, you will be challenged to strip excess line to retain close connection to the fly without inducing drag.

Although a valuable asset in detecting a take, a strike indicator can work against you by pulling the fly along more quickly than is suitable for a perfect presentation. Because current speed at the surface is faster than the current speed on the bottom, the floating indicator is likely to be moving considerably faster than a trailing fly drifting close to the bottom. When fishing alone, those who are practiced in this type of fishing concentrate on the fish itself and tighten at the slightest indication of a take. A spotter working from a position of visual advantage will issue the command "set" when he sees a take. Personally, I often rely on

Understanding subsurface feeding behavior allowed Bonnie to score on this impressive rainbow. This trout was located during a heavy mayfly hatch. Despite great abundance of floating insects, the fish never came to the surface. A weighted nymph fished upstream produced this result.
RENÉ HARROP PHOTO

the old-school technique of greasing the leader to within about six feet of the fly. Treated in this way with a gel-type fly dressing, the leader tracks well and twitches at even the slightest disruption in the drift. It is stealthier than an indicator and does not interfere with the natural drift of the fly. But remember that any mental distraction can cause you to miss the often subtle take of a big nymphing trout.

Detecting a large fish feeding selectively on subsurface food is not necessarily limited to what can be seen beneath the surface. And there are many times when a sizable disturbance on top can be mistaken for a rising fish. This often occurs when a hatch is underway and numerous winged insects are visibly distributed on the water. In my experience, extremely large trout are not usually inclined to focus upward toward the surface when an equal or superior number of edible items are available underneath. And this is often the case during the peak of a hatch. Organisms lifting from the bottom or from submerged aquatic weed are targets that trout can identify from a far greater

The CDC Palmered Caddis is a practical choice when the natural insects are active on the water. This buoyant and highly visible fly is ideal for fast water or as an indicator fly for a submerged pattern.
BONNIE HARROP PHOTO

The CDC Last Chance Cripple is a splendid imitation by itself, but its value extends equally as an indicator fly for a suspended nymph.
BONNIE HARROP PHOTO

The CDC Transitional Nymph addresses the extremely difficult times when trout become exclusively selective to emerging PMD nymphs. BONNIE HARROP PHOTO

distance than those floating overhead. It is inefficient for a trout to make an impulsive selection from the surface when a deliberate and far more accurate decision can be made by concentrating on what is drifting beneath.

Emerging insects rise to the surface to shed the exoskeleton or shuck and assume their winged form before leaving the water. Trout in pursuit of emerging nymphs may intercept the target at any point during the ascension. And when they eat it at or very near the peak, it can appear as though the trout has taken something drifting into view on the surface. A keen eye can detect the size of the fish, but the selection of a floating imitation is not the correct choice in this situation. The solution is sometimes as simple as drifting a slightly weighted pattern that represents the underwater stage of insects observed floating on the surface. A take may be revealed by a flash underneath or the appearance of a dorsal fin, tail, or other disturbance on top. It may also be practical to duplicate the ascension of the natural with a gentle lift of the rod tip. You can usually feel a take on a tight line and occasionally the fish will hook itself. The greased-leader method of strike detection works well for a dead-drift presentation, which in the right circumstance can be executed from nearly any angle as long as you do not spook the fish with your presence.

There are several reasons for using an indicator fly when fishing weighted patterns during emergence, not least of which is the constant possibility of an impulsive take on top. This likelihood is enhanced when the indicator fly duplicates a disabled or partially emerged insect in the winged stage. The Last Chance Cripple was developed for this purpose, and it looks like a helpless mayfly while floating well enough to support a nymphal pattern fished as a dropper. The same applies to a CDC Palmered Caddis Adult when emerging caddis are the object of attention. When the dropper fly is connected to the bend of the indicator fly with an improved clinch knot, you can control the depth at which the subsurface pattern drifts by adjusting the length of tippet connecting the two flies. Here, the key is finding the correct subsurface zone where a trout is concentrating its attention and then adjusting the length of the dropper accordingly. This can range from a foot or more to only a few inches beneath the surface. From an upstream position, the nymph can be made to rise toward the surface by stopping the drift of the indicator fly somewhat in advance of the trout's position. I have watched my friend Masa Katsumata execute this technique to deadly perfection during the perplexing PMD hatches of the Henry's Fork.

The Pale Morning Dun nymph is just beginning to emerge—note the split wing case. TOSHI KARITA PHOTO

Perhaps no living person has influenced my perception of subsurface selectivity than the noted entomologist and photographer Toshi Karita. In a disciplined and scientific manner, Toshi's extensive studies have revealed formerly undiscovered secrets of aquatic life, and they are translated in his remarkable photos and informative writings. Applying this information to creative fly tying has resulted in a significant improvement in my ability to successfully deal with large nymphing trout that were previously thought to be uncatchable. Transitional subsurface patterns are important contributors to a personal hatch-matching system that provides imitative solution to the full range of life stages. This system also includes emergers and cripples that depict developing or disabled insects.

The famed Pale Morning Dun hatches of the western United States provide a graphic example of how acute trout selectivity during subsurface emergence can be. I distinctly remember the day Toshi showed me a collection vial filled with the stomach contents of a single large trout taken during an intense hatch of PMDs—each of the several dozen ingested nymphs displayed exactly the same condition of partial emergence. Specifically, the only variation from a functionally intact nymph was a split in the dark wing case revealing the yellowish coloration of the emerging dun in the first phase of escape. Carrying a healthy supply of nymph patterns that address this discovery has led to many fruitful encounters since that event-

ful day of sharing with Toshi Karita, and it is only one of many. He is a special friend.

Combining the colors of both subsurface and winged stages is a prerequisite for any transitional mayfly pattern, and this often applies to caddis and midges as well. Variations in the proportion of nymphal characteristics to those of the emerging dun are often justified. And it pays to use soft and yielding materials such as marabou, chickabou, and CDC to generate the movement that goes along with nymphs in transition. But we are far from perfection in this regard. Any fly can only represent a single aspect of a rapidly changing image that shows several variations of color and configuration before the process is completed. It is unlikely that a single perfect fly will ever be found, but we can have a lot of fun trying.

It is not my intent to encourage anyone to put aside all other approaches to fly fishing in favor of selective nymphing. Certainly, there are times when the situation dictates a different method, and some waters do not possess the conditions that make it practical. There is value, however, in conditioning ourselves to be alert to opportunities that can increase our productivity on the water, and to be prepared to capitalize on those gifts made available only to the truly observant. A new awareness combined with requisite tools and skills can be added to those we already possess with minor effort or expense. And the days rescued from futility are more than a fair return on the investment.

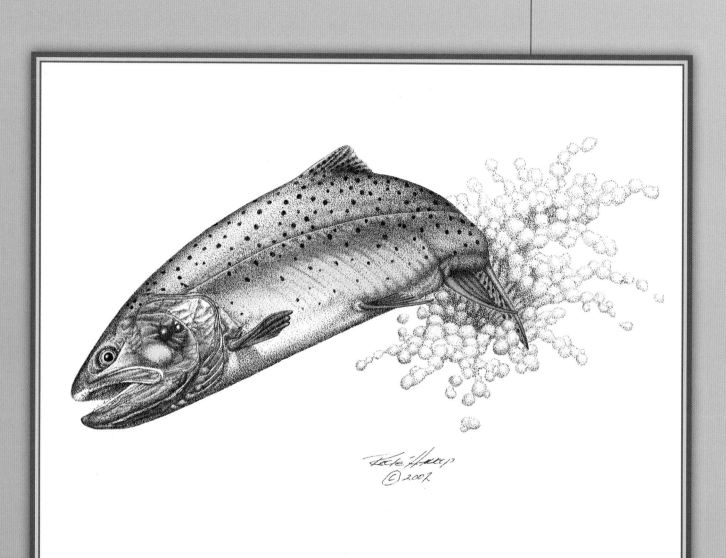

The Native **(Yellowstone cutthroat)**
pen and ink with watercolor tint
14 x 16 inches

The Value of Versatility

Eight Flies for Yellowstone Country

Yellowstone holds many meanings for the international community. Both within and just outside its boundaries are countless natural wonders that range from spectacular mountains and lush forests to thundering waterfalls that can take your breath away. The diversity of wildlife that graze the open meadows is unmatched anywhere on the North American continent, and the towering geysers and other thermal features are nearly indescribable. For the casual visitor, Yellowstone country is an incomparable destination of sights, sounds, and sensations, but for the fly fisher it is Mecca. Vast winter snowfall piles high during the cold season, but in summer it becomes cold, pure water that feeds a multitude of fertile lakes and streams, where trout are the primary residents and countless insect varieties support their numbers. Here in the high Rocky Mountain West, fly fishing is a call heard round the world and amazing are the numbers who heed its voice.

In a lifetime nearing seven decades, I have devoted the vast majority of my time probing the mysteries of legendary waters like the Yellowstone, Firehole, Madison, Snake, and the Henry's Fork. Numerous lesser-known rivers and lakes have cooled my legs but not my enthusiasm as I roam this region with a constant spirit of anticipation and discovery. In a single lifetime, it would be impossible to fish all the water in and near the park, and a close relationship with even a handful is a significant accomplishment.

With the advantage of spending my entire life near this expansive area of prime angling opportunity, I have gained a level of intimacy that has taught me which flies to carry that will cover a substantial portion of the various situations that can be encountered during the principal season that runs from mid-June through mid-September. Accumulated over dozens of years, my collection of flies number in the thousands, and my vest is always heavily weighted with as many fly boxes as it will hold. Specific imitation of known hatches is the primary focus of the majority of my tying because most of my fishing is timed to coincide with the appearance of these insects. Through experience I have learned to recognize the conditions that provide the best assurance of being on the water when the trout are active, although there is never a guarantee of complete accuracy in this regard. In general, the odds are good that I can find a fly in my vest that will meet the requirements of any given situation.

But I enjoy a luxury not extended to short-term visitors who must fish with the limitations of time and the inability to cover all possibilities of fly requirement. Most traveling anglers have ten days or less to absorb the pleasures of a fly-fishing adventure in Yellowstone country. Regardless of the conditions of weather or water, visitors will likely spend every hour possible on the water to maximize their potential for a successful trip. In advance of departure, many will

The Firehole River in Yellowstone is host to numerous aquatic hatches. With geyser activity in the background, Zach Wheeler fishes to a subtle surface feeder. BONNIE HARROP PHOTO

The abundant wildlife of Yellowstone add interest to any day spent in the park. This young bull elk seemed disinterested in the anglers fishing the Madison nearby. BONNIE HARROP PHOTO

spend hours researching the insects most likely to be encountered and tying flies to match them. In fishing, however, timing is everything, and seldom do even the best laid plans mesh precisely with the actual experience. This especially applies to the reliability of encountering the hatches you expect and having the flies that work. In many instances, avoiding large-scale disappointment is dependent upon flies that do not necessarily match a specific insect or those that duplicate a food form that is consistently recognizable to trout over a long period of time. Often these are patterns that one would not think to use, and many times they might even be omitted from the vest.

Even a resident of the Yellowstone area is subject to the advantage of carrying versatile flies that for reasons often unexplained can save the day. This is most prevalent during the warm months of summer when insect activity is most diverse and the complication of correct fly selection is at its peak due to abundance of insects and anglers. Experienced anglers on these waters have a relatively short list of flies that over time have proven themselves in a variety of situations during this period.

I recommend the following list of patterns because I have frequently caught fish with them in situations where I could not clearly identify what the fish were feeding on or I did not have an accurate imitation. Recommended sizes are stated in parentheses in the patterns. None are intended

to replace specialized patterns that specifically imitate known aquatic or terrestrial insects that are likely to be encountered during a short-term visit to the Yellowstone area. Neither should these flies be expected to perform miracles or cancel the futility of poor technique in approach and presentation. Instead, I suggest that you carry the eight patterns in this chapter in addition to a well-researched selection of flies that have relevance to the timing of the visit and the waters upon which they will be fished.

Black CDC Flying Ant

From the beginning of summer through its end, there is rarely a day that I will not tie on a Black Flying Ant when fishing the Henry's Fork. And while there are numerous times when a breeze or some other natural factor can cause these common terrestrials to be the principal food form, their value is not limited by a predominance of numbers. On warm mornings, it is common to find a sparse scattering of winged ants mixed with an assortment of mayfly spinners and caddis that give variety to the summer menu. And though these ants are often outnumbered by their aquatic counterparts, trout seem unusually willing to favor the ant when given a choice. Although unproven in my experience, it has been theorized that ants possess a type of acid that trout find to their liking and that taste may play a role in their attractiveness.

Unlike many insect types, winged ants are not subject to the limitation of a short span of availability, and they are widely distributed throughout the waters of the Yellowstone region. This means they are recognized as a food source throughout the summer months, and it is this familiarity that sustains the trout's unusual interest in them. Because of their mobility, it is appropriate to fish a winged ant imitation at midstream as well as closer to the banks where the wingless variety are found. Except during the coolest hours of early morning and evening or on an unusually cold day, a flying ant pattern is a sound option on nearly any lake or stream I have ever fished, and it has come to my rescue on more occasions than I can count. Though I stock a range of sizes in my box, I use a size 16 the most. Winged ants size 20 and smaller can also perform credibly as a midge imitation, thus adding to their versatility.

Black CDC Beetle

Like winged ants, beetles are a near constant staple throughout the warmer season. Relatively weak in flight, their mobility is generally limited to a distance of forty feet or less from shore, but their appearance is no less exciting to trout than their more mobile terrestrial cousins. Other than during breezy conditions, you should fish a beetle pattern near lush streamside vegetation where the naturals congregate. A fat, squirming beetle is a familiar and tempting sight for big trout that prowl these areas in full awareness that an easy meal can drop to the water at any time.

Highly conditioned to beetles as a daily food source, it is not uncommon for a trout to interrupt intensive focus upon heavy numbers of a different insect to accept a solitary beetle from among the mass. This inherent weakness for beetles is frequently called upon by river guides who need an option for clients who cannot handle the difficulty presented when trout are feeding selectively on mayflies or other aquatic insects. While far short of a guaranteed alternative, a beetle pattern has delivered many otherwise failed anglers from a fishless day.

In the heat of a summer day when the water seems devoid of trout and insect activity, I often extend my fishing by patiently stalking stretches of open stream bank where shallow water will often reveal a resting but alert trout. Working upstream and casting from shore, it is possible to avoid disturbance that would alert a wary trout. In this situation, a beetle can be just as likely to be of interest to the fish as any other pattern. Presenting a fly in this condition requires a gentle and accurate delivery that can be enhanced with a long, delicate leader. Crouching low or kneeling will reduce the likelihood of spooking the fish with either your body or the motion of casting.

Warm and bright conditions can send large trout to the shaded areas where beetles also find comfort. Occasionally,

Black CDC Flying Ant

Hook:	TMC 206BL size 14-22 (16)
Thread:	Black 8/0 UNI-Thread
Abdomen:	Black TroutHunter Pro dubbing
Stabilizers:	One black moose hair on each side of abdomen
Wings:	Paired medium dun CDC feathers
Hackle:	Black Whiting dry fly
Thorax:	Black TroutHunter Pro dubbing

Black CDC Beetle

Hook:	TMC 206BL size 12-18 (14)
Thread:	Black 8/0 UNI-Thread
Wing cover:	2-4 black TroutHunter CDC feathers over peacock herl
Body:	Peacock herl
Legs:	Black CDC fibers

you'll spot a rise in the shadows, but blind fishing a beetle imitation beneath overhanging vegetation can also be productive. And although difficult to always avoid, surprise should never result when a trout rises to a beetle.

CDC Adams Biot Parachute

Perhaps no single dry fly is better known worldwide than the Adams. This timeless classic has been modified in a variety of ways by many tiers, and I am not an exception in this regard. It is generally believed that the original Adams was originated as a caddis imitation, but when tied parachute style with several alterations of the materials, the Adams becomes a versatile mayfly imitation.

Specific to none but suggestive of many, the CDC Adams Biot Parachute assumes a more accurate profile of a mayfly than the bulky overdressed creations we have grown accustomed to seeing over the years. A slender biot body creates a realistic impression of the segmented abdomen of an actual mayfly, which can lend a more realistic image when fished to finicky trout on slow, clear water. Parachute-style hackle in modest quantity duplicates the natural position of a mayfly's legs while providing adequate flotation on all types of water. A vertical wing post of white CDC provides superior balance and visibility with-

out sacrificing the correct wing profile of a mayfly dun. By trimming the wing post to about one quarter of normal height, the fly is transformed into a low-floating emerging style, which can be enhanced by trimming the tail about 50 percent as well.

Most experts in the sport place color of the fly behind size and shape in the order of importance when imitating a particular insect. For this reason, I suspect that many trout will accept neutral coloration when the natural insect of interest is a different shade. And while often short of ideal, the subtle gray of the CDC Adams Biot Parachute has proven adequate in many situations when a closer imitation could not be found.

CDC Rusty Paraspinner (Trusty Rusty)

There is a good reason why the CDC Rusty Paraspinner is fondly referred to as "Trusty Rusty" by many river guides in Yellowstone country. Finding a fly that consistently produces day in and day out through a long season of guiding is a rarity for these hard-working men who survive by helping others catch trout. Most learn right away that while mayfly spinners are among the most common sources of trout food they also represent severe frustration for a client

Streamside vegetation can be loaded with terrestrial insects. Fishing a CDC Beetle along the shaded bank on the headwaters of the Snake is not generally wasted effort. BONNIE HARROP PHOTO

Leslie Harrop fishes a delicate CDC Parachute during a mayfly hatch on this lovely spring creek near Yellowstone.
BONNIE HARROP PHOTO

CDC Adams Biot Parachute

Hook:	TMC 100 BL size 12-22 (16)
Thread:	Gray 8/0 UNI-Thread
Tail:	Brown hackle fibers or Whiting Coq de Leon
Abdomen:	Muskrat gray TroutHunter goose or turkey biot
Thorax:	Muskrat gray TroutHunter Pro dubbing
Wing post:	Paired white TroutHunter CDC feathers trimmed to length
Hackle:	Cree or mixed brown and grizzly Whiting hackle

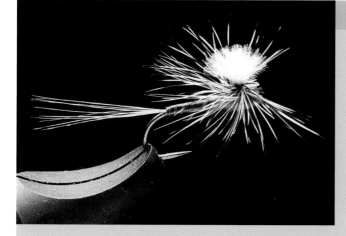

CDC Rusty Paraspinner

Hook:	TMC 100 BL size 12-22 (16)
Thread:	Rust 8/0 UNI-Thread
Tail:	Grizzly hackle fibers or Whiting Coq de Leon
Abdomen:	Rust TroutHunter goose or turkey biot
Thorax:	Rust TroutHunter dubbing
Wing post:	Paired white TroutHunter CDC feathers trimmed to 1/3 usual length
Hackle:	Whiting grizzly hackle two sizes larger than usual trimmed in a wide V over hook eye

The Madison River in Montana is a quick-moving stream that must be waded with great caution. Fast currents make it more difficult for a dry fly to stay afloat. Here, Bonnie works the edge with a CDC Tailwater Special that does a credible job of riding the choppy surface. RENÉ HARROP PHOTO

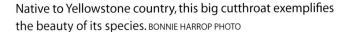

Native to Yellowstone country, this big cutthroat exemplifies the beauty of its species. BONNIE HARROP PHOTO

who must fish a low-floating imitation that is extremely difficult to see on the water. Developing an imitation that provides suitable visibility to the angler while retaining the vital characteristics of a mayfly lying flush on the water with wings outspread was made possible by a complete departure from conventional spinner design.

It was Bonnie's idea to incorporate grizzly hackle tied parachute style into the configuration of spent wings. The hackle is two sizes larger than normal and trimmed over the eye to form a fanned effect reminiscent of veined spent mayfly wings. Like the Adams CDC Biot Parachute, the wing post for the Paraspinner consists of paired white CDC feathers. Trimmed to only about a third of the usual wing height, the CDC wing post is concealed from view beneath the fly by the dubbed thorax and radiating fibers from the base of the parachute hackle. Though only a small white dot when viewed on the water, it is remarkably easy to follow the drift of the Paraspinner at common casting distance. Superior flotation from the parachute hackle and CDC makes this a suitable pattern for even the Madison, where other spinners disappear in the chop.

Mayfly spinners are recognized by trout as a vulnerable food source due to their inability to leave the water.

While the color can vary from species to species, no fewer than six prominent mayflies are matched in the spinner stage by a reddish brown or rust-colored Paraspinner during the course of the summer season. It is a color that is associated with food to trout grown accustomed to the consistency with which it appears on the water. "Trusty Rusty" has earned its reputation as one of the most reliable patterns for waters within and beyond the boundaries of Yellowstone.

Olive CDC Tailwater Special

The CDC Tailwater Special is a crossover pattern that bridges the visual similarities of a variety of naturals that fall into the general category of down-wing insects, from caddis to stoneflies to terrestrials. It was created to address the diversity of conditions associated with rivers that flow from lakes or reservoirs known to anglers as tailwaters. Tailwaters are typically prolific with populations of both trout and insects that exceed what is commonly encountered on many other streams. Current speed and surface characteristics can range from long, slow glides, through soft shallow riffles, to rushing stretches where wading becomes a precarious act. To be uniformly effective, an artificial must possess a degree of realism that will withstand the scrutiny of a seasoned trout in clear, moderate current while retaining the flotational capacity to ride a fast moving current as it bounces over a boulder-strewn bottom. The CDC Tailwater Special meets this criterion.

Black CDC Bubble Back Caddis

The CDC Bubble Back Caddis was designed to duplicate the elusive image of a caddis as it begins its transformation from pupa to adult. As a specific imitation, it is tied in a variety of sizes and colors to match an assortment of individual caddis species, and its productivity during emergence is difficult to equal. Its value, however, is not limited to those situations where trout are interested in only exact imitations.

During a quiet period on the Firehole, I stumbled upon a situation that revealed a broader application of the Bubble Back Caddis as a fill-in fly for times when I didn't have

a more correct imitation. In water warmed by thermal inflow, a sparse hatch of fairly large, dark midges had attracted the interest of several browns that enjoyed complete immunity from everything contained in my box of midges. It was of near desperation that I tied on a size 16 Black Bubble Back Caddis and drifted it over the first of a string of sipping rises. The trout took on the second cast, and I played it quickly to net. The process was repeated until four more browns in the 12- to 15-inch range had been landed, and then the activity stopped. Thirty minutes later, I spotted a solitary rise that showed discreetly against the far bank. Working my way into casting position, I noticed a few PMDs drifting on water unaffected by the geyser activity near the side of the river I had just left. Not bothering to change flies, I made a good cast that drifted only inches from the overhanging grass, and the trout took the little Bubble Back without hesitation. While never heavy, the hatch of PMDs continued for nearly an hour, but I never did change to a corresponding pattern. Apparently, the low profile of the pupa pattern was a close enough match to convince a half dozen or so browns and two rainbows that the fly was an emerging PMD.

Since that memorable day on one of my favorite rivers in Yellowstone, I have come to rely on the CDC Bubble Back Caddis for a number of situations that do not include

Olive CDC Tailwater Special

Hook:	TMC 200R BL size 12-18 (14)
Thread:	Olive 8/0 UNI-Thread
Abdomen:	Olive TroutHunter Pro dubbing
Rib:	Palmered Whiting grizzly hackle
Wing:	Paired natural light brown (tan) TroutHunter CDC feathers
Thorax:	Peacock herl
Hackle:	Brown Whiting

Black CDC Bubble Back Caddis

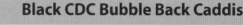

Hook:	TMC 206 BL size 14-20 (16)
Thread:	Black 8/0 UNI-Thread
Shuck:	Sparse black TroutHunter CEN dubbing over 3 wood duck fibers
Abdomen:	Black TroutHunter CEN dubbing
Wings:	Paired black TroutHunter CDC feathers cupped over abdomen to create a domed effect
Legs:	Brown Hungarian partridge fibers tied as a collar
Thorax:	Black TroutHunter CEN dubbing

This small mountain stream is loaded with wild trout of rather modest size that are seldom disturbed. A small CDC Bubble Back Caddis produced well despite limited insect activity. BONNIE HARROP PHOTO

Brown trout inhabit many waters both inside Yellowstone and nearby. BONNIE HARROP PHOTO

the very insect it originally was intended to imitate. Although I cannot explain why this fly will at times produce during a mayfly hatch, it is not difficult to understand how it can easily be mistaken for a small beetle or ant by an alert trout. Perhaps it is the compact form and its low-floating profile that suggest a generalized portrayal of emergence that bring a positive response. But for whatever reason, it is a fly that trout seem to like, and I fish it often.

CDC Lime Trude

The Trude fly is attributed to A. S. Trude, who was among the earliest anglers to fish the Henry's Fork. Although now relegated to history, the Trude fly and its originator survive in what is now referred to as the Trude style of tying a dry fly. Described in simple terms, a Trude consists of a tail, body, and hackle, with its most distinctive characteristic being the wing, which is tied low over the body of the fly. Modern tiers have substituted white calf hair for improved visibility over the original squirrel-tail wing, but little else has changed since Mr. Trude first fished the fly early in the last century. Tied in a variety of body colors, the modern Trude is not a specific imitation but rather a suggestion of life and, therefore, food to an unsuspecting trout. This is especially true on quick, broken water where trout do not get a clear view of the fly before it is whisked away by the current.

For years I had been skeptical of flies that most would consider to be attractor patterns. However, my resistance in this regard quickly ended on a June day of fishing with my friend Rick Smith on the Madison River just outside of Yellowstone. As knowledgeable as anyone on this riffled section of prime trout habitat, Rick provided a daylong demonstration with a lime-colored Trude that has forever changed my opinion of this historic fly design. I watched in amazement as he probed the likely holding water, raising trout after trout during a two-hour period when surface activity was nonexistent. Later during an impressive caddis hatch that lasted until dark, Rick continued to take trout at a remarkable pace without ever changing flies.

Taking the lesson to heart, I began fishing a revised Trude featuring a biot body and CDC wings not only on the Madison but other waters where flotation and visibility are of primary concern. While not always the answer, the Trude has proven itself worthy of a place in my fly box. Usually fished during quiet periods on faster water, it has contributed to an extension of my productive time when I might otherwise have taken a nap. However, a case can also be made for fishing the fly during periods of pronounced caddis activity.

Turkey Tail Nymph

Although purely a guess, I would not be surprised if the majority of anglers worldwide carried some version of the renowned Pheasant Tail Nymph. Proven beyond question to be effective in virtually any location where trout are found, the PT Nymph is unique in its simplicity of design and construction, with the original tied with only wire and pheasant tail. Like the Gold-Ribbed Hare's Ear, the Pheasant Tail is somewhat generic in terms of its application to nymphal forms, but the latter seems generally superior in the waters of Yellowstone country. But while it is certainly a reliable pattern, there is a reasonable argument for an alternative to the Pheasant Tail on waters where it has become too popular.

Highly productive rivers like the Madison and Henry's Fork are the target of experienced anglers and professional river guides who rely heavily on the Pheasant Tail Nymph for subsurface action. Subjected to a near constant barrage of suspended Pheasant Tail Nymphs, caught and released trout can become conditioned to associate this familiar image with danger. On many occasions, I have observed impressive trout actually spook away from a carefully presented PT Nymph with nothing more than its presence to explain the alarm. Counteracting such negative reaction is often as simple as fishing a pattern that differs in color while retaining key elements of nymphal configuration.

The Turkey Tail Nymph uses the beautifully marked brown fibers from a wild turkey tail feather, which distinctly contrasts the reddish brown hue of the Pheasant Tail Nymph. Ribbed with fine gold wire, the Turkey Tail Nymph provides further separation from its more familiar counterpart, which is ribbed with copper wire.

Carried as a companion rather than a replacement for the time-honored Pheasant Tail, the Turkey Tail Nymph is a dependable general nymphing pattern as well as a specific imitation for a number of important mayflies that inhabit waters both near and far from Yellowstone.

CDC Lime Trude

Hook:	TMC 100 BL size 12-18 (14)
Thread:	Olive 8/0 UNI-Thread
Tail:	Whiting Coq de Leon or brown hackle fibers
Abdomen:	Lime-green TroutHunter biot
Wing:	Paired white TroutHunter CDC feathers
Thorax:	Lime-green TroutHunter Pro dubbing
Hackle:	Brown Whiting

Turkey Tail Nymph

Hook:	TMC 200R BL size 12-20 (14)
Thread:	Brown 8/0 UNI-Thread
Tail:	Brown turkey tail fibers
Rib:	Fine gold wire
Abdomen:	Brown turkey tail fibers
Thorax:	Brown turkey tail fibers
Wing case:	Brown turkey tail fibers

Deep Water Decision
acrylic
18 x 24 inches

A Lesson in Humility

On glossy paper, the fish could have been easily mistaken for a salmon. Dark spots the size of small coins covered a length of more than two feet, and the long, hooked lower jaw was more than slightly menacing. But the magazine article said it was a brown trout, and a closer examination of the photo verified the caption. Vivid hues of bronze, gold, and deep copper set its broad flanks ablaze with the colors of autumn, and in the process identified the season. Although rather vague on details, the article described spectacular streamer fishing on a remote river only one state and about a day's drive away. And of course, the temptation to go after those giant browns was simply too strong to resist.

Impulsive decisions are often risky, but I was too young at the time to consider the perils of a hastily planned trip into unfamiliar territory. In mid-October, the timing seemed to be right, and my imagination had no room for problems or failure. I packed my gear and headed for Wyoming at about five p.m. on a Friday. My plan was to fish the weekend and return home in time for work on Monday morning. As is typical with youth, I felt confident that my skills and two full days were adequate to achieve my objective, and the miles melted away as imagined scenes of fly-fishing victory filled my head.

At no time during the drive did I anticipate a problem so severe as failing to find my destination, but that is what happened. I expected to arrive at the recommended campground around midnight. At four a.m. I was still wandering the back roads of the barren desert searching for access to the river until a nearly empty fuel tank forced me to sleep in the car in the middle of nowhere. It was ten a.m. before I found a place to refuel and get directions to the campground. After backtracking more than sixty miles on the highway, I spotted the small access sign I had missed the night before, and a few minutes later I could finally see the river. Anticipation quickly replaced the anguish of losing a half day of fishing when I saw a male brown of enormous proportions launch itself over a slow deep run adjacent to where I stood assembling my tackle.

Filled with expectation, I eased into the water at the head of the campground run and shot a sixty-foot cast through the crisp autumn air. Five hours and three hundred yards of river later, I was still waiting for the first strike. At last, as the sun left the water and the temperature began to plummet, I felt a sharp tug and the weight of a fish. But the exhilaration of the initial pull lasted only through the first short run as it became quickly apparent that the fish was not of exceptional size. Although respectable by most standards, the eighteen-inch rainbow was actually almost a disappointment. Trout of similar size and species were plentiful in my home waters and also available with far less effort than the hundreds of fruitless casts required for

A spill in the frigid waters of autumn can prove deadly. Always important, careful wading saves you from more than simple discomfort. Hypothermia is a serious matter.
BONNIE HARROP PHOTO

Like brown trout, big rainbows are a prime target in the fall. There was no disappointment in catching this autumn beauty despite the fact that it took a nymph rather than a streamer. BONNIE HARROP PHOTO

a single fish. With now chilled fingers, I slipped the size 6 streamer from the rainbow's jaw and watched it disappear into the darkening water.

Clearly underdressed for the conditions, I decided on a warm fire as the first item of business back in camp. But I was again shivering by the time I pitched the small tent and put my gear in order. The difficulties of the preceding twenty-four hours had taken their toll, and I settled for a hastily warmed dinner of soup eaten directly from the can before crawling wearily into the down sleeping bag. Undaunted, however, by discomfort and minor disappointment, my hopes ran high for the following day as I quickly drifted into sleep.

Not surprisingly, the sun had climbed well into the morning sky when I emerged from the frost-encrusted tent two hours later than planned. A fire and hot coffee were out of the question, and like the firewood, my wading shoes left outside the tent were frozen solid. A stream thermometer clipped to a vest pocket read 15 degrees F as I moved my wading gear inside the tent to thaw by the heat

of a gas lantern. In my haste to hit the road, I had not considered the possibility of such frigid temperatures. With no extra insulation between the old-style latex waders, I was chilled before ever entering the water. A thin apron of ice crackled beneath my feet and my unprotected fingers were numb before ever making a cast.

Anchored by the memory of the single big brown trout that had shown himself the day before, I began fishing the same run at about nine a.m. Less than a dozen casts later I was rewarded with a twin of the first rainbow, but the rest of the run yielded nothing more. Hungry and discouraged, I returned to camp for a beer and a quick sandwich. With only a few hours of fishing time remaining, my optimism for a big brown was now only a faint glimmer.

A quarter-mile downstream from the deserted campground, the near bank lifted sharply fifty feet above the river. With fading energy and enthusiasm, I headed for the high bank to scan the water for one final attempt at finding what I had come here for. Random groups of what appeared to be whitefish and an impressive school of small kokanee salmon were all that came to eye in more than an hour of walking and watching. But the water became more interesting as the river began to bend back to the north. Still, I could see nothing of serious interest until I reached the tail of a deep, green pool. There, silhouetted against a white clay bottom, lurked the dark shapes of four very large fish.

Trembling with excitement, I gingerly picked my way down the almost vertical bank to the river below. Crouching low, I eased into casting position and with a roll cast deposited the streamer about forty feet out into the current. Adding two looping upstream mends to allow the fly to sink, I waited a few seconds before beginning a pulsing retrieve using short, quick strips with the line hand and an occasional twitch of the rod tip. After a half dozen repetitions of the same presentation went ignored, I quickly added two small split shot about eighteen inches above the leader and then dropped the fly six feet farther upstream to achieve a deeper drift. About midway through the second pass, the streamer stopped. An instinctive lift of the rod tip met solid resistance, but there was nothing to indicate life at the end of the line. For several seconds I stood with the rod bowed against unyielding weight, and then it began to move. Slowly at first, it began to travel in a quartering direction downstream, and then the spool began to revolve more rapidly as line melted from the reel.

Soon only backing showed in the guides, and there was no sign that whatever I had hooked had any intention of stopping. Leaving the water, I scrambled along the cobbled bank, applying moderate pressure and occasionally retrieving a little line as I followed clumsily behind a still hidden combatant. Finally, nearly a hundred yards distant, a great golden form materialized in a sparkling spray that glowed in the lowering sun. In gentler water, it seemed to lose some of its stubborn strength that had taken me nearly

a quarter mile downstream from the point of contact. Encouraged, I began to lean more heavily on the rod in the hope of working the brute closer to my side of the river, but he still had enough juice left to keep the conflict in high gear. It was not a spectacular fight with searing power runs or head-shaking leaps above the water. Instead, it was a dogged battle conducted close to the bottom but punctuated periodically with an angry thrashing at the surface that continued to confirm the massive bulk. Gradually, the resistance began to weaken and the struggle was now against just sheer weight as the fish rested in the shadows that now darkened the river beneath the towering bank.

Beaching the monster was the only viable landing option, but that meant leading it into knee-deep water that would almost guarantee a violent reaction. Gambling that the 1X tippet would withstand a final forceful surge, I moved to a point parallel to its position. With an aching forearm and cramped fingers, I reeled tightly against the weight and then pulled hard toward the bank, keeping the rod low. My plan seemed to be working as I stepped from the water and began to lead the fish toward the sloping bank.

Inevitably, there is a moment of truth in any engagement with an exceptional adversary. In fishing, we must depend upon our mind and perfectly functioning tackle in order to prevail. Getting the fish on shore meant lifting a massive head nearly six inches above the surface to clear a slight ledge between water and land. There was no surprise at the violent eruption of panic and fury as the 6-weight was bowed to nearly double over the thrashing weight. The powerful thrust of a broad tail demanded instant line release, but the undersize reel was jammed tight. Only a second separated a cracking sound from the collapse of the butt section just forward of my hand. In panic, I threw the shat-

'09

Big trout demand strong tackle. The size of this trout is indicated by the bow in the 6-weight rod, which was close to being overmatched. BONNIE HARROP PHOTO

A brown like this is a suitable reward for the sacrifices in comfort that can accompany autumn streamer fishing.
BONNIE HARROP PHOTO

tered rod to the side and pounced on the slippery, struggling form. It was a wrestling match for the ages with no clear indication of a winner for several minutes. Eventually, I was able to get both arms around my muscular opponent, and I crawled from the shaded water clutching the prize. But sometime between that point and the collapse of my rod, I realized that something was definitely out of place.

At 30-plus inches, the great fish was certainly large enough to equal or exceed anything my imagination might have produced prior to that time. However, instead of the magnificent brown trout I was expecting, my hard-won trophy was a massive carp in obvious excess of 10 pounds. It had been foul hooked in the dorsal fin, which provided even greater advantage during the twenty-minute battle. With confused emotion, I freed the streamer and pushed the gasping creature back into the dark current. Wet, cold, and thoroughly dejected, I gathered the pieces of the broken rod and headed back to my car.

A heavy mist settled over the river as I packed my gear in preparation for the long drive home. There would be more than eight hours to ponder the events of a poorly planned trip and a river that seemed to have the last laugh on an enthusiastic but ill-prepared visitor. The temptation was to blame a generalized magazine article and its author for my failings, but deep inside I knew the fault was mostly mine.

Less than a year later I met the river guide who had introduced that writer to the fall migration of brown trout in the Green River above Flaming Gorge Reservoir. After listening to the pathetic tale of my ill-fated visit to the same location, he patiently explained that I had arrived about ten days too early to hit the peak of the run. Fishing the bright period of the day was pointless while the trout rested in the deep pools, although one could expect to see the occasional sporting rise that would reveal their presence. (Contrasted with a feeding rise, a sporting rise is something male trout, steelhead, and salmon do during spawning season.) The special streamers he showed me were about double the size of anything I had tried there the previous fall and were tied on hooks more often associated with saltwater species. He chuckled when I told him about the big carp and broken 6-weight rod and then

Sunset comes early, and the temperature can plummet in a Rocky Mountain autumn. It pays to dress warmly, even when the day begins on a comfortable note. It is almost certain to change. BONNIE HARROP PHOTO

added that his personal choice was a 10-weight for the lake-run browns that could run in excess of 15 pounds. All of this was information not included in the article, along with the fact that temperatures approaching 0 degrees F were not uncommon even in October. Feeling progressively more uncomfortable as my story went on, I omitted the part about getting lost on my first night there. We shook hands and I thanked him for the information and advice. He has been a good friend ever since.

I returned to the Green the following autumn in the last week of October. A larger tent warmed by a catalytic heater had enough space to keep me and all my gear ice-free during the frigid nights along the river. I had at least one extra of every item of cold-weather clothing that might be needed and a new pair of insulated waders as well. I had a new 9-weight graphite rod with an 8-weight fiberglass backup, both fitted with oversized reels containing loads of extra backing, and two large fly boxes jammed with brightly colored bucktails and streamers up to size 2/0—with tools and materials to tie more. I also brought along, but never used, a five-gallon container of extra gasoline and several detailed maps.

With enough time and provisions to fish for five days, I concentrated my efforts on the three hours just before and after dawn followed by an equal amount of time from dusk to darkness. Fishing was never fast, as I worked the quicker runs between deep pools, but the trout I caught were all impressive browns. A male taken on the third

This has been a productive style for fall streamer fishing where ever it is fished. The same configuration tied in brown and olive are also useful in this season. BONNIE HARROP PHOTO

evening was a duplicate in dimensions and weight to the giant carp of the year before and remains the largest trout I have ever landed on a fly.

My annual pilgrimage to the Green lasted for more than half a decade, during which time I came to love the special beauty and energy of the place despite its harshness and desolation. Sadly, however, a change in fisheries management in the late 1970s brought an abrupt end to the greatest trophy brown trout fishery I have ever known. But despite the glorious exhilaration that marked the ensuing years, the memory of greatest personal value and influence is of my first trip to the Green and its lesson in humility. From that point on, any adventure into new territory has always been preceded by disciplined planning and preparation aimed totally at avoiding failure. And because this policy has paid off, I suppose that old carp deserves at least some of the credit.

Rainbow and Mayflies
carbon pencil with watercolor tint
18 x 20 inches

A Formula for Success

It could be said, I suppose, that enjoying a trip to the Rocky Mountain West or elsewhere is not necessarily dependent on catching fish. However, most traveling anglers expect something more for their time and expense than just viewing magnificent scenery and enjoying the spacious landscape. Traveling anglers not only want to catch some fish, but they often want to catch fish that are larger than those found on their home waters. Often standing in the way of accomplishing this objective are the seemingly whimsical forces of nature. Add to this a wild and free-living trout whose comfort and even survival are dependent upon a constant ability to avoid capture. Confronting uncontrollable factors is a feature of any day spent on the water, and the ability to counter these intrinsic aspects is what separates success from failure. And though nothing is guaranteed, the odds of a fulfilling experience favor the resourceful individual who leaves as little as possible to chance.

Today's fingertip access to instant information gives little excuse for a poorly planned trip to virtually any location on the planet. With assumption as a prime risk factor in any journey of unfamiliarity, it is important to answer the key questions well before you depart. Specifics pertaining to travel are often available directly from the internet with commercial and governmental web sites providing logistical assistance to groups and individuals. Perhaps the most reliable source of current and accurate information relating directly to your destination is on-site businesses that specialize in hosting visiting anglers. The most progressive outfitters and fly shops are accustomed to providing service to foreign travelers, and some even employ bilingual staff members to further enhance the comfort of their customers. Establishing an identity and a relationship with a reliable fly shop is an effective way of accessing accurate and current information both before and during your visit. Do not hesitate to ask questions regardless of how foolish or basic they might seem, remembering that it is their job to provide assistance. Also, request and then check out references that can verify that you have selected the right lodge, outfitter, or fly shop.

Ideally, any first visit to remote locations lacking services is made in the company of someone who is familiar with that area. This could be in the form of an experienced friend or professional river guide, either of which can simplify the exploration of lesser known waters. Without this assistance, it pays to fully research every conceivable detail that might influence the adventure. Safety as much as comfort should be considered central to any plan that takes you away from the security of civilization. Wild country possesses beauty and special opportunity, but it is not

A guided float trip allows the visiting angler to capitalize on local knowledge and expertise. Floating the remote canyon water of the South Fork of the Snake can be an unforgettable experience. BONNIE HARROP PHOTO

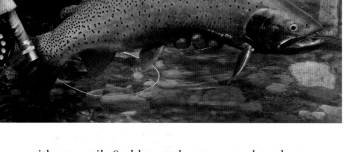

This big Yellowstone cutthroat was caught on an early September day when the maximum temperature reached only 40 degrees F. The temperature reached 80 degrees on the following day. The prudent angler will plan for such extremes when preparing a trip to the states of Montana, Wyoming, and Idaho. BONNIE HARROP PHOTO

without peril. Sudden and severe weather changes can bring danger to an unprepared visitor who assumes the reliability of seasonal conditions. This applies especially to areas of high elevation where winter-like conditions can occur at any time. The onset of hypothermia can be quick and deadly. Protective clothing should be a primary component of any angler's gear bag, and no fishing vest should be without a water- and wind-resistant wading jacket.

Difficult access seems to go hand in hand with most attractive fishing locations where human activity is light. Rough and unimproved roads are best negotiated with a high-clearance all-wheel-drive vehicle that provides passage over rocky and deeply rutted stretches where precarious mud holes can also be a problem. The value of a detailed map backed up with a GPS and a cellular phone should be clear to anyone who ventures off the beaten path in search of undisturbed water. And finally, let someone know where you are headed and when you plan to return.

In my line of work, I am subjected to a constant flow of visitors from all parts of the world. The Rocky Mountain West boasts an international reputation for bountiful waters and fishing opportunity that most can only dream of. And although the famous waters in and around Yellowstone can justify this lofty position, this trout-rich region is no longer in the primitive condition that it was just a few decades ago. In prime time, the most accessible and popular rivers are loaded with anglers of varying degrees of experience and skill, and because of this near constant attention, only the most qualified actually fulfill the expectations commonly derived from vast publicity aimed at drawing business to the region. And while it is true that many obstacles confronting the inexperienced can be removed by using the services of a highly competent professional guide, many cannot afford or choose not to take this route. Despite the added challenge of dealing with unfamiliar waters, anyone who prepares well can have a satisfying experience.

Perhaps the most neglected aspect of preparing for a trip to the Rocky Mountain West is physical conditioning. On the Henry's Fork for example, one should be prepared to spend hours walking the open riverbank in search of a trophy fish. At more than a mile above sea level, this necessity can be exhausting to even those accustomed to the same activity at lower elevation. Wading big and often forceful rivers can place excessive demands on those not accustomed to such physical exertion. A strength and endurance program is good insurance against fatigue and mishap that can subtract from the pleasure and efficiency of a long day on the water.

Timing is everything, and matching the appropriate season to the type of fishing you hope to experience is an effective way of minimizing the surprise element. Careful

The chance for a splendid rainbow like this attracts hundreds of expectant anglers to the bountiful waters of the Rocky Mountain West. Success in this regard is dependent upon thoughtful planning and preparation. BONNIE HARROP PHOTO

research can reveal what to expect in terms of hatches, weather conditions, tackle requirements, and other pertinent information. Since severe weather and other temporary problems can disrupt even the best-laid plans, you should fortify your visit with an alternative strategy in the event something goes wrong with your first priority. This

June snow on the Centennial Range is a vivid reminder that extreme weather can occur at any time in the Rocky Mountains. Regardless of the season, it pays to bring warm clothing when visiting this region of the United States. RENÉ HARROP PHOTO

Colorado angler Jim Bartschi was greeted by nearly a foot of snow when he arrived on the Henry's Fork in early October. Despite the harshness of the day, Jim found plenty of big trout rising to a heavy hatch of *Baetis*. He was fishing in shirt sleeves a few days later. BONNIE HARROP PHOTO

means identifying in advance those close-by options that may serve to salvage an otherwise lost opportunity.

Once committed to the water, it is too late to make radical changes in just about everything except the spot you are fishing. With sadness, I recall one particular group of Japanese visitors to my home water who spent nearly an entire week fishing the same limited piece of water where they had spotted a single good fish on the first day. Going nearly fishless from that point on led to a very disgruntled foursome who left the Henry's Fork in bitter disappointment. Asking for advice can often mean putting pride aside, even though most accomplished fly fishers are quick to provide tidbits of helpful information to a struggling fellow angler. Shyness or ego should never be allowed to interfere with an opportunity to gain advantage when time is limited and success becomes elusive. Walking and watching is inherent to the Henry's Fork experience and any other broad water where the fish are dispersed by the nature of opportunity. Individual trout prosper and grow large in uncrowded habitat, and the largest are often reclusive. Exceptions, of course, do exist, but it is wise to expect

considerable difficulty in recognizing subtle and secretive behavior that eludes the casual or inexperienced observer. With this in mind, you should come prepared to cover a relatively large amount of water in each day of fishing and to search diligently both above and below the surface. And bear in mind that you must also be prepared to fish the correct imitation in a manner appropriate to the trout's location and behavior.

Unless you live and fish in an area of big water, wind, and the constant potential for large trout, it is unlikely that your favorite tackle will meet the demands of a typical western river. Longer casts in less-than-ideal weather conditions are not necessarily the rule, but they will factor into virtually any day on the water. Failing because you are fishing a rod of short-range capacity on water where a forty-foot presentation or even longer can be needed at any given time is an avoidable problem if you plan ahead. The same applies to the struggle of trying to punch an effective cast into a stiff breeze with a weak-action rod. Playing a fish in excess of 20 inches can place severe mental pressure on one who is not accustomed to such things. A responsive rod with enough backbone to withstand the rigors of a heavyweight battle that may stretch on for several minutes has clear advantage over one more suited for enjoying the limited tenacity of small trout. A rod significantly shorter than 9 feet in length will generally subtract from its ability to cover the wide variety of presentation requirements of most waters common to the Rocky Mountain West. I prefer a rod with crisp action but without the extreme rigidity that tends to be restricted to only long-range efficiency. When dry-fly fishing, my policy is to approach the fish as closely as is possible with something in the neighborhood of twenty-five feet being the ideal casting distance. A long cast should be reserved for only those situations when no other choice is available, which on deeper waters can be frequent.

A smooth-running reel with good backing capacity is the best insurance for successfully bringing an exceptional fish to net. I am fond of large-arbor reels that seem to minimize tangling or jamming of the line on the spool. A reliable drag system becomes highly important when you are engaged with a large fish on light tippet or when it is more than a hundred yards into the backing. A cheap or poorly designed reel has no place in the serious fly fisher's arsenal,

and sympathy will not come to those who try to use it as an excuse for having the trip of a lifetime go wrong.

Advantages stemming from modern fly-line technology have been surprisingly overlooked by many who could benefit by specially designed tapers that conform to specific types of fishing. Performance is the bottom line on many western spring creeks and tailwaters where precise accuracy and control are as critical as any place on earth. Trout in these insect-rich waters are not forgiving of even the slightest mistake. Correct line performance for this kind of fishing is entirely different than when shooting long casts with a nymph or streamer. The prudent dry-fly angler will match his rod and reel with a line that will float high, mend smoothly, and turn over a long leader.

No one on their first visit to strange water will be naturally prepared with all the right fly patterns, but it is important to research the insect hatches and other predominant trout foods, whether you purchase or tie your own flies. Again, the best source of information is a trustworthy local fly shop that is accustomed to providing this service either directly or online. Pertinent fly patterns purchased on-site are usually the most effective whether actually fished or used as models for your own tying. A

The serenity of the Henry's Fork can be fully enjoyed by the well-prepared angler. Few trips go exactly as planned, but major difficulty need not occur if the right precautions are taken. BONNIE HARROP PHOTO

Masa Katsumata has made the five-thousand-mile trip from Japan to the Henry's Fork numerous times. Special assistance to foreign travelers is readily provided by local fly shops and outfitters. These services are easily accessed online, and some even provide foreign language translation. RENÉ HARROP PHOTO

portable fly-tying kit can be an invaluable asset for those times when you encounter something not covered by the existing contents of your fly boxes or in remote areas where commercial flies cannot be obtained.

Success with nymphs or streamers on deep rivers and lakes often depends on fishing recommended patterns or experimenting. However, wadable waters provide much better opportunity to take the guesswork out of fly selection. This applies especially to dry-fly fishing and sight nymphing to feeding trout. A small aquarium net makes simple work of capturing drifting insects both on and below the surface. Fly selection based upon up-close examination is much more reliable than looking at moving insects on or in the water. Select an artificial that matches the natural in size, shape, and color. A critical mistake is to shy away from fishing extremely small imitations even when the fish are obviously feeding on insects size 20 and smaller. Tiny mayflies, caddis, and midges are typically more available than larger specimens throughout the year. This reality is recognized by even the largest trout in many western waters, and they respond accordingly. A deviation

of one hook size from the natural can go completely ignored by anything more significant than a juvenile fish.

From my days as a river guide and later as an angler who is on the water more than one hundred days a year, I can state with full certainty that nothing is more assured to bring defeat than poorly developed casting skill. It is sad to watch a frustrated angler struggle in an attempt to learn something on distant water that could have been accomplished at home. Improving your ability to present a fly to a fish does not require travel, rising trout, or even water for that matter. An open grassy place such as a lawn or community park will suffice just fine as a practice area for casting. Hands-on instruction from an experienced individual will speed the process of developing the ability to deliver a fly to a minimum distance of thirty to forty feet with accuracy and control. Excellent instruction manuals or videos are available in the event a qualified instructor cannot be found.

It is always wise to practice with the same rod, reel, line, and leader that you expect to use during any visit to new water. A duplicate setup or at least something close should be included in your practice sessions as well and then taken along as backup insurance against a broken rod or other equipment failure. Clip the point from a fly and practice hitting a target about two feet in diameter from a variety of distances and angles. Remember that a straight-line cast made directly upstream is the easiest presentation to master and probably the most versatile for dry-fly fishing and sight nymphing in shallow water.

There is something truly pleasurable in the time we spend preparing for a new fly-fishing adventure. Studying the peculiarities of a far-off and unfamiliar destination selected on the basis of reputation is a discovery unto itself as mental images begin to develop. The long hours of planning accumulate into a heightened sense of anticipa-tion as the time for departure draws near. In our minds, we see ourselves fully engaged with beautiful water, perfect casts, and splendid trout. Repeatedly we inspect our gear and frequently find ourselves repacking to add some forgotten item or just to double-check. Late into the night we tie more flies than could ever be used in a single trip and watch as they become organized into boxed rows of fur, feather, and steel. It is in this time of contemplation that we find joy in simply thinking about fly fishing, and this preserves hope and sanity in an otherwise pressuring world. Advance preparation is a formula for converting dreams to reality, which later become treasured memories that can last a lifetime.

Fly selection becomes more complex when two or more different insects are available simultaneously. Flavs, Brown Drakes, and caddis were all available when this big hen took the largest of the three naturals. RICH PAINI PHOTO

Twenty Inches
pen and ink with watercolor tint
9 x 11 inches

Men of the Water

Beyond his red suspenders, there was nothing really different about the sturdily built man in late middle age standing waist deep in one of my favorite runs. It was late spring on the lower Henry's Fork where giant Salmonflies clung to the blossomed branches of a tall chokecherry tree that shaded a weathered wooden drift boat hitched to an old International utility van bearing Montana plates. The Henry's Fork is a big river down low where it enters the upper end of the Snake River plain and courses across the southern width of Idaho. In the mid-1960s, there were no crowds and no reason to begrudge the stranger's possession of the water my brother and I had intended to fish that day. But as we rigged our rods and pulled on waders, my attention kept drifting out toward midstream where the left-handed angler probed the riffled run with the most impressive display of fly-casting skill I had ever witnessed. At a distance of more than fifty yards, I could see the wire-rimmed spectacles beneath a battered felt hat that did not conceal the look of determination on the face of a man who truly knew what he was doing. There was no sound but the old Hardy reel as his rod bowed against a heavy rainbow. Distracted by the demonstration, we delayed a short hike to unoccupied waters while the man worked his way toward the near bank where he quickly netted and released the 3-pound fish. Impressed by the obvious expertise, I complimented him on the fine trout as he rested briefly along the rocky edge. Our conversation was short but friendly, and over the ensuing years I would see him on many occasions both on the water and in his fly shop in West Yellowstone. His name was Pat Barnes, and he was the first river guide I ever met.

Finding Pat Barnes on the water without a client was a rarity until his very last days of operating a legendary fly shop and guiding operation. And even though he was fishing for himself on that memorable June day, it was a scouting mission for the benefit of those who would employ his services in the coming week. Unlike today, there was no electronic source of accurate fishing information to assure opportunity on distant water, and guesswork was not in Pat's makeup. He staked his sizable reputation on the ability to put his clients on the best water at the optimal time, and failure was not an option. As a man of the water, Pat Barnes was the consummate professional and the model for many who would follow in the enigmatic trade. Gone are the red wader suspenders that identified river guides of that generation, but the profession is flourishing in numbers that would astound those old-timers.

The West Yellowstone I remember in the mid-twentieth century bore little resemblance to the modern bustling community we know today. It was mostly a tiny commu-

Rich Paini put aside his ambitions as an anthropologist to start an outfitting business on the Henry's Fork. Rich splits his time between guiding and managing his successful operation. BONNIE HARROP PHOTO

Results like this 10-pound Henry's Fork rainbow have made Bob Lamm one of the most sought-after guides in the Yellowstone region. Now in his fourth decade of professional guiding, Bob commands as much respect as anyone who ever entered the profession. MIKE LAWSON PHOTO

nity built in the pine forest where rustic cabins lined unpaved streets. The downtown sector was mainly a random mixture of quaint souvenir shops, nondescript restaurants, and raucous honky tonks. Just as today, however, the economy of this gateway community was essentially driven by visitors to our nation's oldest park, with fly fishing among the notable attractions. Although the current population of anglers dwarfs what existed in that era, West Yellowstone had already established itself as the epicenter of the modern fly-fishing movement. Men like Jim Danskin, Bud Lilly, and Wally Eagle joined Pat Barnes as the earliest human influence on many who would forsake a conventional lifestyle for one dictated by the vagaries of water, hatches, and rising trout. Knowing those pioneering river-guide and fly-tackle entrepreneurs provided a road map of sorts for a young man in his early twenties who would leave the cor-

porate world and never look back. Although guiding fly fishermen has never been my primary occupation, the number of days I have spent in the employ of expectant and sometimes demanding clients over the past four decades has provided a window on this enduring profession.

It was not long after Bonnie and I started our fly-tying business in 1968 that I got my first taste of guiding. Will Godfrey had just recently established the first fly shop and guide service on the Henry's Fork in the community of Island Park just south of the Montana and Idaho border, and he was one of our earliest fly accounts. Like other outfitters of the day, guiding was somewhat incidental to Will's primary business of selling flies and tackle to traveling anglers. The season was short and guides who doubled as store clerks got a lot of time off between clients. Most were students who by Labor Day would be back in school leav-

Though not a paying client, Bonnie capitalized on the ready net of Pat Gaffney on Henry's Lake. Pat left a promising Massachusetts law practice to work full-time as a guide in Idaho and Montana. RENÉ HARROP PHOTO

Guide and fly shop owner Jon Stiehl is an example of a younger generation of guides who have made a career in the business of fly fishing. Educated as a geologist, Jon left Maryland right out of college to make his home on the Henry's Fork in Idaho. BONNIE HARROP PHOTO

ing Will shorthanded after early September. Although not especially comfortable or qualified, I began filling in for departed staff members when the occasional opportunity for a guide trip arose. Fortunately for me, many of those early guide clients were elderly but reasonably competent anglers mainly interested in boat transportation down Box Canyon or through the then-private Railroad Ranch.

Some of them were well-heeled friends of the Harriman family who sported elegant bamboo rods and expensive English reels. Aloof to a certain degree, they were seldom interested in the opinions or advice of an upstart local guide even when the trout were less than cooperative.

Although I was uninspired by the work, guiding provided a break from the tying vise and allowed me to spend the day outdoors and always in a beautiful place. For the next fifteen years, I guided part-time for a variety of outfitters from the general area. During that period I became acquainted with others of my generation whose approach to guiding was far more serious than my own. Men like Bob

Jacklin, George Anderson, Mike Lawson, and George Kelly followed closely in the footsteps of Will Godfrey, branching out on their own to establish operations that were patterned after the West Yellowstone examples from whom they learned the trade. Fueled by writers such as Joe Brooks, Ernest Schwiebert, Doug Swisher, and Carl Richards, the fly-fishing movement gravitated westward to the fertile and uncrowded waters of Yellowstone country, and its growth would have a profound effect on not only the rivers but the men who worked them as well. Within less than three decades, the number of fly shops in West Yellowstone more than doubled, and most would employ up to a dozen guides on their staff. Sold in the mid-1980s, Will Godfrey's original tackle and outfitting business on the Henry's Fork was joined by three more operations of similar function in a community of less than three hundred residents. Once a short-term job of modest income, guiding has become a well-paid seasonal trade that employs literally hundreds of individuals around the periphery of Yellowstone Park. For

A true professional in every sense of the word, Travis Smith assists a young Japanese client during a Flav hatch on the Ranch water of the Henry's Fork. In winter, Travis runs his own outfitting business in Patagonia. His summers are spent guiding in his home state of Montana and in Idaho.
RENÉ HARROP PHOTO

I never miss a chance to fish with Marty Reed. A consumate pro, Marty guided full-time in Idaho and Argentina for nearly a decade. This proud young father now guides only part-time while studying to become a pharmacist. RICH PAINI PHOTO

the destination states of Montana, Wyoming, and Idaho, fly fishing was now a leading economic contributor with benefits spread throughout the business community. For example, a recent study revealed that the Henry's Fork fishery alone generates nearly fifty million dollars in revenue annually for the communities through which it flows.

Comparatively speaking, guiding was easy in the days when seeing more than a dozen other anglers on the water was an unusual occurrence. For the most part, trout fed in peaceful seclusion with little conditioning to the almost relentless pressure they receive today. Unsophisticated by today's standards, fly tackle and the skill to use it effectively were shared by a relative handful of eccentric practitioners who enjoyed their sport in privacy, and even those who employed guides were reasonably self-sufficient. The primary responsibility of the old-school river guide was to

put his client over rising fish and to provide good company when the water was quiet. Before 1970, it is doubtful that a few guides could put a proper name on even a small percentage of the multitude of aquatic insects that bring trout to the surface. Perhaps more interesting is the fact that extensive hatch-matching knowledge was not considered an essential qualification in the days before specific imitation became common.

With limited historical accuracy, the heavily hackled hairwing dry flies that dominated sales in the Rocky Mountain region were known as western flies. The popular Wulff, Humpy, and Trude-style patterns were mainly designated by color rather than a name associated with an actual insect. With drift-boat fishing on burly water as their mainstay, river guides placed primary emphasis upon flotation and visibility when it came to selecting a fly for their

Montana outfitter Bob Jacklin is known worldwide as one of the most accomplished guides in the Rocky Mountain West. This Madison River brown came on one of Bob's rare days off. BOB JACKLIN PHOTO

Right: Will Godfrey was the first Henry's Fork outfitter in the late 1960s. WILL GODFREY PHOTO

Above: For more than forty years, the name Mike Lawson has been synonymous with the Henry's Fork. Now the senior outfitter on the Henry's Fork, Mike's guiding is giving way to more personal pursuits on his home water. MIKE LAWSON PHOTO

clients, and the larger the better. It was not uncommon for a guide to rely almost exclusively upon a single fly pattern for weeks on end, varying only the size when a change became necessary. Jim Danskin, for example, loved the Royal Wulff, and he fished it almost exclusively during the summer months. Varying from size 14 up to a gigantic size 6, Jim maintained an abundant stock of his favorite pattern in his fly shop, and I'm not certain he truly believed that much else was needed. Superstition played strongly into how many guides of his generation selected their flies.

Although slower waters like the fabled Henry's Fork did not accommodate the bulky profile of the conventional style of western dry flies, there were few if any commercial fly patterns that specifically addressed the multitude of regional hatches prior to the early 1970s. Guides and anglers waded the shallow flows armed with flies developed by

eastern tiers for waters and hatches several thousand miles away. The familiar Pale Morning Duns, for example, were imitated by a Light Cahill, and a simple Adams worked about as well as anything else available at the time for the commonly encountered *Callibaetis*.

With plenty of water and trout to go around, river guides of the time were aided by the absence of angling pressure and the fact that catch-and-release had yet to become a significant influential factor in the behavior of trout. The luxury of simplified fly selection would rapidly become a relic of the past, however, as the population of fly fishers increased and the competition among guides began to intensify.

By the mid-1980s, the client base of most outfitters had shifted from mostly self-reliant and realistic individuals who demanded relatively little and returned each year to

A group of guided anglers at the end of a float trip through Box Canyon enjoy a Henry's Fork sunset. River guides occupy a special role helping visitors fulfill their fly-fishing dreams. Uniquely dedicated to their profession, these passionate men of the water often put personal fishing aside in favor of sharing their knowledge and expertise with others. BONNIE HARROP PHOTO

fish with the same guide to a class of highly dependent anglers of dubious skill and often unreachable expectations. Among this new breed of modern and frequently uncommitted participants were those who were unwilling to accept any responsibility for disappointment or failure. Seldom willing to learn or even listen, they would shift to a different guide whenever a day's experience failed to produce a satisfactory number of trout, which for many was a very frequent occurrence. And it was at this time that I gave up a personal involvement with guiding in favor of preserving a personal connection to the sport that had been placed at risk. A partnership in a new outfitting operation brought me temporarily back to the trade about fifteen years later when the common client was a more patient, respectful, and realistic person. My last years as a river guide were spent with clients of various age and background but who to an individual were fairly well prepared, polite, and eager to learn. Perhaps it is the mellowing of age that allows me to reflect somewhat fondly upon those bygone days when the fishing success of a stranger was allowed to become more important than my own.

Always a reluctant participant, my time as a river guide was spread over nearly twenty-five years but actual time with clients would total only a few hundred days. In the twenty-first century, this is in sharp contrast to some younger guides who will work that many days in a single year. Major outfitters in the Yellowstone region may run as many as fifteen hundred guide trips in a six-month season. Top river guides will log a minimum of one hundred days on the water, and some may exceed that number by twenty-five to fifty days per season. Some regional guides like Travis Smith of TroutHunter on the Henry's Fork are full-time professionals who will add another hundred days in the off-season operating on the relatively pristine waters of South America.

To say that providing guide service to traveling anglers has become a big business is a gross understatement of fact. Rather new to the western fly-fishing scene are elegant and often exclusive lodges that promote fly fishing as a corporate retreat. Made fashionable by the movie *A River Runs Through It*, fly fishing has become a must-do experience for young professionals, who may try it only once. Raw beginners comprise a sizable portion of the outfitter's clientele, and the real profit comes from the sale of tackle, wading gear, and clothing. The guides typically receive more than half of the daily fee, and it is certainly money well-earned. Regardless of their level of expertise, few guided anglers will lay out three hundred to five hundred dollars per day without the expectation of catching fish, and no guide worth his salt is ever satisfied with anything less. Unreliable weather, water conditions, and insect activity are factors beyond a guide's control, but they pale when compared to the difficulty and frustration of trying to produce for a newcomer who has never cast a fly rod. It is not uncommon for a guide to spend as much time retrieving flies from streamside vegetation and untangling the client's line than the actual work of catching a fish. Diligent and resourceful, modern guides have devised ways to compensate for a client's inadequacies, especially when fishing from a drift boat.

Although impossible to prove, I am convinced that the innovative technique of fishing weighted nymphs below a large strike indicator is the brainchild of a tormented river guide. Although it resembles nothing even close to what is conventional, indicator fishing allows the artificial to be placed in a position where it can be spotted by a trout without executing a well-coordinated cast. From outside the boat and in often hostile currents, a strong and athletic guide can position the angler and manipulate the fly drift in such a way that little actual fishing skill is involved. But a hookup is only the beginning, and it often takes a near miracle to coach a beginner through the intricacies of playing and landing a fish of significant size. But remarkably, these miracles do happen with enough frequency to allow a frazzled guide to face another day.

It should come as no surprise that guides from the old school confront considerable difficulty adjusting to the diverse client base of recent times. Unlike the past, guide trips do not often entail a leisurely float on uncrowded water in the company of competent anglers. Few past forty years of age can match the endurance and physical conditioning of a younger guide class. An exception, however, is the well-respected Henry's Fork Angler's guide, Bob Lamm. Coming to Yellowstone country from Missouri in his late teens, Lamm began his guiding career under the expert tutelage of Jim Danskin in the mid-1970s. Impressive in all phases of the trade, Bob is as comfortable and efficient wading clients on the challenging fly-only water of the Henry's Fork as he is at the oars of a drift boat on the Madison.

It is this competency on diverse waters combined with near matchless knowledge of trout and their habits that have established Bob Lamm as perhaps the most sought-after guide I have ever known. The majority of Bob's days on the water are booked well in advance of the season, and there is a waiting list of those who seek his services. Most of his clientele are individuals who have fished with him for years, and he accepts no uncommitted or unskilled applicant. Fly rods and drift boats are replaced by fine shotguns and retrieving dogs in the late fall when Bob's talent as a waterfowl guide takes over. This off-season business continues through late winter, beginning in Idaho and finishing in his home state of Missouri. Bob Lamm is an impressive man.

Historically, river guides have been viewed as eccentric and romantic characters hooked on life in the outdoors and exhibiting only disdain for sophisticated ways. Many have endeavored to assume this role, but the percentage who actually succeed is small. It takes a special personality and disposition to deal with the pressures of a diverse and ever-changing clientele committed to an eight- to ten-hour day with no turning back once the trip begins. A guide is compelled to project nonstop enthusiasm and positive outlook regardless of what is happening at any given point in the trip. Remembering that most people who hire a guide really do need a guide, one can easily imagine the patience and resiliency required to handle the skill limitations and personality defects of what can be as many as one hundred different clients in a single year.

An experienced and capable fly fisher understands that fishing can be difficult even in ideal conditions and on the best of water. The most productive waters are invariably the most popular as well, and angler competition, both professional and private, is a constant. During the salmonfly hatch on the Madison, it is common to wait in line at a busy launch ramp for as long as an hour before following several dozen boatloads of like-minded fishermen. It is in this type of situation where knowledge and experience separate the truly accomplished from the pretenders. Although pride is a driving force, a professional guide knows that the size of the gratuity usually hinges on the number or size of the fish his clients are able to land under his supervision. The cost of fuel and specialized equipment run high, with a custom-fitted drift boat and trailer that must be replaced about every other year, valued at as much as $8,000, at the top of the river guide's expense list. A one-hundred-dollar tip is not uncommon when the day goes well, and the best guides consistently earn this extra compensation.

To my knowledge, no successful river guide has ever entered the profession without a deep love and appreciation for fly fishing and all that it represents. In the early years, many of the guides I knew were societal dropouts who wanted to work a little and fish a lot. Today's practitioner is more likely to be an educated businessman with a formal degree and a head full of empirical knowledge of all things pertaining to trout. Succeeding in the field is almost entirely dependent upon accumulating a group of satisfied repeat customers who choose his services over those of his

Henry's Fork guides prepare to make an early season float on the Box Canyon section of the Henry's Fork. Though late in May, snow still clings to the shaded banks of this popular stretch of water. BONNIE HARROP PHOTO

competitors. As his reputation grows, so too does the quality of his clientele. The majority of river guides burn out long before their client base is dominated by accomplished and committed anglers. Rookie guides are almost always relegated to high-maintenance beginners whom they may never see more than once. There are dues to be paid in any endeavor. At the peak of the profession are a few elite river guides who gain near-rock-star status in the local saloons and other gathering places where conversation is ruled by the idiom of fly fishing. In general, they are relatively youthful men of impressive physical stature and engaging personalities.

On the surface, the rugged lifestyle of the modern river guide may project a somewhat glamorous image that belies a strenuous reality that few can duplicate or sustain. Although rowing skills are a fundamental of float fishing, it is not uncommon for a guide to spend as much time walking or holding the boat in heavy water as actually at the oars. A new pair of waders is frequently worn out within a month during the prime season, which gives clear indication of the wear and tear on the man's body. Repeated consecutively for two and three weeks at a time, the

rigorous days of a full-time river guide would be physically devastating to most who envision themselves as potential candidates for the trade. Wade fishing eliminates the burden of managing a heavy drift boat, but long days of walking the banks and wading the currents during all extremes of weather make guiding even on gentler flows a physical demanding routine.

Understandably, assuring the safety of the client plays no small role in the responsibility any guide assumes when he enters the profession. River guides in Idaho, for example, must be certified in advanced first aid and CPR training, which must be renewed every other year. More than one unguided angler owes his life to a benevolent river guide who possessed the skills and physical ability to perform a water-related rescue.

Historically, river guides have always been vocal advocates for conservation of trout and their habitats, and guides are also largely responsible for promoting the modern fly-fishing ethic. But the predecessors of the new breed were never as challenged to learn and understand the complexities of a highly pursued quarry made vastly more elusive by the relentless attention of a higher quality of angler.

Although the number of guided anglers has grown radically in recent decades, the number is dwarfed by an army of extremely qualified participants who fish without the need for on-stream assistance. And although the practice of catch-and-release has prevented adverse impact on trout populations, the impact has been felt in the way trout respond to an artificial fly. Conditioned by experience to detect a fraudulent offering, a sizable trout on pressured water is seldom the victim of an incompetent angler.

Substantially qualified from the beginning, the exceptional river guide continues to improve his skills and knowledge with each day on the water. To the prudent client, a guide selected for his instructional capabilities becomes a far more valuable investment than one who is simply able to catch fish. River guides at the highest level possess the ability to teach physical and intellectual skills that are required to become self-sufficient in one of today's most challenging sporting endeavors. The lasting benefit of time spent with a truly accomplished guide exceeds the memories of trout brought to the net or the pleasure of entertaining company.

Any credible river guide can assist in correcting flawed mechanics in casting, and most are capable of explaining several ways to correctly present the fly. More important, however, are those who are capable of communicating knowledge gleaned from years of on-stream observation of trout and their living food sources. This is especially valuable to those individuals who live far from trout country and pursue their sport with limited time on the water in which to learn the natural complexities of fly fishing. Learning and pleasure are not mutually exclusive, and both can be comfortably accomplished in the company of the right guide.

Barring insider status, it is nearly impossible to fully appreciate the extraordinary dedication and commitment that the upper level professional river guides apply to each day on the water. There are also sacrifices involved that will eventually take their toll on a guide's ability to sustain a long-term involvement with the trade. They enjoy no paid holidays and any day off is easily measured in lost income. Compelled to deliver a quality experience, the pressures of thirty or more consecutive days between breaks can make personal relationships nearly impossible to maintain. For some, this is where the line is drawn when a choice must be made between a family and career. But perhaps the most consistent and predictable casualty of life as a river guide is the exchange of personal enjoyment of fishing with a fly rod for the vicarious pleasure derived from another's success. And sadly, it is somewhat rare for a retired river guide to ever succeed in fully reconnecting with the private fly-fishing community. Perhaps this relatively short professional lifespan can be compared to that of high level athletes who give everything to a passion then fade into obscurity when their playing days have ended.

In a life subjected almost constantly to the characters of fly fishing, I know of none who perform greater service to the sport or who pay a higher personal price than the men of the water. They are a rare breed who will always be separate from the common but also will never be without value to the integrity of the sport. The legacy of the rugged and independent river guide continues in good hands.

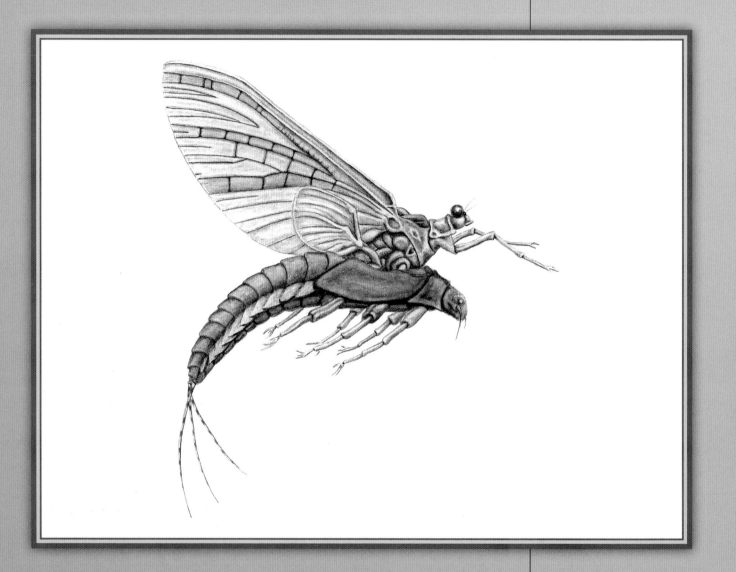

Emerging Mayfly
carbon pencil with watercolor tint
8 x 10 inches

Emergence

The parking lot at Last Chance Access is a legendary gathering place for anglers fishing the Henry's Fork. In the prime season from mid spring through early autumn, it is common to see fifty or more vehicles bearing license plates from across the United States, and the languages overheard are proof of the international fame enjoyed by the great river. But only half a dozen vehicles were parked there on a chilly afternoon in mid-October.

An early morning snowfall had changed to a light mist just before noon, which made conditions ideal for the fall hatches that seem to thrive in this kind of weather. Even from a distance, the voices and figures scattered along the upper Railroad Ranch were mostly recognizable as Henry's Fork regulars from either Idaho or nearby Jackson, Wyoming. A noticeable exception was a river guide who had driven nearly five hours from the Bighorn in Montana, but he too was a familiar face. This guy was playing a nice rainbow, and he answered the question I was thinking before I could ask. "Mahogany Duns," he called out from near midstream. This was in reference to a hatch of deep reddish brown mayflies that was now underway. At a full size 16, this was a gift at a time when most dry-fly fishing involves "squint flies" in size 20 and smaller. Spotting a sizable head a few hundred feet away, I left my friend to enjoy the fight and headed downstream.

Only one large fish among several dozen of modest size was visible in the hundred yards of open water, but there was no guarantee that a longer walk would provide better opportunity. In water that would reach my waist a month or so earlier, I crept cautiously through a slow, knee-deep current to a position that was forty feet away and directly downstream from the busy trout. Though creating minimal disturbance, the broad snout told the story of the size of what lay beneath as it sipped rhythmically from the surface. Moving by as much as a foot from side to side, the big hen was not a stationary target as she intercepted the drifting Mahoganies. It took four casts before timing and alignment were just right, but the rise was a refusal of the dun pattern I had selected to begin the battle. Bumped gently aside by the motion of the aborted rise, my fly had been pegged as a fraud at the last second as it drifted over the trout's position. The refusal was a reaction I had experienced countless times on waters where big, seasoned trout develop an acute sensitivity to flaws in presentation or fly pattern. In many cases it is not unusual for the offended fish to disappear without offering a second chance for a better cast or a different fly. This time, however, the trout reappeared after several anxious minutes, but now the game was different.

From the edge of my vision and perhaps twenty feet away from its original location, a glimmer of silver and the

A floating nymph fooled this rainbow during a fall hatch of Mahogany Duns. Success followed nearly an hour of casting and three fly changes. BONNIE HARROP PHOTO

Bonnie Harrop changes flies during an emergence of midges on a spring creek in eastern Idaho. Despite the chill of November, trout leisurely sipped the tiny insects through much of the day. RENÉ HARROP PHOTO

tip of a spotted dorsal fin punctuated a distinct bulge in the current as the big rainbow again showed itself. Thirty seconds later and six feet to the right, a spotted back and more dorsal marked a second disturbance as the fish moved aggressively to something in the film. Each successive sighting was in a different location and the high floating duns, though growing more numerous, were deliberately ignored. Changing to a low-profile emerging pattern, I began trying to place the fly in a spot where I hoped it might be found, and I worked hard to stay behind the fish as it worked an area about fifty feet in diameter. Four fly changes and nearly an hour later I got lucky.

Only three rod lengths in front of me an impressive form appeared over a submerged weed bed and then lifted close to the surface to take another insect. Noting the direction as it turned to the side, I shot a quick cast three feet to the right, and the fish took the Mahogany floating nymph as quickly as it settled on the water. Angered by the sting of the hook, the heavy fish bored forcefully toward the far bank nearly a hundred yards away. Freedom might have been gained on that initial run, but the sight of another wading angler caused a change of direction that brought her in a quartering angle back toward my side of the river. In a different season the fight would have undoubtedly been more strenuous and animated, but the cold water of a Rocky Mountain autumn had a subduing effect that allowed me to slide my net under the 20-inch fish after less than five minutes of spirited, though temperature-impaired, resistance. Toward the western horizon, clearing skies prepared to greet a sinking sun, and a rapid drop in temperature quickly followed. At close to freezing, it was simply too cold for the hatch to continue, and the fishing ended with that single splendid trout.

A light mist began to spread from the edges of the river as I lingered on the bank to admire a trio of trumpeter swans as they settled on the now still water. After walking less than a hundred yards back toward the parking lot, I was overtaken by a lone angler who obviously wanted to talk. Polite but certainly not timid, the young stranger spoke with a soft southern accent that I immediately connected with a battered old station wagon with Mississippi plates that sat by itself in the mostly empty parking lot. Fishing a short distance downstream, he had watched my hourlong engagement, and he now complimented the reward of the effort. A conversation developed as we walked the quarter of a mile together, and it continued as we sipped a welcome cup of hot coffee on the tailgate of my truck.

With three years of fly-fishing experience, it was the young man's first trip to the Yellowstone region. His plan was to hit several of the famous trout streams in the three states of Idaho, Montana, and Wyoming, and the Henry's Fork was his starting point. Impressed by the beauty of the country and water only seen in photographs, he had begun the day filled with excitement and optimism as the hatch of Mahogany duns appeared and trout began to rise. Enthusiasm was rather quick to fade, however, as each respectable trout he tried to approach from upstream would disappear before he could make a single cast. After thirty minutes and three blown opportunities, it became apparent that the only anglers who were having success were those who would avoid spooking the fish in this extremely thin water by presenting the fly from a downstream position. By duplicating this approach he was finally able to get within range of a 14-inch rainbow that eventually accepted a dun pattern tied parachute-style, which also hap-

pened to be the only Mahogany imitation in his fly box. His next chance was against a significantly larger fish that he approached with renewed confidence and a similar upstream presentation.

There is a certain arrogance connected with a big trout that continues to feed uninterrupted while seeming to know of a pursuer's intent. This seems to have been the case for the young angler who sent cast after cast over a highly desired objective that would not accept his fly but also would not stop rising. Though only assumption, it is likely that the newcomer had experienced a situation comparable to what I had encountered with a fish of similar size and behavior, but with a far less favorable outcome. Notably different, however, was a trout that remained somewhat passive as it waited for an insect to float over its position rather than aggressively pursuing something that had not yet reached full flotational capacity. This separation in feeding behavior prevented the conclusion that the same pattern that had worked for me would have produced a similar result for the disappointed stranger. However, it seemed likely that the high-winged parachute did not match the visual characteristics of the food form being targeted by the big trout. With no alternative, there was little he could do but continue to fish his lone Mahogany pattern until the hatch had ended and the opportunity was gone.

It was a classic example of what happens to many expectant anglers who often travel great distances to test themselves on unique waters known for prodigious hatches

Emerging midge TOSHI KARITA PHOTO

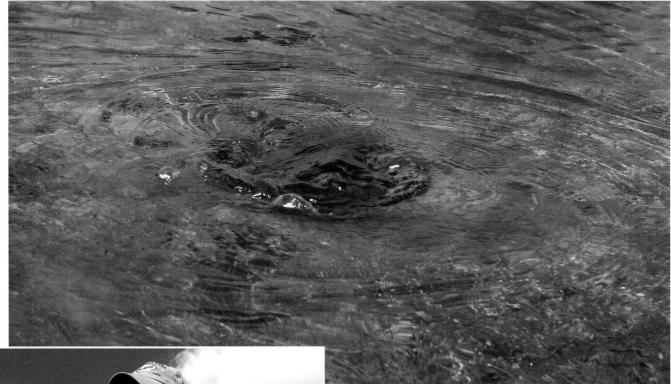

While this disturbance appears to indicate a rising trout, the fish was actually taking emerging nymphs just beneath the surface. A dry fly would be the wrong choice in this situation.
BONNIE HARROP PHOTO

The complexity of emergence can dictate numerous fly changes during the course of any hatch of aquatic insects. It pays to carry a variety of patterns when attempting to deal with the changing appearance of emerging organisms.
BONNIE HARROP PHOTO

and large trout. Many who fail in their objective have a tendency to place the blame on an overrated fishery or something other than their own lack of preparation for a goal that is not easily accomplished. Young fish that have not endured years of near constant disruption to the act of feeding do not display the same resistance to an artificial fly as those grown wise in the ways of survival, and it is this division in behavior that dictates the degree of difficulty one must expect when large seasoned fish are the sole objective.

By coming to the surface, large trout reveal themselves as a target for those in search of a special prize, and it is this feature that draws anglers to rivers like the Henry's Fork. But finding that special fish is often only the beginning of what can be a prolonged engagement with a single adversary. This is especially true during an emergence of aquatic insects such as mayflies, caddis, or midges, and those who do not understand the complexity of this event are frequently faced with the frustration of failing to find

the correct imitation at a time when the possibilities are multiple.

Eggs deposited in the water by winged adults hatch into nymphal or larval forms, where they exist in a subsurface condition for up to a year or more. As these underwater stages reach maturity, they undergo changes that prepare them for what is typically a relatively short existence in the winged stage. Caddis and midges enter a pupal phase following the larval stage, and they remain in this condition for a brief period of time before emerging on the surface. Mayflies do not pupate but instead progress directly from the nymphal to the winged stage. It is this transition from wingless water-dwelling organisms to air-breathing creatures of flight that has come to be known as a hatch, and the varieties are many.

For decades, matching the hatch was centered on the imitation of freshly emerged insects with highly visible floating patterns and nothing else. But while perfectly crafted artificials of this description continue to have their place, they are not always the solution in the problematic situations that have become common on waters of great reputation where trout are compelled to a high degree of selectivity in their feeding behavior. Today, the selection and presentation of a correct imitation is not nearly as uncomplicated as when angling pressure was light and trout were allowed to feed in relative peace. We now know that a big trout has choices within the singular species designation of any hatch, and there is an explanation for any choice that is made.

The duration of a hatch is sometimes too short to allow the assurance that any shot at a big trout is not the day's last. This makes it imperative to correctly assess the situation and then successfully execute the process of approach, fly selection, and presentation in the shortest possible amount of time. This requires complete concentration on the trout and the often subtle clues revealed by its feeding pattern. This is where knowledge and understanding of the process of emergence comes into play.

The process of moving from the nymphal or larval stage to an air-breathing form involves breaking free from the exoskeleton with complete release being the objective if survival to the next stage is to be attained. Ideally, this transformation takes place without excessive difficulty, but there are exceptions that can keep the insect in a state of partial emergence for a significant period of time. A distinct pause at this point can be close enough to the surface to give the impression of a rise when the detained insect is

consumed by a trout. The degree of separation from the exoskeleton, which is often referred to as the shuck, can vary. When applied to imitation, this means that the tier is dealing with an insect in the act of change with the result being a pattern that combines key features of two distinctly different stages. When intended to be fished just beneath the surface, the general shape of the fly would approximate the underwater stage with only suggestive color of the emerging adult showing in the wing case area. A pattern depicting further advancement toward emergence might be tied in a matter that allows the fly to be fished in a complete or partially submerged position. Either configuration would be considered a transitional pattern, and the technique can be adapted to the specific images of mayflies, caddis, and midges.

Transitional patterns are typically most effective during the peak of emergence. When targeting this phase of emergence, trout will aggressively feed across a relatively broad feeding area. Often the nose of the trout will not penetrate the surface, which indicates the need for a sunken pattern. The back or perhaps part of the dorsal fin may be all that is shown in a false riseform that indicates the trout's true intent. Trout are also known to shift into this feeding mode when alerted to the presence of an angler who has disrupted its comfort in feeding on the surface.

Weather factors can delay the departure of fully emerged insects or even render them lifeless in extreme conditions. Cold or damp weather can hinder the drying of wings and warming of muscles that make flight and freedom from the

Emerging mayfly TOSHI KARITA PHOTO

Surrounded by freshly hatched adults, Leslie Harrop found an emerger to be most effective during this evening hatch of Brown Drakes. BONNIE HARROP PHOTO

water possible. A sparsely dressed emerger will float low on the water while duplicating a temperature-impaired insect. An imitation of this type can be the solution when a trout is clearly feeding on the surface but ignores a higher floating adult pattern.

A brisk wind can drown insects that are new to a dependence upon air for obtaining oxygen. This happens when they are knocked down on a choppy surface from which they cannot escape. Dead insects lying spent on the surface are often overlooked by those who casually view the situation from above. But they are clearly visible to a trout that surveys the scene from beneath. A flush-floating pattern may be difficult to see on the water, but it can produce substantial reward for those who accept this inconvenience.

During emergence, it is not usual to observe floating insects that have broken through the film only to find themselves disabled by an inability to completely free themselves from the shuck, which now acts as an impediment to any progress from that point on. While often connected to the shuck by a mere thread of attachment to a leg, wing, or other body part, the hapless victim is doomed to certain consumption by any trout that recognizes the obvious state of vulnerability. Unlike transitional forms, these disabled organisms are not capable of further change

in appearance. There is similarity, however, in the requirement of representing characteristics of both the above and below water stages, as is the case with transitional patterns. Known commonly as cripples, these water-bound casualties can carry an elevated profile that makes a corresponding imitation quite easy to see, but a lower floating and less visible pattern may work better in some situations.

Like any predator when given a choice, a trout will select a prey least likely to escape. Crippled insects conform to this condition of natural availability when compared to unencumbered individuals that flee the water as quickly as possible. Like drowned insects, cripples cannot escape the attention of a hungry trout, but they do not necessarily lie motionless on the surface. Unwilling to give up the fight for survival, cripples squirm and struggle against the encumbrance in a futile effort to fly from the water, attracting a trout's attention to a helpless victim and the certainty of a successful rise. A subtle twitch of the fly with the rod tip can sometimes induce a take when a drag-free presentation does not.

While available to a varying degree throughout emergence, cripples can be most productive at or near the end of the event. Unable to leave the water, those not consumed or pushed to the edges remain an available food source when most if not all of the other forms of the hatch have disappeared. I go to this pattern style frequently when insect and trout activity have become sparse but a few fish continue to rise.

While imitations of fully emerged and healthy aquatic insects still play a vital role in your fly box, it is important to have alternatives from which to choose when a clearly visible high-floating pattern fails to get the job done. The days of simplicity in pattern selection have gone the way of undiscovered waters and common solitude. Carrying an assortment of imitative variations for a host of different hatches has become an established practice based upon the reality of a different world where fly fishing now attracts thousands rather than just a few. But remember we are discussing only the largest and most angler-resistant trout. Treating these highly sought-after creatures as individuals is the starting point, and we should expect none to act or respond in exactly the same way. As a single adversary, each will present a unique challenge in terms of what is required to overcome the peculiar mechanism for survival employed by any seasoned trout. For the observant angler, obscure clues to the puzzle of identifying the correct imitation can be revealed in the behavior of the objective, but success is often dependent upon a thoughtful process of elimination wherein many flies may be tried before a solution is found. Of course, there are instances when simple luck comes to the rescue, but accidental success is not a sound basis for dealing with the complexity of emergence.

Probing the mysteries of emergence is but one aspect of fishing for trout with a fly rod. Other situations involving both aquatic and terrestrial insects are nearly always less complicated and, therefore, somewhat easier to manage. Any insect activity involving movement from land to water, such as in the case of ovipositing mayflies or caddis, do not bring a changing image as part of the imitative requirement. Likewise, land-based organisms such as ants, beetles, and hoppers carry a single respective image when they become available to trout.

While bringing an additional element of difficulty, emergence promotes greater understanding of trout behavior and the respect that must be given to those that survive to impressive size. Though elusive to extreme, they are the forces that motivate advancement in the skill of fly fishing, and there are no better teachers.

BONNIE HARROP PHOTO

Mahogany Transitional Nymph

Hook:	TMC 200 R BL size 14-18
Thread:	Rust 8/0 UNI-Thread
Tail:	Wood duck fibers
Rib:	Fine copper wire
Abdomen:	Gray-olive TroutHunter CEN dubbing
Thorax:	Gray-olive TroutHunter Pro dubbing
Wing case:	Rust TroutHunter CDC
Legs:	Brown Hungarian partridge fibers

BONNIE HARROP PHOTO

Mahogany Short Wing Emerger

Hook:	TMC 100 BL size 14-18
Thread:	Rust 8/0 UNI-Thread
Tail:	Wood duck fibers
Rib:	Fine copper wire
Body:	Mahogany TroutHunter Pro dubbing
Wings:	Mallard wing quill segments
Legs:	Brown Hungarian partridge fibers

BONNIE HARROP PHOTO

CDC Mahogany Drowned Dun

Hook: TMC 100 BL size 14-18
Thread: Rust 8/0 UNI-Thread
Tail: Whiting Coq de Leon
Abdomen: Mahogany TroutHunter goose biot
Thorax: Mahogany TroutHunter Pro dubbing
Wings: Dark dun TroutHunter CDC

BONNIE HARROP PHOTO

Mahogany Biot Parachute Dun

Hook: TMC 100 BL size 14-18
Thread: Rust 8/0 UNI-Thread
Tail: Whiting Coq de Leon
Abdomen: Mahogany TroutHunter goose or turkey
            biot
Thorax: Mahogany TroutHunter Pro dubbing
Wing: Dark dun turkey flat
Hackle: Whiting grizzly dyed brown

BONNIE HARROP PHOTO

Mahogany Hairwing Cripple

Hook: TMC 100 BL size 14-16
Thread: Rust 8/0 UNI-Thread
Tail: Sparse tuft of gray-olive TroutHunter
            CEN dubbing over wood duck fibers
Rib: Fine copper wire
Abdomen: Gray-olive TroutHunter goose or turkey
            biot
Thorax: Mahogany TroutHunter Pro dubbing
Wing: Natural deer hair

BONNIE HARROP PHOTO

Brown Transitional Caddis

Hook:	TMC 100 BL size 14-20
Thread:	Tan 8/0 UNI-Thread
Tail:	Brown TroutHunter CEN dubbing
Rib:	Fine copper wire
Abdomen:	Brown TroutHunter CEN dubbing
Thorax:	Blackish brown TroutHunter CEN dubbing
Wings:	Natural brown TroutHunter CDC
Legs:	Brown Hungarian partridge fibers

BONNIE HARROP PHOTO

Brown Hairwing Caddis Emerger

Hook:	206BL size 14-20
Thread:	Tan 8/0 UNI-Thread
Body:	Brown TroutHunter goose or turkey biot
Wing:	Elk hair
Legs:	Brown Hungarian partridge fibers

BONNIE HARROP PHOTO

Brown CDC Drowned Caddis

Hook:	TMC 100BL size 14-20
Thread:	Tan 8/0 UNI-Thread
Abdomen:	Brown TroutHunter goose or turkey biot
Thorax:	Trico TroutHunter Pro dubbing
Wings:	Natural brown TroutHunter CDC
Legs:	Butts of CDC wings tied back and trimmed to length

BONNIE HARROP PHOTO

Brown Hairwing Caddis Cripple

Hook:	TMC 206 BL size 14-20
Thread:	Tan 8/0 UNI-Thread
Rib:	Fine copper wire
Body:	Brown TroutHunter Pro dubbing
Wing:	Elk hair
Hackle:	Whiting ginger grizzly

BONNIE HARROP PHOTO

Brown Hybrid Caddis Adult

Hook:	TMC 100 BL size 14-20
Thread:	Tan 8/0 UNI-Thread
Rib:	Fine copper wire
Body:	Brown TroutHunter Pro dubbing
Wing:	Paired natural brown CDC over natural elk hair
Hackle:	Whiting ginger grizzly

BONNIE HARROP PHOTO

CDC Gray Transitional Midge

Hook:	TMC 206 BL size 12-24
Thread:	Gray 8/0 UNI-Thread
Tail (shuck):	Grizzly hackle feather
Body:	Muskrat gray TroutHunter Pro dubbing
Wing case:	Natural dark dun TroutHunter CDC
Legs:	Natural dark dun TroutHunter CDC fibers

BONNIE HARROP PHOTO

CDC Gray Midge Emerger

Hook: TMC 100 BL size 12-24
Thread: Gray 8/0 UNI-Thread
Tail: Natural blue dun TroutHunter CDC fibers
Abdomen: Canada goose biot
Thorax: Muskrat gray TroutHunter Pro dubbing
Hackle collar: Natural blue dun TroutHunter CDC fibers

BONNIE HARROP PHOTO

CDC Gray Spent Midge

Hook: TMC 100 BL size 12-24
Thread: Gray 8/0 UNI-Thread
Abdomen: Canada goose biot
Thorax: Muskrat gray TroutHunter Pro dubbing
Wings: Natural mallard CDC

BONNIE HARROP PHOTO

CDC Gray Midge Cripple

Hook: TMC 206 BL size 12-24
Thread: Gray 8/0 UNI-Thread
Abdomen: Canada goose biot
Thorax: Muskrat gray TroutHunter Pro dubbing
Wing: Natural blue dun TroutHunter CDC
Hackle: Whiting grizzly dyed dun

BONNIE HARROP PHOTO

CDC Gray Midge Adult

Hook: TMC 100 BL size 12-24
Thread: Gray 8/0 UNI-Thread
Abdomen: Canada goose biot
Thorax: Muskrat gray TroutHunter Pro dubbing
Wing: Natural blue dun TroutHunter CDC
Hackle: Whiting grizzly dyed dun

Jewel of Japan (yamame)
pen and ink with watercolor tint
8 x 10 inches

Midging
Top to Bottom

When I was younger, I did not prefer one type of fishing over another. If I could do it with a fly rod, that was good enough. If the fish were large and easily obtained, so much the better. There was a time when the rushing turbid flow of spring runoff was an event to look forward to as giant Salmonfly nymphs begin to stir. It is possibly the best opportunity to score a truly exceptional trout, as every fish in the river gorges itself on submerged insects more than two inches long. Action can be fast and furious as fish throw caution to the wind in a feeding frenzy of astounding proportions.

However, time has taken its toll on my once powerful legs and the fearless abandon of my warrior years. Now I am not nearly as inclined to brave the swollen flows of May on my home river. Although I do take an annual sampling of the opportunity generated by a waterborne feast I can only take so much. A week or so of fighting brutal currents and slinging heavily leaded nymphs as large as size 2 has me longing for a more gentle pastime. It is not often that I am compelled to leave the Henry's Fork. But with two weeks remaining before the river would return to normal, Bonnie and I packed the truck and headed north.

The temperature had been in the low seventies when we checked in at Pine Creek between Gardiner and Livingston, Montana. However, it was a different story when we turned down the gravel road that leads to Nelson Spring Creek the next morning.

A heavy mist enveloped a tree-lined pool no more than fifty feet across, and the dimples that appeared on the placid surface were not caused by trout. Sparse but heavy droplets of rain fell gently on the valley floor, but through the overcast I could make out a faint snowline on the sloping foothills a few hundred feet higher. Shivering just a bit while peering beneath the hood of the waterproof jacket, I thought wistfully of the fleece wading pants and other foul-weather gear left thoughtlessly back in Idaho. Rocky Mountain weather is as changeable as a woman's mind, and I knew better than to leave home unprepared. With no fish movement as a distraction, my thoughts drifted back to other days on this same pool when vigorous hatches and voracious trout gave full explanation to why they call this valley Paradise.

Over the years I have learned a lot from the miniature rivers known as spring creeks, where trout and insect behavior can be observed in the wild as nowhere else. I do not recall a day when something interesting and unique did not happen, and it was no surprise when I was drawn from my nostalgic reflection by a slight disturbance upstream.

The trout held in shaded water with barely enough depth to cover its dorsal. There was no urgency in the subtle

Spring creeks in the Yellowstone region provide midge-fishing opportunity throughout the year. The air temperature was barely 40 degrees on this chilly November day. BONNIE HARROP PHOTO

rise, and the rhythm of its feeding was relaxed and deliberate. At first there appeared to be nothing on the surface, but as I bent closer to the water I could see a scattering of tiny gray insects. The minuscule reward of each rise clearly necessitated economy of effort in the accumulation of a meal. Both the insects and the riseform they generated were difficult to discern in the restricted light. Equally difficult were the casting requirements they presented to the expectant angler who watched from thirty feet downstream.

Although the rain had now ceased, there remained a chill on the slight breeze, but it was more than the temperature that caused my hands to tremble. It was five full minutes of exasperation before my fumbling fingers could secure the size 22 fly to the 7X tippet. The trout had stationed itself along the inside edge of a current that broke around the end of a massive cottonwood log angling into the stream. There was virtually no current directly below the log, and the drift line was a thin seam between quick and dead water. It was here, only a foot below the tip of the log, that a blunt nose continued to appear about every ten seconds. The situation dictated a perfectly timed straight-line cast delivered tightly against the sheltering protrusion.

A tardy sun found a crease in the leaden clouds that cloaked the looming peaks of the Absaroka Range, shedding radiant light and welcome warmth on the unfolding drama. It was not a short or simple cast for the little 3-weight, but I did not make the three-hour drive for easy fishing. The first throw looked good, but the fly landed too far outside and was quickly swept away from the trout's view. My second effort was an overcompensation to the left, and the fly rested motionless on stillwater. Cringing at the miscalculation, I stripped the floating emerger back alongside the busy fish. An alarming swirl told me it was alert to the unnatural disturbance.

Minutes ticked by with no indication the trout intended to feed again. I cursed the blunder, but just as I was about to shift my attention to the next pool upstream a nose reappeared in the same spot. The rises were more widely spread, indicating that the fish was nervous, and I knew that further error would not be tolerated. It is tempting to claim skill alone for the next cast that gently nudged the coarse bark and then fluttered softly to the water. Centered perfectly in the narrow corridor, the fly was exactly where it needed to be. There was a brief hesitation before the drift

Midges as large as size 12 are common in many stillwater fisheries. Trout up to 15 pounds include midges as part of their diet in Henry's Lake. BONNIE HARROP PHOTO

kicked in, and I knew in that instant that luck had played strongly into what appeared to be a perfect presentation.

The emerger appeared briefly as a tiny white dot before vanishing in a take that was a mere wink in the shadows. I tightened to the weight of the fish, which at first seemed puzzled as to what had happened. But I knew what was coming. The delayed reaction was a violent boil below the log, followed by a searing upstream run terminating in a twisting eruption that shattered the placid pool. Illuminated in the late morning sun, the trout was a suspended blur of copper, bronze, and scarlet. Madly, I stripped slack as it rocketed back by me and then winced an instant later at the shock on the reel as the line abruptly slammed against the spool. There were two more jumps below, and another short burst to where the tiring fish proceeded to slug it out in a knee-deep riffle.

Fearing excessive stress on the fragile connection, I did not attempt to bring it 70 or 80 feet back upstream, preferring instead to reel my way down to the riffle. Lifting high with the delicate 8-foot rod, I brought a sizable head up over the rim of the net and down into the mesh. It was a robust male brown, heavy jawed and perhaps slightly more than

18 inches in length. No monster, of course, but certainly respectable by small-stream standards. I plucked the tiny barbless hook from the corner of the mouth and then slipped the gift back into the gentle current. The struggle had lasted fewer than five minutes, and he rested only briefly before gliding back to the old sheltering log, and home.

The big brown was the first of many splendid trout Bonnie and I would take over two days spent on the pastoral spring creeks of the Paradise Valley. A serious spring storm driven by vicious winds cut short our visit, but we enjoyed more than a dozen combined hours of delightful fishing on the Nelson and DePuy Ranches. We had accomplished our objective and were not saddened by an early weather-forced departure.

Although the famed mayfly hatches that frame the reputation of the private waters made no significant appearance, our rod fees had not been squandered. Trout fed almost constantly on one stage or another of the midge lifecycle, and though the majority of activity took place on or near the surface, we did not go fishless when the trout were not looking upward. Tiny, weighted larvae patterns fished deep in the riffles accounted for more than a few victims, while a lighter version twitched delicately or suspended without motion over weeded water with almost indiscernible current did impressive damage to lazily cruising targets. The fishing was exactly what we had hoped to encounter, and we returned to the Henry's Fork refreshed and ready for the summer season that lay directly ahead.

That spring creek experience was not an isolated incident, for the days when midges have come to the rescue are nearly countless. These minute two-winged insects exist in virtually every water I have ever fished, and their value as an almost constant food source for trout cannot be overstated. To ignore or fail to understand midges is to invite failure when success could otherwise be had. Although the skills associated with fishing midges effectively are not easily attained, the rewards are well worth the effort, and to succeed will make anyone a better fly fisher.

Midges in the larval stage are reclusive bottom dwellers. Although vast in numbers, individually they are of minimal size, which by itself helps to explain why they are overlooked by the majority of anglers. However, for years stillwater specialists have tapped into the value of midge larvae, which populate relatively shallow lakes and ponds. Although the word "midge" is synonymous with "small," some exceptionally fertile environments like Henry's Lake in Idaho are host to populations of midges as large as size 12. This, however, is an exception, and as a rule midges, regardless of the stage, are exactly as the term implies.

Although blind fishing larval patterns in still or very slow moving water is not a complete waste of time, there is

a better way. In these conditions, swimming larvae that move with a sharp, flexing motion are an active and attractive target for trout cruising visibly near the surface. It is only a guess, but I suspect that larvae that periodically collect en masse near the surface are lured from the depths by microscopic organisms that exist as food in that location. This seems to occur during periods of low light, usually in evening or early morning hours, although I have observed the phenomenon on dark overcast days with no wind.

In the absence of current, trout are compelled to move in the food-gathering process. Cruising near the surface, trout can be clearly observed as they ingest great quantities of midge larvae. Occasionally they will swim in a reasonably straight line, but more often the feeding path is somewhat random. Considerable luck and guesswork is added to a high requirement of accuracy in placing a fraudulent fly in the vision of a moving objective. There is no greater frustration than to make a cast that lands the correct distance in front of an approaching fish only to have it veer away at the last moment. This may happen dozens of times before everything comes together just right and a connection is made, but to pull it off is extremely satisfying.

Midge larvae have a distinct wormlike characteristic, and the criterion for effective imitation is quite simple— keep it slender. This can be problematic for patterns intended to be fished deeply in moving water, but it is easy to retain the natural's profile when tying a fly intended to be fished near the surface. In my opinion, small biots do the best job of duplicating the pronounced segmentation that is present throughout the length of a midge larva. One of my favorite stillwater larval patterns features a fairly stout hook covered with tight wraps of goose biot, either natural or dyed to the appropriate color. The only addition is a bit of sparse, sometimes contrasting dubbing to cover the forward tie-down area of the biot. The Biot Midge Larva has enough density to penetrate the film, but the sink rate is such that it will not go too deep to be seen by the trout.

The Hanging Midge was originally intended to be fished as an emerging pattern. Certainly it works well for that purpose, but because the majority of the fly hangs beneath the surface, it doubles as an effective larval pattern. Key in giving visibility and function to the pattern is a short tuft of CDC, which angles out over the hook eye. Additional support and balance is provided by a turn or two of short-fibered hackle wrapped directly behind the CDC. The body is goose biot that hangs vertically beneath the surface. Unlike the Biot Midge Larva, which is fished underwater and sometimes twitched to attract attention, the Hanging Midge is fished on top without movement.

While there is little if any difference in the physical appearance of midge larvae that populate streams and those in stillwater, there is sizable variance in behavior. With the

This beautifully colored brown was found sipping midges along an exposed weed bed. A forty-foot cast across tricky currents combined with a size 22 CDC Hanging Midge to make this a particularly satisfying victory. BONNIE HARROP PHOTO

Though mixed with slightly larger *Baetis* mayflies, midges were the insect of choice on a late autumn day on the lower Henry's Fork. Perhaps this can be explained by an increased vulnerability due to the midges' inability to quickly escape from the pupal shuck. BONNIE HARROP PHOTO

exception of pupation, it is rare if ever that larvae will swim to the surface in flowing water. However, they are active close to the bottom or in submerged aquatic weed beds. Foraging trout root around in the various habitats, consuming larvae dislodged by this activity. Because of their abundance and availability, they are a familiar food source even in waters of substantial depth and current speed.

The largest Henry's Fork rainbow in recent memory was landed by a client of talented river guide Marty Reed. Surprisingly, it did not take place in placid dry-fly water but rather in the brawling, boulder-strewn flows of Box Canyon, just upstream of the Railroad Ranch. In conditions much better suited for heavy nymphs and large attractors, the 10-plus-pound brute took a size 18 Midge Larva.

The most memorable day of the season past was spent with my daughter Leslie and her ten-year-old son Zach. We were fishing a small tributary that flows across a broad meadow before joining the upper Henry's Fork. The water was low, as is typical of late summer, and big cutthroat finned lazily in willow-shaded pools. It is a popular spot, and although the fish were not easily spooked, they resis-

ted the usually reliable assortment of nymphs, hoppers, and ants. The solution to this unexpected selectivity was revealed in a small aquarium net held at elbow depth beneath the water for just a few seconds. Trapped in the fine mesh were more than half a dozen blood-red midge larvae. I did not fish that day, choosing instead to savor the pleasure of my family's excitement. Nearly a dozen splendid natives of the Yellowstone country fell to a larval pattern consisting of little more than a small hook covered with fine copper wire. The highlight of the day was watching my grandson land his first 20-inch trout on a fly rod.

I consider any trout feeding visibly beneath the surface to be a potential recipient of a correctly fished larval pattern. Seining the current is the most effective way to determine if dislodged larvae are present in the flow. Frequently the helpless morsels are nearly microscopic, and it is a mistake to rely on what you see above the water to identify what is happening below.

Conventional sight-nymphing techniques work well for deep-midging trout, although the requirements of accuracy and concentration are tightened considerably.

This riffle on the Henry's Fork was loaded with feeding trout. Zach Wheeler did good business with a Midge Pupa fished just beneath the surface. BONNIE HARROP PHOTO

Midge larva
TOSHI KARITA PHOTO

Scores of drifting larvae are a delivered meal easily consumed with minimal exertion. Therefore, it is not typical for midging trout to show significant lateral movement, something which applies to surface fishing as well. Approach from downstream, and keep the fish in view. Most importantly, do not give up if the fish does not take right away. Persistence pays off in achieving a perfect presentation that comes directly to the trout at precisely the right instant, and it may take dozens of repetitions to pull it off.

In open, moving water it is usually best to present midge larvae as close to the bottom as is possible. However, creating a weighted larval pattern that is heavy

enough to function correctly in deeper water can be a problem. The exceedingly slender profile characteristic of this stage must be retained throughout the length of the body. This combined with the frequent restriction of an extremely small hook places severe limitation on the ways weight can be added. Many tiers, myself included, address the dilemma by using closely wrapped turns of soft flexible wire for the construction of virtually the entire fly. Extremely fine wire specifically suited to this purpose is commonly available in a variety of appropriate colors. An added benefit is a defined segmented effect, which is highly suggestive of the natural.

A relatively long tippet of 6X or finer will produce a quicker sink rate and more natural drift than coarser material. I am reluctant to add split shot unless the water is too fast or deep to allow the fly to enter the correct feeding zone. Often, two larval patterns fished in tandem six to twelve inches apart are better than a single fly. This setup, in addition to being heavier, increases the likelihood that the fish will select your fly from among the competing naturals. Another way of getting a deeper presentation is to represent two or more midge larvae on a single hook. Big trout are not shy about taking multiple midges in a single effort and may get just a little greedy. The ability to use a hook two or three times the size of the actual insect might seem like cheating just a bit, but the increased odds of holding a truly large fish may help to ease the conscience.

Big trout often seek extremely shallow water to feed on small insects. Compressed into a shorter column, the concentration of subsurface organisms is much denser and more easily obtained than in deeper flows. Everything coming down passes directly in front of opportunistic fish who trade a perilous risk of detection for a less labor-intensive food-gathering pursuit. This is also applies to other aquatic life forms. Water a foot or less in depth does not require a heavy fly. The unweighted stillwater style of midge larvae is entirely suitable for this condition.

When sight nymping with tiny midges, you almost have to have a sixth sense—the signs of a take are subtle and may seem to be insignificant to the untrained eye. A glimpse of a white inner mouth or a quick turn of the head are signals to tighten, as is any subtle movement of tail or fins. I find that a leader greased with a gel or paste-type flotant to an appropriate distance from the fly works best when extra visual assistance is desired. Often a strike is so gentle and quick that it will not transmit to a conventional floating strike indicator. A greased leader will react to the most minor disruption in the drift, and I tighten at the slightest twitch. If this technique is not for you, try using a small tuft of bright yarn or CDC as an indicator, or a dry fly of adequate size and visibility. A size 16 or 18 will usually support the relatively negligible weight of the larva, and because casting distance should be kept to a minimum, you should still be able to see a small indicator fly, which won't alarm the fish.

Pupation, or the transition from larval to the pupal stage, can take place near the bottom. In this instance the techniques used when fishing the larval patterns also apply to the next phase of the life cycle. The fundamental difference is in the design of the imitation, which is a radical departure from the wormlike larva.

Midge pupae have a pronounced thorax area, which is considerably larger in diameter than the abdomen. Included in the forward portion is an enlarged head from which protrude plumelike gills. Two stubby wings hang beneath the thorax, enclosing six folded legs. A smaller set of gills are located at the tip of a slender and distinctly segmented abdomen. The overall configuration lends itself to a little more creative latitude than does the preceding stage, but this does not mean the tier can get carried away. Overdressing is perhaps the most common flaw in any unproductive midge pattern, regardless of the stage. A good imitation emphasizes the prominent features without ex-

Though usually of diminutive size, midges are often the target of impressive trout. This spring creek rainbow took a size 24 spent midge pattern. BONNIE HARROP PHOTO

cess in any aspect of construction. Attempting to define all the respective body parts becomes pointless when the fly is much smaller than size 20. Excessive bulk is the kiss of death and should be avoided whether you purchase the fly or tie it yourself.

Unlike the larva stage, which is a growing stage lasting for months, midges remain as pupae for a much shorter duration before emerging as winged adults. When this occurs at the surface, it begins a sequence that produces the most interesting and enjoyable fishing that midging has to offer.

Midge pupae in many lakes and streams rise to the surface to hang in or just below the film. Although they remain in this condition for a relatively brief period of time, it is important to be prepared to fish imitations that duplicate their appearance and behavior in this time of severe vulnerability. I rely upon two styles of pupal imitation. One is a sunken pattern tied without weight but still dense enough to penetrate the film. Goose biots create a realistically segmented abdomen, but I sometimes switch to thread when the hook is extremely small. The longer fibers from the off-side of a turkey flight quill also work well for this purpose. They are more slender than biots from the opposite side and have much greater working length as well. The pronounced thorax of the Biot Pupa is ball-shaped dubbing approximately three times the diameter of the abdomen. A modest amount of CDC fibers over top of the thorax give slight buoyancy to the forward portion of the fly, which helps to maintain a vertical posture in the water and slow the sink rate. For the purpose of strike detection and support, I grease the leader to within an inch or two of the fly. The versatile Hanging Midge with its partially submerged profile oftens works well on trout feeding on pupae.

Emergence into the adult stage takes place in the film as the enclosed insect gains freedom through a split in the pupal skin. This is a time of distinct vulnerability for many aquatic insects, but in the case of emerging midges, it seems to be more prolonged than is generally the rule with such counterparts as mayflies and caddis. Perhaps this is because midges seem to prefer cool temperatures to make the transition to the winged stage. During the warmer seasons, emergence is usually strongest in early morning or evening, or on damp overcast days when temperatures are low. This would also help to explain why emerging midges provide the majority of dry-fly action from late autumn through early spring.

Some difficulty accompanies the act of gaining freedom from the pupal skin (especially since the temperature of the water often exceeds that of the air), and midges can spend more than a minute completely freeing themselves from the confining pupal skin. While the midges are in this helpless condition, trout capitalize upon insects displaying the combined characteristics of two different stages. My imitation of this phenomenon, the Transitional Midge, has undergone considerable revision since I began fishing

it back in the 1970s. While the basic configuration remains the same, I have settled upon CDC as the key component, and the result is a pattern that works as well during emergence as anything I have ever tried. I have always considered simplicity to be the hallmark of a truly great fly, and certainly this describes the deadly little pattern. A single finely barred hackle tip, tied as if it were a tail, gives graphic representation of a segmented trailing shuck. The legs are sparse fibers of CDC, and the body is thinly dubbed or simply tying thread. The key feature is the humped appearance of wings trapped in the pupal skin. It is accomplished with CDC pulled loosely over the entire length of the body and secured at the head. The bubble effect of the CDC positions the fly fairly high in the film, while giving visual reference to its location.

A slightly different version of the same concept allows the use of a larger hook, without losing accurate portrayal of the insect. The Hatching Midge shows a segmented representation of the clinging pupal skin in the form of a biot wrapped about halfway up the hook shank. The front half of the fly is tied almost exactly like the Transitional Midge, using CDC and dubbing to indicate the emerging adult. A minor sacrifice in visibility is compensated by greater holding capacity and a more natural position in the film.

Emerging midge TOSHI KARITA PHOTO

Midge pupa TOSHI KARITA PHOTO

Underside of midge adult

Winged adults, because they can escape by flying from the water, are somewhat less attractive food items. However, like the emerging forms, they are often delayed by the effect of cold temperature. Therefore, it is not uncommon to find success with an imitation that is much more visible than those which address the other stages. Riding high on the surface, midges in the adult stage offer the only legitimate opportunity to elevate the profile of what is usually a very small fly. I have taken plenty of respectable fish on a simple floater consisting of a biot body, CDC wings, and one or two turns of short hackle, usually black, cream, or grizzly. This style is considerably easier to see than the flat-wing midge adult that is tied without hackle. However, because of its more realistic appearance, the latter is often more effective.

Both male and female midges die soon after mating and oviposit. Enough fall to the water at this time to justify carrying a few patterns to cover this event. Sparsely dressed, spent-wing styles tied both with and without hackle will mimic this final phase of a midge's existence.

Occasionally midge adults will swarm in great numbers just barely above the water. Varying in quantity from a few to perhaps hundreds, these drifting balls of living protein are a sharp contrast to the rule of tiny as it applies to imitating midges. Clusters of midge adults are an enticing image to trout, which can consume several rather than one miniature food item in a single rise.

The Griffith's Gnat comprised of grizzly hackle palmered over a compact body of peacock herl is a simple but effective way to imitate midge clusters. However, certain deficiencies in flotation and visibility have prompted me to tie a CDC version of this popular fly. Sparse white CDC tied at the head of the fly corrects the problem. The objective in this simple maneuver is to distribute the CDC fibers through the hackle rather than form a pronounced wing.

The CDC Cluster Midge has given valuable service wherever I have fished it, including a lovely little stream in the mountains of Japan. The beautiful but elusive yamame, or cherry trout, were giving me fits on a cold, blustery day when there was little on the water to bring them up. Accustomed to the deliberate take of larger trout in the U.S. waters, I was usually too slow on the lightning quick strike; however, I managed to make four solid connections before the sparse surface activity came to an end. None of the splendid little jewels exceeded 10 inches in length, but they were among the most satisfying fish I have taken anywhere. It was a memorable experience, and I will always remain grateful to the humble little fly that made it possible.

Slower flowing streams like the Firehole in Yellowstone and much of the Henry's Fork in Idaho are ideal midging water, but the quicker flows of the Madison and other

rivers of similar characteristic should not be ignored, especially in the off-season when currents are gentled by lower flow. Although not always easy to spot, big trout frequently sip midges along sheltered edges or in fairly gentle riffles. Watch the smooth tails of otherwise turbulent pools, or cushioned water around rocks, logs, or other instream structure.

Although fishing midges on or near the surface requires significant skill and concentration, the techniques do not deviate radically from those which are fundamental to fishing other small flies to shy and selective trout. The best rod for this purpose is the one you can cast with the greatest accuracy and control. My preference for bigger water and longer range is an 8½- to 9-foot quick action 4-weight. I complete the setup with a 15- to 18-foot leader, adjusting the tippet length to accommodate the situation. A presentation made upstream or on writhing current is best accomplished with a tippet length of 36 inches or sometimes longer. In wind or when making tight curve casts upstream or to the side I keep the tippet length at about 30 inches.

Spring creeks and smaller rivers often do not invite a cast much longer than 30 feet. An 8-foot 3-weight and 14-foot leader facilitate the tighter requirements of such conditions. Bonnie, on the other hand, sticks with a 5-weight and a leader just shy of 16 feet for all her trout fishing. She forces no cast beyond her competence and seldom fails to catch fish on the demanding waters we both prefer. Stealth in wading and deft presentation more than compensate for a line weight many would consider too heavy for fishing small flies. Wise anglers choose function over fashion, and results always speak louder than anything.

For many years, a tippet of 6X or finer was shunned as impractical for landing anything larger than a 12- to 16-inch trout. Now, however, technology has given us modern material of remarkable strength, which is especially valuable in hiding the tippet from the prying eyes of a leader-shy trout. Lower visibility is not alone in justifying the selection of an extremely fine tippet in demanding small-fly situations. The ability of the fly to follow drag-producing eccentricity in the current is improved in each step down in tippet size. Now it is routine to fish a 7X tippet when midging, and I do not hesitate to drop to 8X if the fly is smaller than size 24 or if the fish is less than 16 inches. The bite of an exceptionally small hook is usually a weaker link to the trout than a fine tippet. It is wrong, however, to risk harmful effect by playing a fish for an excessive length of time. The strength and resolve of even a fairly large trout is often weakened enough to allow it to be landed after a fight of five minutes or so. Surrender line when the fish wants to run, but apply maximum pressure when it wants to rest. Get it to the net as quickly as possible, remembering that the satisfaction of fooling a big trout on a fragile tippet and tiny fly should always exceed the pleasure of landing it.

Bear in mind that you are doing well to see most floating midge patterns 50 percent of the time. Setting the hook on a midge take must be a gentle lifting of the rod and should be executed when the rise appears in the area where you believe your fly to be when it is lost among the naturals.

Art may be best defined as the beauty that is excellence. There is excellence to be observed in the refined skills of midge fishing, which at the highest level becomes an art. There are no shortcuts to attaining master status as a midge fisherman, only endless practice, determination, and patience. It is a place to grow to over time, and those who persevere will catch the difference.

Triple Brassie

Hook:	TMC 2487 BL size 14
Thread:	Black 8/0 UNI-Thread
Body:	Alternate bands of fine copper wire interspaced with black TroutHunter Pro dubbing

Note: This fly simulates three midge larvae.

Deep Midge Larva

Hook:	TMC 100BL size 18-26
Thread:	Black 8/0 UNI-Thread
Abdomen:	Soft wire to match color of natural
Legs:	Sparse partridge fibers
Thorax:	Black TroutHunter Pro dubbing

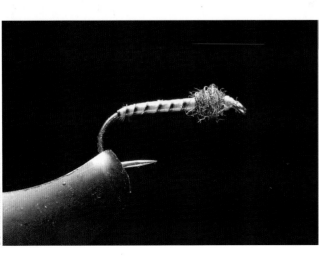

Biot Midge Larva

Hook:	TMC 100BL size 18-26
Thread:	8/0 UNI-Thread
Abdomen:	TroutHunter goose biot to match natural
Thorax:	Black TroutHunter Pro dubbing

Note: For ease and durability, soak biot in water, then cover hook shank with water-based head cement prior to forming body.

BONNIE HARROP PHOTO

Biot Midge Pupa

Hook: TMC 100BL size 18-26
Thread: 8/0 UNI-Thread
Abdomen: TroutHunter goose biot to match natural
Thorax: Trico TroutHunter Pro dubbing
Wing case: Dun TroutHunter CDC
Gills: Butts of CDC wing case clipped slightly
              beyond hook eye

BONNIE HARROP PHOTO

CDC Biot Midge Adult

Hook: TMC 100BL size 18-26
Thread: 8/0 UNI-Thread
Abdomen: TroutHunter goose biot to match natural
Wing: Paired TroutHunter CDC feathers tied
              short over abdomen
Thorax: TroutHunter Pro dubbing to match
              natural
Hackle: Whiting, no more than 3 turns

BONNIE HARROP PHOTO

Flat Wing Midge

Hook: TMC 100BL size 18-26
Thread: 8/0 UNI-Thread
Abdomen: TroutHunter goose biot to match natural
Wing: 1 or 2 TroutHunter CDC feathers tied
              flat over abdomen
Thorax: TroutHunter dubbing to match natural
Legs: 3 or 4 CDC fibers on both sides of
              thorax

BONNIE HARROP PHOTO

BONNIE HARROP PHOTO

CDC Spent Midge (with hackle)

Hook:	TMC 100BL size 18-26
Thread:	8/0 UNI-Thread
Abdomen:	TroutHunter goose biot to match natural
Wing:	Paired TroutHunter CDC feathers tied spent
Abdomen:	TroutHunter Pro dubbing
Hackle:	Whiting, no more than 3 turns

BONNIE HARROP PHOTO

CDC Spent Midge (no hackle)

Hook:	TMC 100BL size 18-26
Thread:	8/0 UNI-Thread
Abdomen:	TroutHunter goose biot to match natural
Thorax:	TroutHunter Pro dubbing
Wing:	CDC fibers pulled over thorax, then divided to form V shape and clipped to body length

BONNIE HARROP PHOTO

CDC Cluster Midge

Hook:	TMC 100BL size 16-24
Thread:	8/0 Black UNI-Thread
Body:	Peacock herl
Hackle:	Grizzly Whiting palmered length of body
Wing:	White TroutHunter CDC tied no longer than body. CDC fibers should mix with hackle rather than form a distinct wing.

CDC Hanging Midge

Hook:	TMC 100 BL size 18-26
Thread:	8/0 UNI-Thread
Abdomen:	Canada goose biot
Thorax:	Muskrat gray TroutHunter Pro dubbing
Wing:	White TroutHunter CDC trimmed short
Hackle:	Whiting grizzly

CDC Hatching Midge

Hook:	TMC 100 BL size 18-26
Thread:	8/0 UNI-Thread
Tail (shuck):	Sparse dun CDC fibers trimmed to ½ body length
Abdomen:	Canada goose biot
Thorax:	Muskrat gray TroutHunter Pro dubbing
Wing case:	Dun TroutHunter CDC cupped over thorax
Legs:	Dun CDC fibers

CDC Transitional Midge

Hook:	TMC 100 BL size 18-26
Thread:	8/0 UNI-Thread
Tail (shuck):	Small grizzly hackle tip
Body:	Muskrat gray TroutHunter Pro dubbing
Legs:	Dun CDC fiber tied center of body
Wings:	Dun TroutHunter CDC cupped over body

Cutthroat and Caddis
carbon pencil
16 x 20 inches

Caddis System

Because of their rarity, things that remain reliable gain increased significance to an aging angler who finds only discomfort in most change. But near the end of each long winter, I continue to find renewal as the pulse of the river begins to quicken and once again the trout begin to rise.

Hatches during the cold season are invariably comprised of tiny midges or *Baetis* mayflies that challenge the eyesight as critically as the casting arm. As a younger man, I ignored the discomfort of cutting winds, chilled fingers, and the labor of trudging through knee-deep snow to reach the water in the hope of finding a hatch of tiny midges or *Baetis* mayflies. Even then, however, my thoughts would eventually turn to the pleasure of warmer days and the return of insects that could be matched with a fly larger than size 20. In my part of the world, there is never a hard date that can be relied upon for the first appearance of any hatch. But nature provides its own signals for the arrival of spring, and when nighttime temperatures cease to fall below freezing and the willows at streamside begin to bud, it is time to look for the first caddisflies of the year.

In my early days of fly fishing, I did not know a caddisfly from a leafhopper. However, I was quick to learn that the often annoying swarms at river's edge could translate to rising trout and that a simple Adams dry fly was a close enough match. It would be at least a decade before I began to understand the complexity of the caddisfly's existence, but there was bliss in my ignorance. Local waters were never crowded, and the fish were far more charitable in their willingness to take a fly in those days. More than forty years later, the budding willows and the insects they harbor are still a dependable announcement of a new season, but the behavior of trout and the humans who pursue them have altered the simplicity I enjoyed in my youth. Although caddisflies continue to signify opportunity, increased fishing pressure has changed the way trout respond to an artificial fly.

As fly fishers, we praise ourselves by choosing to release rather than harvest our catch, and there are positives in this civilized mentality. It is good that trout populations are not significantly depleted by our actions and that individuals are allowed to grow large. The downside to this enlightenment is a conditioned ability among larger and seasoned specimens to avoid capture. Countering this enhanced elusiveness is dependent upon several factors, not the least of which is a firm understanding of their food sources. And for as much as we wish fly fishing could be a less complicated affair, this is a reality we all must face as its popularity continues to grow.

Caddis are a key member of a diverse community of aquatic insects that includes mayflies, stoneflies, and midges, among others. In most trout waters, they are no

Swarms of mating caddis mix with Brown Drake spinners over Millionaire's Pool on the Henry's Fork. Despite an obvious size advantage, the big mayflies were not the first choice of the impressive surface feeders that were cruising the placid waters. A size fourteen CDC Fertile Caddis fooled the lead fish on the last cast of the day. BONNIE HARROP PHOTO

less important than any other hatch-producing organism, and the complexity of their life cycle equals or exceeds those of their aquatic cousins. Distinct in both appearance and behavior, caddis in their varying stages are an available and attractive nutriment for trout throughout the year.

In retrospect, it is now clear why caddis gained almost instant endearment to an aspiring fly rodder with little knowledge or finesse. Among the most notable characteristics of caddis is a propensity for movement both on and beneath the water. Like most beginners, I struggled in situations when a drag-free drift was required such as during a mayfly emergence or spinnerfall. Little did I know that a fly moving in opposition to the current could actually be duplicating the natural behavior of a caddis adult on the surface. In the beginning this would happen by accident, but I would later learn to entice a response by intentionally twitching my dry fly in the area of a caddis feeding trout. Later still would come specially designed patterns that would lend themselves more efficiently to this technique.

My father loved fly fishing, but he never progressed beyond swinging or stripping wet flies across the current and would quickly switch to bait if the trout proved unrespon-

sive. Like most of that generation, he depended primarily upon undisturbed waters for his catch, and it didn't hurt that most of the trout in his day were the relatively gullible cutthroat. He did not know and probably didn't care that his unsophisticated method and nondescript patterns were most likely imitative of caddis pupae rising quickly toward the surface to hatch. The same procedure worked for me as well until I began to explore other waters where a larger number of participants pursued haughty rainbows and secretive brown trout. By necessity, I began to refine my tactics as my obsession grew and predominant failure became an unacceptable outcome. Although painfully slow, my understanding of underwater aspects of caddis began to expand, as did my ability to contend with those elusive factors both with a fly rod and at the tying vise.

Growth in fly fishing is proportionate to time spent on the water, and observing may be the most important component. Close scrutiny of the water taught me that just prior to emergence most caddis pupae propel themselves rapidly to the surface. Release from the pupal shuck occurs rather quickly, and they become airborne as winged adults in a matter of a few seconds. A hungry trout must react quickly to intercept an escaping prey, and the accelerated action of their feeding is a distinct tipoff that emerging caddis is their likely objective. Much of this activity takes place close to the surface to produce what is often mistaken for a rise to a floating insect. One must also be alert for times when an emerging pupa in the act of changing to a winged adult becomes the primary target. This brief condition of immobility takes place in or just below the film, and the image of the artificial must mimic what is taking place. In neither instance is a fully-winged adult appropriate. However, an ascending pupa is a swimming fly that must be imitated by a sunken pattern that looks like the natural. The metamorphosis from pupa to adult requires a pattern that has elements of both stages. This is not a fixed image for more than a few seconds unless the insect is somehow injured in the process. I have found that a compact and portly configuration does the best job of portraying the bulging of the thoratic area as the enclosed adult begins to push its way through the confinement of the pupal skin. A loop of CDC over the back of the body forms a bubble that supports the fly in the correct position in the film while duplicating this tempting image.

The fledgling caddis is another style that can be used to imitate a hatching insect that is not quite able to fly. The paired CDC wings are about one-third shorter than is typically applied to fully-emerged adult imitations, and a partial collar of partridge fibers creates the lifelike impression

Bonnie Harrop took this opening day hen on an Olive CDC Henry's Fork Caddis. Cool temperatures kept the usually fleet insects riding low on the water and easily available to the fish. RENÉ HARROP PHOTO

of a freshly hatched or crippled adult as it struggles to take flight. Buoyant CDC dubbing makes this pattern equally efficient on quick or slow currents.

The conventional approach to imitating caddis emphasizes the natural characteristic of fluttering movement often observed when adults are on the water. Material used

Cased-caddis larva

Hydropsyche *pupa*

Underside of a caddis adult TOSHI KARITA PHOTOS

Henry's Fork guide Rich Paini coaches Gareth Jones during an evening caddis hatch. One of the finest anglers I have ever met, Gareth routinely scored with a CDC Spent Caddis fished as far as sixty feet from the boat. RENÉ HARROP PHOTO

in the wings will sometimes vary, but most will agree that nothing is better for keeping the hook elevated above the surface than high-quality hackle palmered over a dubbed body. Physically, CDC is softer and lighter than elk or deer hair, and I sometimes add a sparse amount of partridge or other mottled fiber to bring a more realistic appearance to the wings. Correctly tied, this style can be manipulated on the water in a manner that reflects the behavior of the actual insect. Drag, which is the inevitable result of poor presentation, is not necessarily a curse when trout are feeding on active caddis adults. This can make caddis an ideal hatch for a beginning angler of undeveloped casting skill. Cool, damp days or the chill of evening can delay the escape of freshly hatched caddis and are prime opportunities for fishing a palmered dry fly. Swarms of caddis along the banks tell us that this is a current and familiar food source. Therefore, a high-floating imitation will often tempt an opportunistic trout even during times when few caddis are actually on the water. Knowledgeable river guides frequently capitalize on this during slow periods of the day, especially when fishing from a drift boat.

The mating ritual is an intensely active period that can bring caddis back to the water despite the fact that it takes place mainly in the air or on land. Although this is purely speculation, I suspect that, like other creatures, the rigors of reproductive activity can take a physical toll on adult caddis. Since a significant portion of mating takes place in overhanging vegetation, it is only logical to assume that the isolated presence of caddis close the bank can be attributed to exhausted or weakened adults that have fallen to the water. This theory is further supported by the inert posture of the insects as they drift with the current. This situation can be encountered throughout the warmest season and usually occurs at dusk.

Unobservant anglers can disregard concentrated feeding activity along the edges of even the burliest of rivers. On the Madison, for example, trout congregate around sunset in water little more than ankle deep. The objects of their attention, as often as not, are immobilized caddis at or near the end of their existence. Subtle sipping rises are a striking contrast to the urgent assault that is normally associated with emergence. The same applies to gentler waters like the Henry's Fork where fishermen prowl open bank-side trails, completely oblivious to what they might be missing right at their feet. Big bank feeders find comfortable seclusion in undercuts where their feeding activity is concealed from predatory attention. It takes a practiced eye to discern the discrete rise, and the technical requirements are as demanding as anything in fly fishing. No less exacting is the need for accurate replication of the natural. The depth, clarity, and speed of the water combine with the behavior of the insect to determine the degree of realism needed in an artificial fly. Trout may be drawn as much to the motion as to the image of a caddis skittering across the surface. Quick, broken water can obscure a trout's view and reduce the opportunity for critical inspection of the fly. As the end draws near, caddis lose their mobility and become helpless on the water. The feeding behavior of the trout reflects this condition of vulnerability as the pace becomes much more deliberate and relaxed. Instinctively, they know the prey cannot escape, and there is usually adequate time to bring close scrutiny to the authenticity of a prospective food item.

Resistance to flawed presentation or a poor fly pattern is greater on popular catch-and-release waters where the artificial must not only appear but also behave as much like the natural as possible. Like mayfly spinners, spent caddis are at or beyond the point of expiration, which means they are completely subject to the vagaries of the current. Even minor drag is a red flag to a trout conditioned to notice the slightest discrepancy in the offering. Visually, the caddis is not an especially complicated creature, but fly fishers must pay keen attention to the key characteristics. Clouded water or a choppy surface may bring limited forgiveness from the trout for a clumsy or overdressed imitation, but otherwise, a thoughtfully constructed pattern will always be a more reliable producer.

Resting or spent caddis ride low on the water and are inherently more difficult to see, especially in smaller sizes. Like others, I have attempted to elevate the profile for the sake of improved visibility but with mostly disappointing results. Conceding to reality, I tie flies that conform as closely as possible to what I am trying to imitate. When the fly cannot be seen on the water, I compensate by concentrating on where I think it is and tighten at the sight of any rise that appears near that spot.

In the early years, discovery came rapidly because there was so much that I didn't know about water-dwelling insects. That which happened above the surface was quite easily observed, but periodically a situation would reveal something that I had overlooked. For example, I had fished caddis imitations for several years before recognizing the relevance of egg-bearing females to surface-feeding trout. It was the frustration of failure during a strong evening appearance of what were obviously low-floating caddis that led to the revelation that most were encumbered by a distinct greenish colored egg sac that was prominent in the hand but not when viewed on the water from above. Several lessons were delivered during that period of enlight-

Caddis adult TOSHI KARITA PHOTO

ening futility, not the least of which is to give foremost consideration to the trout's view of a floating insect, which is the underside. Needless to say, I am never without a good assortment of what I refer to as fertile caddis when there is a chance that egg laying might occur.

More elusive is the subsurface activity of all aquatic insects. We are conditioned to understand that their span of existence is dominated by the various underwater forms, and we have become accustomed to fishing submerged patterns that imitate these stages. Less widely understood, however, is that some fertile female caddis dive to the bottom to deposit their eggs and then return quickly to the surface. The technique for fishing a diving caddis pattern is in some ways similar to fishing a rising pupa, but it requires a winged pattern that is heavy enough to penetrate quickly into the depths. A strike can occur during the downward plunge, but it is much more likely when the fly is lifted briskly back toward the surface with the rod tip. This method is best executed with an upstream cast, and the take can be violent when it happens during the lift.

A considerable number of years had elapsed before caddis larvae found their way into my personal fishing picture. To me, it seemed rather illogical that this sedate bottom-dwelling stage could be of more than minor significance in the diet of a trout. I credit George Anderson, the noted Montana outfitter, with showing me the error of my ways when we were fishing the Madison together back in the 1970s. It was midafternoon on a hot August day, and fishing was slow. Switching from drys to a weighted imitation of a caddis larva, George nailed fish after fish in the rapid flow, while I went fishless. His simple yet deadly pattern was inspired by a common tendency of many caddis to build a protective case around themselves while in the larval stage. His technique was to bounce the fly along the

Caddis are an evening staple for much of the season on many Rocky Mountain waters. Natural insects hovering over streamside vegetation indicate that caddis activity is underway. BONNIE HARROP PHOTO

bottom at a speed equal to the current without applying action with the rod during the drift. It was a lesson well learned and one that I fall back on quite frequently throughout the year. I will also fish an imitation of the wormlike free-living larva using the same procedure, though I use this less often than its cased counterpart.

The history of my evolution as a fly fisherman and tier is revealed in a systemized approach to dealing with a single type of insect. The organized rows of specific imitations that address the varying forms of caddis are a far cry from the random assortment of mixed patterns that I carried as a youth with far more enthusiasm than reasoned effort. In the season when they are appropriate, I carry two boxes of caddis patterns, each containing at least one hundred flies. This is a good indication of just how much opportunity caddis provide on the waters I frequent. Since the beginning, I have been compelled to tie better imitations, and as my understanding has expanded so too has the effectiveness of my flies. There is no pattern in my vest that is without a predecessor, and most have many. And although there are some who might view this attitude as exceeding

the need, there is comfort in knowing that I can take something close to full advantage of what caddis have to offer, which is considerable.

A fully functional caddis system is structured to address the specific stages of the insect with attention also given to interim or emerging phases. For the waters of the Rocky Mountain West, shades of cream, tan, brown, green, and black will cover the body colors of most hatches. I rely primarily on tan, brown, gray, or black CDC for the wings on patterns that imitate the adult stage. Hooks in size 20 through 12 target the essential range of natural insects, with the exception of the giant October caddis in size 8.

There is no rule in fly fishing that requires anyone to adhere to another's approach to the sport. But I do not believe it is possible to know too much about trout and their behavior. Food is the essential motivator for the activity that produces opportunity, and as anglers we can only be as successful as our understanding will allow. In addition to correct presentation, prevailing on the water is as simple as having the right fly at the right time. A good system of imitation goes a long way toward making that happen.

BONNIE HARROP PHOTO

Caddis Larva (Green)

Hook:	TMC 200R BL size 12-20
Thread:	Olive 8/0 UNI-Thread
Weight:	Tight turns of copper wire in thorax
Abdomen:	Caddis green TroutHunter goose or turkey biot
Legs:	Black CDC fibers trimmed to ⅓ length of fly
Thorax:	Blackish brown TroutHunter CEN dubbing

Note: This weighted fly is fished deep with no action.

BONNIE HARROP PHOTO

Cased Caddis Larva (Green)

Hook:	TMC 200R BL size 12-20
Thread:	Olive 8/0 UNI-Thread
Rib:	Copper wire with extra tight turns in thorax for added weight
Case:	Pheasant tail fibers over tapered dubbing to form conical shape
Abdomen:	Narrow band of caddis green TroutHunter Pro dubbing
Legs:	Black CDC fibers trimmed to ⅓ length of fly
Thorax:	Blackish brown TroutHunter CEN dubbing

Note: This weighted fly is fished deep with no action.

BONNIE HARROP PHOTO

CDC Ascending Caddis (Tan)

Hook:	TMC 206 BL size 12-20
Thread:	Tan 8/0 UNI-Thread
Rib:	Gold wire
Back:	Brown marabou
Abdomen:	Tan TroutHunter CEN dubbing
Legs:	Brown partridge fibers tied as a partial collar
Antennae:	2 wood duck fibers
Thorax:	Brown TroutHunter CEN dubbing

Note: Fish this fly beneath the surface on a tight line quartering downstream. Twitch the fly with the rod tip, and retrieve at the end of the drift with a short, quick, stripping action.

BONNIE HARROP PHOTO

Bubble Back Caddis (Tan)

Hook:	TMC 206 BL size 12-20
Thread:	Tan 8/0 UNI-Thread
Shuck:	Sparse tuft of tan TroutHunter CEN dubbing over three wood duck fibers
Abdomen:	Paired natural tan TroutHunter CDC feathers looped over tan TroutHunter CEN dubbing to create a humped effect
Hackle:	Brown partridge fibers tied as a collar
Thorax:	Brown TroutHunter CEN dubbing

Note: Fish this fly dead-drift in the film or twitch it with the rod tip.

BONNIE HARROP PHOTO

CDC Caddis Emerger (Olive)

Hook:	TMC 100 BL size 12-20
Thread:	Olive 8/0 UNI-Thread
Shuck:	Olive CDC fibers trimmed to length of abdomen
Abdomen:	Olive TroutHunter goose or turkey biot
Wings:	Paired natural blue dun CDC feathers
Overwing:	Four to six natural blue dun CDC fibers ⅓ longer than wings
Legs:	Brown partridge fibers
Antennae:	Two wood duck fibers
Thorax:	Blackish brown TroutHunter CEN dubbing

Note: Fish this fly dead-drift in the film or twitch it with the rod tip. You can also fish it beneath the surface on a tight line quartering downstream. Twitch the fly with the rod tip and retrieve at the end of the drift with a short, quick, stripping action.

BONNIE HARROP PHOTO

CDC Fledgling Caddis (Tan)

Hook:	TMC 206 BL size 12-20
Thread:	Tan 8/0 UNI-Thread
Shuck:	Sparse tuft of tan TroutHunter CDC dubbing
Abdomen:	Tan TroutHunter CDC dubbing
Legs:	Brown partridge fibers tied as a partial collar
Wings:	Paired natural tan TroutHunter CDC feathers
Antennae:	Two wood duck fibers

Note: Fish this fly on the surface either dead-drift or twitching it with the rod tip.

BONNIE HARROP PHOTO

CDC Palmered Caddis Adult (Brown)

Hook:	TMC 100 BL size 12-20
Thread:	Tan 8/0 UNI-Thread
Hackle:	Whiting cree or grizzly dyed tan
Body:	Brown TroutHunter Pro dubbing
Wings:	Paired natural brown TroutHunter CDC feathers
Antennae:	Two wood duck fibers

Note: Fish this fly on the surface either dead-drift or twitching it with the rod tip.

BONNIE HARROP PHOTO

CDC Henry's Fork Caddis (Olive)

Hook:	TMC 100 BL size 12-20
Thread:	Olive 8/0 UNI-Thread
Abdomen:	Olive TroutHunter goose or turkey biot
Wing:	Paired natural blue dun TroutHunter CDC feathers
Overwing:	Brown partridge fibers
Thorax:	Peacock herl
Hackle:	Whiting grizzly dyed dun trimmed on bottom in a wide V

Note: Fish this fly dead-drift on the surface when caddis adults are at rest on the water.

BONNIE HARROP PHOTO

CDC Fertile Caddis (Brown)

Hook: TMC 100 BL size 12-20
Thread: Tan 8/0 UNI-Thread
Egg sac: Single caddis green TroutHunter CDC
            feather trimmed to ¼ body length
Abdomen: Brown TroutHunter goose or turkey biot
Wings: Paired natural brown TroutHunter CDC
            feathers
Legs: Butts of CDC wings tied back and
            trimmed to ½ body length
Thorax: Blackish brown TroutHunter CEN
            dubbing

Note: Fish this fly dead-drift on the surface when egg-bearing female caddis are on the water.

BONNIE HARROP PHOTO

CDC Diving Caddis (Olive)

Hook: TMC 3761 BL size 12-20
Thread: Olive 8/0 UNI-Thread
Egg sac: Single caddis green TroutHunter CDC
            feather trimmed to ¼ body length
Rib: Gold wire with extra tight turns in thorax
            for added weight
Abdomen: Olive TroutHunter CEN dubbing
Legs: Brown partridge fibers tied as a partial
            collar
Wings: Paired natural blue dun TroutHunter
            CDC feathers
Antennae: Two wood duck fibers
Thorax: Blackish brown TroutHunter CEN
            dubbing

Note: This is a weighted fly that is allowed to sink and then lifted back toward the surface with the rod tip.

BONNIE HARROP PHOTO

CDC Paracaddis (Brown)

Hook: TMC 206 BL size 12-20
Thread: Tan 8/0 UNI-Thread
Body: Brown TroutHunter CDC dubbing
Wings: Paired natural brown TroutHunter CDC feathers
Post: Butts of CDC feathers
Hackle: Whiting cree or grizzly dyed tan and trimmed in a wide V from front of hackle

Note: Fish this fly dead-drift on the surface when spent adults are on the water.

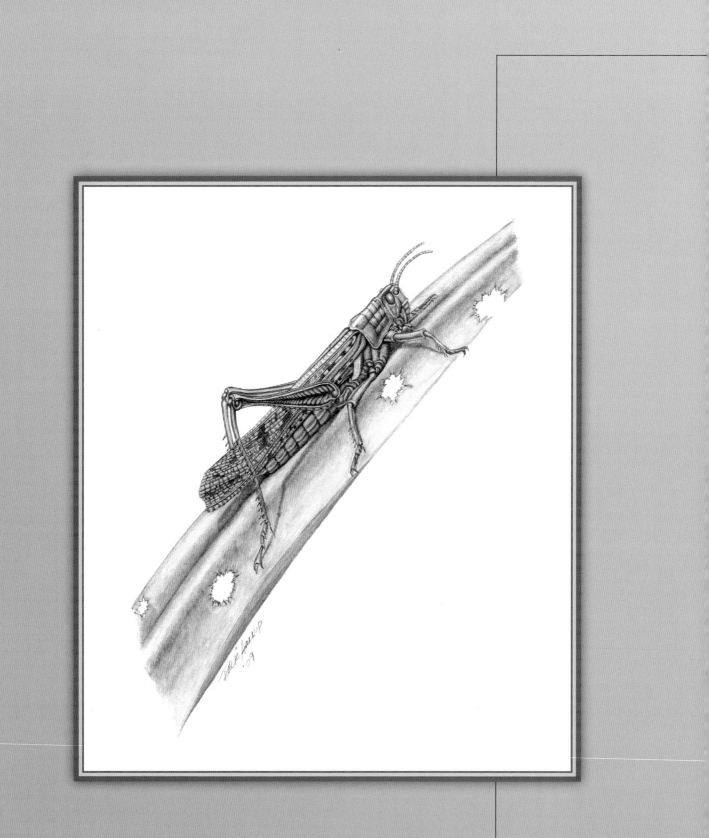

Hopper
carbon pencil with watercolor tint
9 x 11 inches

Hoppers

Large and Small

My attraction to fishing began at a very young age. As a farm kid in eastern Idaho, I was surrounded by a variety of waters just waiting for a fat night crawler or some other common bait. Even local irrigation canals held prospects, and I would sit for hours waiting for a fish to bite. The species did not matter and a fat sucker brought as much excitement as its more attractive and edible relatives. Mostly, I sank my hook into deep, mysterious pools where only the heft of the fish could be identified before it came into view. And it was at such a place that I first recall seeing an identifiable insect struggle across the top of the water only to be engulfed in the swirl of a large trout. Even as a raw beginner, I was aware that fish would periodically splash at the surface, but until that day I did not understand what was actually going on. Identified from a distance of little more than a dozen feet, it was clearly a grasshopper that had tempted the big cutthroat up from the depths. This was a turning point in the life of a young angler who would eventually lose himself to the charms of rising trout and the insects that make it happen.

I did not instantly become a fly fisherman on that fateful summer day in the early 1950s, but my mind opened to possibilities that far exceeded sitting in the shade of streamside willows while waiting for something to happen at the end of my line. For the next several years, I would wait in anticipation for the drying winds of midsummer and the irresistible flying bait that came with them. Invariably, this season produced the best fishing of the year, and I carried the knowledge that trout love hoppers beyond the bait fishing days to the time when artificial flies began to dominate my mentality.

For the most part, my beginning years of fishing with a fly rod were spent not knowing what my flies were imitating. Hoppers were the rare exception, and my earliest attempts at fly tying produced clumsy and vague representations of the one insect I knew would attract trout. Skill and understanding increased with the passing of time, and many childish ideas and attitudes were cast aside. At no time along the way, however, have I forgotten that early lesson from the water.

For most devotees of the dry fly, size does matter. Mention a size 22 Trico hatch and more often than not you will get a painful grimace in response. Conversely, news that the Salmonflies are hatching on the Big Hole is guaranteed to light up the face of anyone who has sampled the gorging frenzy evoked by the giant bugs. Big flies are synonymous with big fish and, to some degree, easy fishing. Witness the mass of expectant anglers who gather along the Henry's Fork in mid-June each year for an event that often fails to meet expectations. For some, however, just the chance of hitting a hatch of the oversize mayflies known as Green Drakes is justification enough to drive

Any angler with experience will carry a selection of hopper patterns during the warm days of summer. Patterns as small as size 16 depict younger insects, which are available to trout as early as June. Growing as the season progresses, these tempting terrestrials are often imitated with artificials as large as size 4. BONNIE HARROP PHOTO

hundreds of miles. And while it is true that large aquatic insects often deliver on the promise of spectacular fishing, they can be fickle and short-lived. Influences of weather and water conditions can disrupt the timing and duration of their appearance, making it difficult to plan a trip intended to intercept such events.

Land-based insects known a terrestrials do not seem as vulnerable to the vagaries of nature as their waterborne counterparts, and ants, beetles, and other non-aquatic organisms can be as vital to dry-fly opportunity as mayflies or caddis. And although most are relatively small, some possess the size and substance to motivate almost reckless response from trout. Their added advantage is a reliability of population, which combines with a prolonged period of availability. Although symbolic of hot, dry, and windy weather, hoppers are not nearly as limited as their stereotype would imply.

Hoppers become more available to trout as their habitat begins to shrink. The vegetation of unirrigated fields

Underside of hopper TOSHI KARITA PHOTO

and meadows begin to lose their nutritive value when seeds mature and stalks, stems, and leaves wither in the heat of mid to late summer. This occurrence coincides with the maturing of the lively, crackling insects that migrate toward sources of water where plant life remains fairly lush. By early September, hordes of hoppers concentrate tightly along the banks of rivers and streams as both they and their requisite forage prepare to fully complete their respective life cycles.

It takes something special to break through the secretive behavior of large brown trout. This early autumn brown could not resist the tantalizing action of a rubber leg hopper on the lower Henry's Fork. BONNIE HARROP PHOTO

For as long as eight weeks before they succumb to freezing temperatures, hoppers can be successfully imitated with dry flies as large as size 4. Stream banks that lie in favorable orientation to prevailing breezes are oftentimes lined with lusty trout just waiting for a grasshopper wind to distribute the meal. Animals, both wild and domestic, are considered allies by hopper-hungry fish that associate their streamside activity with the arrival of food. Even anglers strolling close to the water are not an alarming sight if their presence causes hoppers to scatter across the surface.

Some experienced anglers hunt the fabled hopper banks of Rocky Mountain meadow streams almost exclusively during the prime season. River guides relish the tim when a big, high-floating hopper pattern may be the only fly his client will need for an entire day on the water. On choppy water, it often doesn't matter if the fly drags. Trout quickly become accustomed to seeing the struggling, kicking motion of desperate creatures that are completely out of their element when they find themselves on the water.

Also, a delicate presentation does not duplicate the audible sound of a hopper crashing into the surface, which is something that may attract rather than frighten a fish. Hoppers blown too far from shore are subject to drowning before making it back to the safety of land. And although it is undoubtedly better if the imitation is floating, a sunken hopper is not automatically rejected. Such cushions against flawed techniques are a rarity on any popular public water where trout are subjected to a near constant barrage of artificial flies. Bear in mind, however, that on slower currents where clear water magnifies all errors, trout can be as critical of an imperfectly presented hopper as of any other artificial offering. Fast water patterns, for which flotation receives primary emphasis, do not always possess the requisite features to make them effective in more exacting conditions.

A live hopper attempting to flee the water is partially submerged, and trout in spring creek-like conditions have every advantage in visually assessing the validity of a fly.

A favorable wind can deliver exciting action when hoppers concentrate along the edges of nearly any stream in the Rocky Mountain West. This Henry's Fork rainbow took a size 16 Spring Creek Hopper in early July. The same pattern two sizes larger would be more appropriate a month later.
BONNIE HARROP PHOTO

My grandson Zach Wheeler found himself without a hopper pattern when he spotted a nice rainbow near the famous log-jam on the Henry's Fork. He picked this old deer-hair hopper that had been in my fly box for more than thirty years and promptly nailed the 20-inch bank feeder on the first cast.
BONNIE HARROP PHOTO

When angling pressure is heavy, seasoned trout apply stern scrutiny to not only how the fly looks but also how it behaves. The larger the fly, the more blatant the flaw. Foam hoppers, while ideal for brisk, heavy currents, may actually float too high to duplicate the half-sunken image that I believe must be present to be a realistic and dependable slow-water pattern.

With a heavy, plump abdomen as the dominant feature of a natural, I find it practical to use reversed elk hair to form the extended body of my hopper imitations. Realistic segmentation is created with crisscrossing turns of thread that gather the individual elk hairs as they leave the hook shank to produce the necessary length of the abdomen. Although somewhat buoyant by itself, the elk-hair body seems to float in, rather than on, the surface. I keep the pattern floating low by applying floatant only to the wings, which support the fly in a natural position on the water. When probing quick water along the shoreline from a boat, I grease the entire fly, giving special attention to the abdomen to assure a long drift and good visibility. Two or three snappy false casts will dry the fly and keep it floating high. I rinse the fly after landing a fish to remove any slime and then blot it dry between the folds of a buckskin drying patch. Amadou also works well for this purpose.

Realism in the wings of the hopper pattern must be balanced against their flotation properties. Straight, hollow elk or deer hair is a good choice for the latter purpose. However, the flaring of these commonly used wing materials when tightly secured to the hook is a drawback to realistic hopper wings. I solve this problem by enclosing the hair under-wing with overlapping segments of turkey wing quill. This over-wing comes from matching right and left feathers that have been reinforced with an art fixative called Tuffilm, which prevents the individual fibers from separating. I trim the segments in equal widths, and snip the tips diagonally to a taper that is similar to real hopper wings. After installing each wing segment individually with the upper edge rolled slightly over the top of the body, I trim the butts of both the under-wing and over-wing just behind the eye to form a pronounced head that resembles the real thing. Recently, I have replaced the hair underwing with two or three CDC feathers, which seem to provide enhanced flotation.

Simplicity in the design and construction of an artificial has always made sense to me. This somewhat traditional philosophy of fly tying is applied to all aspects of the way I tie hoppers, including the all-important legs. Lively rubber strands flecked with contrasting color are ideal for hopper legs. When knotted, the jointed rubber legs resemble the powerful hind legs of a live hopper, a prominent characteristic in both the appearance and behavior of the insect. Trout are attracted to the motion as much as the image of hoppers, which means that equal consideration must be given to both factors. In many instances, the kicking motion induced by subtle manipulations of the rod tip will entice more strikes than a motionless drift.

The presentation of any large fly involves certain adjustments on the part of the angler. Slow-action rods and light lines do not give casting advantage in situations where the excessive bulk and air resistance of larger hopper patterns dictate the results. Likewise, a relatively short and heavy leader will more easily handle the task of punching sizable imitations into the wind that typifies ideal hopper-fishing conditions. Such contrasts to conventional dry-fly strategies are of little consequence on big, brawling water, but in slow, clear-water situations that demand finesse, such a coarse setup can be highly problematic. Although I take pride in the fact that even my largest hoppers are designed to minimize the resistance to ease of casting, they do present a problem for the 4-weight rod and 16-foot leader that I favor for the majority of my dry-fly fishing.

On the Henry's Fork, my home water, the very best hopper fishing takes place in areas that are widely known for requiring highly developed presentation skills because of

Perhaps no insect is more capable of bringing large trout to the surface than a fat hopper. The weakness of trout for a good hopper imitation can bring welcome relief to the normal selective feeding behavior of a big Henry's Fork rainbow.
BONNIE HARROP PHOTO

the extremely discerning trout. With minor exceptions, the big rainbows demand no less precision when taking a fake hopper than in any other selective surface-feeding situation. This applies to casting proficiency as well as realism in the imitation. The forceful arrival of a hopper on quiet water is accepted as a perfectly normal occurrence unless accompanied by the overhead presence of a fly line. Such motion, or the shadows it creates, are warning signs that the trout know all too well. So too is a stiff and visible tippet that betrays the fly as a fraud. A solution to the problem of delicate hopper presentation on demanding water did arrive—but it took some time.

In fly fishing, growth is often dictated by one's ability to penetrate the obvious. Hoppers become obvious during a rather narrow portion of the season when they are large and concentrated close to water. This, however, describes only a brief portion of their existence. Hoppers begin as tiny miniatures of what we later see as they approach the conclusion of their life. This differs from many aquatic organisms that begin life in an underwater environment as creatures largely unlike the winged insects we fly fishers are accustomed to seeing on the water. Physical growth of mayflies, caddisflies, and stoneflies occurs during the underwater phase over a period of several months. Trout will not see a mayfly adult from a single hatch become any larger than at the time of its emergence from the final submerged stage. Although not as frequently as later in the season, hoppers can become the target of a hungry and opportunistic trout in late spring and early summer. Their size, at this time, is but a fraction of what they will later become, but their appearance and behavior is essentially the same whether still developing or fully mature.

I had fished for a number of years before learning that I did not have to wait until late July or August to capitalize on the benefits of fishing hoppers. Like ants or beetles, hoppers do not intentionally locate themselves on water. Fateful accidents can happen to hoppers at any time during the course of normal activity, but wind is most often the culprit. Carrying ant and beetle patterns ranging from size 12 down to size 20 and smaller had become a habit long before I thought of fishing hoppers smaller than size 10. However, it only required one experience on the Madison to alter that practice. It happened on a late June day when the river was devoid of normal surface activity. However, livestock feeding close to the river's edge were stirring up tiny size 16 hoppers that were being blown onto the water by the stiff breeze. Half a dozen sizable trout were lined along a sixty-foot stretch of bank where drifting hoppers provided an easy afternoon meal. With nothing in my vest that came even close, I left those fish unmolested if not undisturbed. Not left behind, however, was a lesson I have never forgotten. From that point on my box of terrestrials contains as many hoppers below size 12 as above.

Although it is somewhat unusual to find hoppers as the primary objective until a month or so later than my experience on the Madison, small hoppers can successfully be fished with the same approach as an ant or a beetle. This is usually as a searching pattern when action is slow, or as an option during a hatch when the fishing simply gets too tough. Perhaps the greatest advantage of fishing hoppers smaller than size 12 is the ease with which they can be presented on a long leader and light tippet. This is of tremendous advantage when fishing the clear, tricky currents of late summer and early fall when the water is low and the fish are especially wary. Though real hoppers are much larger on average, and a size 14 imitation is not nearly as enticing as a size 8, a spooked trout will never take an artificial—and a 9-foot, 3X leader will almost certainly assure that result. Therefore, I fish with far greater confidence with an undersized pattern and a long, fine leader. Trout seem willing to respond to a reduced image of a hopper as long as it is well-defined in the key areas, which are the abdomen and hind legs. Also, remember that a size 14 or 16 hopper is much larger than the majority of aquatic insects that hatch during the same peak period of availability. A hopper pattern need not be large to attract trout away from much smaller aquatic insects.

Hoppers, whether large or small, definitely deserve a place in a fly fisherman's heart. They are as reliable as the wind on a summer day, and as welcome as the season in which they appear. It is a time of plenty when gifts from the land are distributed on the water, and both trout and angler can partake of the bounty.

BONNIE HARROP PHOTO

Foam Hopper

Hook:	TMC 5212 size 6-10
Thread:	Olive 3/0 monocord
Body:	Green closed-cell foam
Under-wing:	Sparse Krystal Flash
Wing:	Olive elk hair
Indicator:	Paired fluorescent orange TroutHunter CDC feathers
Legs:	Chartreuse rubber legs

CDC Rubber Leg Hopper

Hook:	TMC 100 BL size 8-16
Thread:	Brown 3/0 monocord
Body:	Tan elk hair extended over heavy monofilament core
Under-wing:	Paired natural tan TroutHunter CDC feathers
Wings:	Paired mottled turkey quill segments
Legs:	Tan rubber legs

Black CDC Cricket

Hook:	TMC 100 BL size 8-16
Thread:	Black 3/0 monocord
Body:	Black elk hair extended over heavy monofilament core
Under-wing:	Black elk hair
Wings:	Paired black TroutHunter CDC feathers
Legs:	Black TroutHunter goose biots

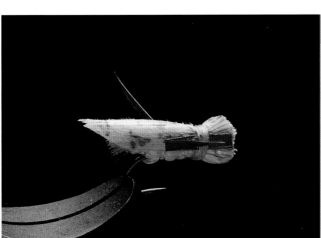

Spring Creek Hopper

Hook:	TMC 100 BL size 8-16
Thread:	Yellow 3/0 monocord
Body:	Yellow elk hair extended over heavy monofilament core
Under-wing:	Natural elk hair
Wings:	Paired mottled turkey quill segments
Legs:	Rusty spinner TroutHunter goose biots

Beetle
carbon pencil with watercolor tint
11 x 14 inches

Beetles
Plan B

The idea of a magic fly is as old as fly fishing. And it is a safe guess that most of those who pursue the sport would be delighted to exchange the complexity of fly selection for a single pattern that would tempt trout to the surface in all situations. While it is said that any fly will catch fish if it is fished long enough, we learn early on that our success hinges primarily upon the ability to identify and match insects that happen to gain the attention of trout at that particular moment. In the best habitat, it is typically mayflies, caddis, or some other aquatic organism that induces the highest level of interest. For the extreme dry-fly enthusiast, hatches of these insects both familiar and otherwise seem to be an ever-changing complication that is manifested in vests heavily laden with fly boxes that seem to expand until they reach full capacity. As a willing member of this rather obsessive group, I confess to an objective of having the right fly at any given time on the wonderful and diverse waters near my home not far from Yellowstone.

At the expense of a usually aching back, the fifteen or more fly boxes I carry on most days do an acceptable job of handling what I might encounter over one-hundred-plus annual days of fishing. While viewed as excessive by some, I consider the rewards of a fly-heavy vest to be well worth the discomfort, which always vanishes when I am playing a big trout. With familiar, quality water only minutes away, my fishing time is usually planned to coincide with the reasonably predictable appearance of certain hatches. But on a river like the Henry's Fork, you learn to expect the unexpected, and no day seems to be without a surprise of some kind. Despite having a multitude of proven patterns close at hand, there are plenty of times when my best efforts at fooling a particular trout are met with complete disdain. Most frustrating are the times when the trout's objective is clearly identifiable and everything seems perfect, from the cast to the choice of fly pattern. Finding oneself in a heated engagement that may last up to an hour can mean a repetitious marathon of casts beyond count and numerous fly changes. Surrender is not an option when the trout is especially large or when pride comes into play, but success in this situation can sometimes be had by an alternative plan that falls outside common logic.

My inside vest pocket contains a relatively small fly box with the contents marked as plan B. And though humble in comparison to its more sophisticated companions, this assortment of flies plays a distinct and valued role in many trout encounters when a favorable outcome is dependent upon an unconventional solution to an otherwise hopeless situation.

In the minds of the fly-fishing majority, beetles are a purely terrestrial enticement to trout. Grouped with other

This angler took a nice rainbow from Millionaire's Pool on the Henry's Fork during a strong *Callibaetis* hatch. He later told me that he chose to use a size 12 Black Beetle rather than trying to match the speckled mayflies. BONNIE HARROP PHOTO

land-based insects such as hoppers and ants, they are typically considered a food source of short seasonal availability. Developing through larval and pupal stages, terrestrial beetles at high elevation generally attain adulthood in the warmer months of mid to late summer. At the driest time of year, the mobile adults seek alternative habitat close to water, where natural vegetation remains lush until everything begins to wither with the frost of autumn. During this period of lower water levels and higher than ideal temperatures for aquatic insect activity, beetles are at their most active along the edges of streams that flow through open terrain. Wind, rain, and other influences, such as grazing livestock, are capable of sending sizable numbers of this known delicacy to the water, where trout quickly seize upon the easy meal. Fishing a beetle imitation along shaded edges where streamside vegetation is present helps to fill quiet times when insect activity is sparse. Opportunistic trout take up residence in these areas and are constantly on the lookout for food items dropping on the water from above. Unsuited to this situation and

Beetle   TOSHI KARITA PHOTO

completely helpless, beetles float low on the water, and a gentle, sipping motion may be the only indication of a trout's presence.

As winged insects, beetles can fly away from the banks, which means that a beetle imitation can be appropriate for midstream trout as well. A trout that rises randomly when no particular hatch is underway can be a receptive target for a drag-free beetle imitation. As a recognized form, the trout's rise to a beetle in this situation is nearly always con-

This bank feeder ignored every pattern I tried during a Brown Drake hatch on the Henry's Fork until I switched to a CDC Beetle that was two sizes smaller than the big mayflies. It was dark by the time the fish was hooked and landed. BONNIE HARROP PHOTO

fident and sometimes quite energetic if the trout is moving some distance in the process of collecting the morsel. Larger beetle patterns can also raise the excitement level, resulting in an enthusiastic and showy take. Modern beetle designs of buoyant foam and lively rubber legs are especially known for evoking this type of response.

Although it is not common practice, it is probably possible to fish a beetle exclusively in the proper time frame and location with results acceptable to those with less than advanced knowledge or interest in other trout foods. With no rules to the contrary, anyone is free to simplify his fishing by ignoring the complexity of trout behavior. I know plenty of Henry's Fork regulars who will not fish a different fly until they are completely satisfied that a beetle will not get the job done. Most, however, base initial fly selection on what is observed on the water when fishing to a trout that is seriously involved in feeding. There are certainly times when beetles dominate the available food source, and a close imitation can be the appropriate choice. This is often the case on breezy summer days when substantial numbers of beetles are blown onto the water. Personally, I have never witnessed an occasion when the

volume of these insects was adequate to create anything close to a feeding frenzy, but I do recall times when a beetle was the top-producing fly of the day.

It is difficult for me to contemplate the subject of beetles without recalling one of the genuine characters of the past. Through most of the summer months, Chuck Gash made an almost daily hike of more than a mile into the interior of the Harriman Ranch on the Henry's Fork. He was elderly when I met him in the 1980s, and we never did become closely acquainted. I was impressed, however, by the deliberate pace at which he fished and his obvious love of the river. While always separated on the water by some distance, I watched his patient approach and the simple downstream presentation he seemed to always prefer, but we talked only in passing on the worn trail along the river's edge. On most days, his catch seldom seemed impressive, but he usually took a fish or two, which seemed to satisfy his need. Although I have never confirmed it, many believed that Chuck fished a simple, black deer-hair beetle, regardless of what was actually on the water. It is also said he believed that given a choice, a trout would always select a beetle over anything else that

A foam beetle is most suitable on fast, choppy water. This Madison River brown was feeding along a grass-covered island in current that would drown most beetle patterns. RONNIE HARROP PHOTO

might be available. And though this theory has never been completely proven to my satisfaction, there is definitely something unique in the way trout respond to beetles. And like others who knew him, I credit that old gentleman for bringing a greater awareness of this behavior to light. I carry and fish beetles a lot more since knowing Chuck Gash.

On spring creeks and slow-moving meadow water, a trout's fondness for beetles does not minimize the need for careful presentation. And while there are certain exceptions, the requirements differ little from those that apply to other situations where the trout are wary and very skeptical of drag. A standard setup usually includes a long leader of 12 or more feet with a tippet averaging about 6X. A size 14 or smaller beetle pattern will not generally require a major adjustment in this leader when switching from a delicate mayfly or caddis imitation. I especially like CDC for its lightness, and use it almost exclusively for beetles intended to be fished in these conditions. A drag-free presentation is most typical when imitating beetle behavior on the water, where the usual movement of the natural is only an occasional wriggling of the legs. Soft fibers of CDC will move subtly with the current or a gentle twitch with the rod tip if needed.

Although brown and olive are also included, black beetle patterns dominate my fly box. Iridescence is a key feature of many beetles, which explains why peacock herl shows prominently in some of my most effective patterns. Ring-necked pheasant tail fibers, either natural or dyed, can also yield a desirable effect. Above size 12, dyed elk hair is usually substituted for CDC, although sadly at the cost of extra weight and a tendency to become waterlogged rather quickly. Although far from an advocate of closed-cell foam, I concede to its advantage in tying larger beetle patterns. Although infrequently encountered in big numbers, beetles up to size 4 are not rare. Any viable food item of such size will not be ignored by a hungry trout, particularly when the insect is struggling on the surface.

Big, foam bugs with plenty of rubber legs are a favorite tool of river guides when drift fishing during quiet periods on medium to very fast water. Fished tightly along the banks or on other logical holding water, these virtually unsinkable flies do not require much finesse. Alighting heavily on the water is not usually a problem when "crash-landing" describes the arrival of the natural. Ordinarily the kiss of death, drag can be a positive when it activates the lively rubber legs that can generate a savage response from beneath.

Big trout in slow, clear, and relatively shallow water show zero patience for clumsiness even when the presentation delivers an oversize beetle. Although the pattern can be similar to that which is appropriate for heavier flows, a longer, more refined cast is the general rule. Subtle manipulations administered with the rod tip will bring the artificial to life without alarming the fish, if executed correctly. Twitching the fly with the rod tip is an intentional and controlled act, but allowing the fly to be dragged contrary to the current is the result of a bad cast. Remember, however, that very large beetles are the exception to what is commonly viewed by trout. On most water in my experience, a size 14 beetle is somewhat larger than average. Smaller sizes are invariably more numerous, and therefore more familiar to trout.

Anglers tend to know less about aquatic beetles than they do about their land-based cousins. Perhaps this can be explained by the scarcity of research as it applies to aquatic beetles and their role in the diet of a trout. Few fly-fishing publications provide separation between aquatic and terrestrial beetles, which leaves us guessing to a large extent. With limited scientific information, it is most practical to address the similarities of the two types of beetles, with specific emphasis on their collective ability to bring trout to the surface.

The hard wing covering creates a domed effect on the back of most beetles, whether aquatic or terrestrial, and the size of both types can range from small to large. They can vary in color, although most seem to be quite dark. I think aquatic beetles are more mobile on the water than terrestrial beetles. Observation will dictate how individual behavior should be duplicated in fishing situations. However, a dead-drift presentation seems to out-fish any other method of presenting a beetle pattern.

Still or slow-moving water with a silted bottom is the home for aquatic beetles, and adult activity is not limited to just the warmer months. Where populations are present, a beetle pattern can be appropriate even in winter when air temperatures reach a reasonable level. For fly fishermen, this is probably the most important difference between aquatic and terrestrial beetles.

A box of beetles stays in my vest regardless of the season. Its contents are based upon observation without regard to the origin of the naturals they represent. A beetle pattern comes into play when naturals are observed on the water, and I try to match what I am seeing at that time. There are times, however, when a trout's love for beetles is incorporated into a different strategy.

Prowling upstream along the banks of a clear trout stream has become a habit during quiet times between hatches. Watching for big, resting trout outside the main flow can add considerable productive time when others

Beetles join hoppers, ants, and other terrestrials to draw trout to the water's edge. Fishing a beetle pattern close to streamside vegetation is a productive way to fill time between aquatic hatches. BONNIE HARROP PHOTO

have given up for the day, with the added advantage of having a lot of water to yourself. The real challenge is to spot the fish from a far enough distance to prevent it from being spooked by the motion of casting. Entering the water can be an option if you need to lower your profile, but this often comes at the risk of alerting or loosing sight of the trout. When practical, I prefer to kneel on the bank while keeping the objective in constant view. A long, fine leader will minimize the likelihood of the line or its shadow bringing a premature end to the game. Few are the times when something edible is not in motion with the water even though the number may be sparse. The trick is to show the trout something recognizable as food, and it helps when a known attractiveness can be capitalized upon. In many situations, a beetle fits this criterion, which is why it is often the first fly I will try when an opportunity presents itself.

A cast made from downstream must be gentle and accurate because the fly and leader must travel over and beyond the fish, and there is no way to manipulate the drift once the fly is on the water. When not actively involved in feeding, a trout may require more time than usual to recognize a floating food item, and it is impossible to predict its response. At times, a startling rush to the surface will occur the instant the fly comes into view, but a trout can also ponder the decision well beyond the time when the fly passes overhead. I have watched trout turn, likely sensing that a beetle is not about to escape, and follow the fly six or more feet and then take it while going downstream. My policy when fishing beetles in this situation is to drop the fly at least four feet beyond the trout and to delay the pickup until it has drifted eight to ten feet below. In my experience, three or four good drifts without a response reveal the need to change from a beetle to a different fly. A subsurface nymph is the most logical alternative when trout ignore a beetle.

Perhaps the strongest evidence of a trout's weakness for beetles is displayed at a time when most anglers would not think of trying one. And while far from being foolproof, more than one highly resistant trout has succumbed to a tactic I refer to as plan B. Speaking personally, nothing in fly fishing is more enthralling than a one-on-one show-

down with an exceptional fish. Countless are the hours I have spent locked in on a single trout that defies my best efforts, both physically and intellectually. I love the challenge of not one but many perfect casts, and the mysteries that can accompany the identity of the right fly. Personal pride and respect for the adversary usually prevent any weakening to the temptation of finding a way to short-circuit the hatch-matching scenario when facing defeat by a superior opponent. In reality, fishing a beetle at such a time is the equivalent of surrender for one who treasures the magic of a hatch. On a river like the Henry's Fork, one becomes accustomed to disrespectful treatment from big savvy trout that can seem invincible. To become a sore loser even in times of belittlement is never considered to be a mark of strong character, but a man can only take so much. Although never absolutely assured, more than one trout has submitted to a black beetle fished solely as an act of utter desperation.

Although highly prized by trout, beetles are not a substitute for solid knowledge of other food sources, and simply fishing a beetle imitation will not make up for poor physical skills. In general, a beetle will be rejected at least as often as it is accepted, even with perfect presentation. Through a significant portion of the season, however, fishing a beetle can make as much sense as anything, and failing to acknowledge this fortunate reality is an avoidable mistake.

Black CDC Beetle

Hook: TMC 206BL size 12-20
Thread: Black 8/0 UNI-Thread
Body: Peacock herl
Legs: Black CDC fibers
Shellback: 2-4 black TroutHunter CDC feathers cupped over body to create a domed effect

Brown CDC Beetle

Hook: TMC 206BL size 12-20
Thread: Rusty 8/0 UNI-Thread
Body: Pheasant tail fibers
Legs: Reddish brown CDC fibers
Shellback: 2-4 reddish brown TroutHunter CDC feathers cupped over body to create a domed effect

Black Elk Hair Beetle

Hook: TMC 100BL size 8-14
Thread: Black 8/0 UNI-Thread
Body: Peacock herl
Shellback: Black elk hair
Legs: Black elk hair

Big Foam

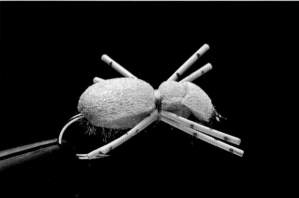

Hook: TMC 5212 size 4-12
Thread: Olive 3/0 monocord
Body: Peacock herl
Shellback: Green closed-cell foam
Legs: Gray and black rubber legs

BONNIE HARROP PHOTO

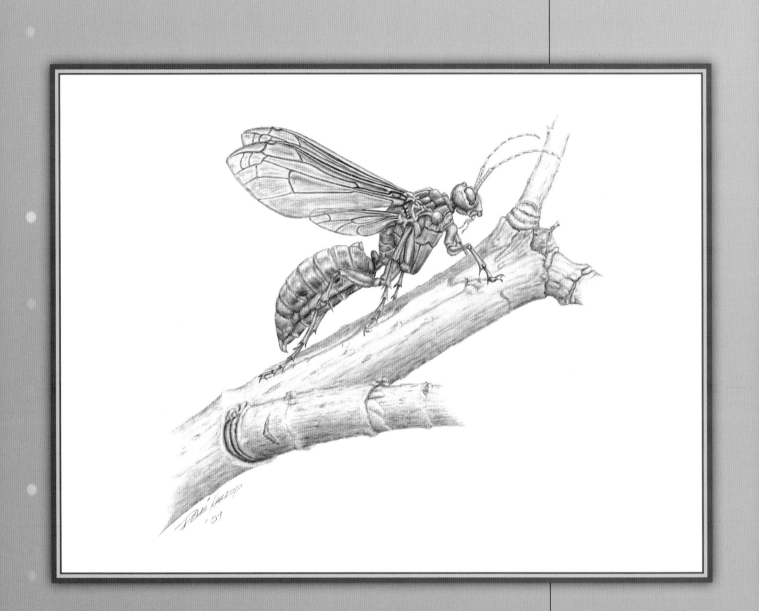

Aquatic Wasp
carbon pencil with watercolor tint
9 x 11 inches

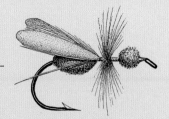

Aquatic Wasps

A Mystery

Like several other prolific trout streams in the Rocky Mountain West, the reputation of the Henry's Fork is forged by an abundance of insects that cause trout to rise. Success on such waters is largely dependent upon the ability to identify and imitate key forms while accurately predicting the timing of their appearance. Aided substantially by the research and subsequent writings of notable angler/entomologists during the 1970s, many, if not most, who fish the prominent waters of the Yellowstone region have a relatively firm grasp on the identity of major aquatic insect populations and know when to expect to see them on the water. Although less complex in their relationship to trout, terrestrial insects have not been overlooked as a food source of considerable significance.

Historically speaking, mayflies take center stage in terms of producing bank-to-bank attention on the surface. Caddis are a close second in this regard, followed by stoneflies and midges in the usual order of importance. Barring the occasional exception, land-based insects, such as hoppers, beetles, and ants, do not provide expansive feeding opportunity on big water. In the proper season, however, trout stay alert along the edges, where terrestrials can become available at nearly any time of day. Trout display a consistent fondness for any food source unable to escape capture, which fits the description of most insects not born of the water. Excepting conditions of a strong wind that can carry the naturals a considerable distance from their habitat, it is normally practical to fish a terrestrial pattern within 20 or 30 feet from the bank.

For a fly fisher, nothing is more stirring than the sight of a blanket hatch or spinnerfall and the accompanying attention it can receive. We plan and hope for those times when everything comes together to produce the kind of opportunity dreams are made of. However, hitting the major insect hatches—such as giant Salmonflies or legendary Green Drakes, which are famous for their ability to elicit reckless abandon in the feeding behavior of trout—is often the result of luck rather than correct predictions. In general, hatches of insects larger than size 14 are short-term happenings of inconsistent reliability. More often than not, we find ourselves squinting to follow flies size 16 and smaller, while dealing with the often brutal selectivity that comes with longer-term hatches such as Pale Morning Duns or *Baetis*. Resistant to anything short of perfection in presentation and fly pattern, big, defiant trout can represent more work than pleasure two months into the season. By midsummer, terrestrials begin to take a stronger role in the diet of trout, while bringing some relief to the intensity of dealing with aquatic hatches.

Wind ceases to be an enemy during the dog days from mid-July through early September. Even a modest breeze can relocate terrestrial insects onto the water, extending

Whether winged ants or aquatic wasps, the appearance of these familiar forms assures the attention of the largest trout of the Henry's Fork. Even the famed Green Drakes will not do a better job of attracting fish to the surface despite their superior size. BONNIE HARROP PHOTO

Fishing a winged ant or aquatic wasp pattern need not be limited to water close to the bank. This angler did good business on the open water of Harriman Ranch with a CDC Water Wasp. BONNIE HARROP PHOTO

dry-fly opportunity well into the heat of late afternoon as streamside vegetation begins to load with trout-attracting morsels. While hoppers and beetles represent a more substantial meal, ants are most numerous in their availability to trout. In varying quantities, ants are constantly dropping on the water throughout the summer season. Although often unseen or ignored by some anglers, they do not go unnoticed by trout that learn quickly to recognize a consistent food source.

I am convinced my early success with ant patterns can be at least partially attributed to a lack of interest by most others in fishing what was often a very small fly. For well over a decade, my pet ant pattern was almost foolishly simple. Usually all black, it consisted of a portly abdomen and a similar but smaller thorax. The two dubbed body parts were separated by a narrow waist and two or three turns of hackle. This humble pattern was not easy to float or see on the water, but it delivered consistently on my home water and with equal results on the spring creeks of southwestern Montana. Adding wings to the patterns was intended as much to improve flotation and visibility as to duplicate the characteristics of a natural counterpart. It was not uncommon, however, to see winged ants among the other terrestrials at streamside, and the new version of the original pattern accomplished its purpose.

A budding fly fisher in those days, Bonnie loved the improved ant pattern and would not hesitate to show it to any rising trout, regardless of its location in the stream. Fishing the fly within a more logical range of terrestrial activity went out the window for us both as Bonnie's success at midstream began to rival the results found closer to the edge. Although innocent of any intentional experiment, Bonnie's discovery was responsible for expanding the practical application of a winged ant to situations not normally associated with terrestrial imitation. Early on, we simply enjoyed the benefits of a fly that produced with relative consistency rather than seeking understanding of its uncommon attractiveness to trout feeding far from terrestrial habitat. But on a river with width often exceeding two hundred yards, one should question the reasonability of fishing a land-based imitation at its center point, and eventually someone did.

A man of limited academic qualification, Bing Lempke was a longtime friend and fishing companion who possessed impressive knowledge of trout-related insects. Sharing observations and opinions on fishing and fly tying was a continuing element of a relationship that extended through the final three decades of his life. Twenty-five years my senior, Bing brought expanded historical perspective to our collective understanding of the Henry's Fork and the diversity of insect communities for which it is so well known. At first, we agreed that trout could retain memory of winged ants induced into feeding areas far from the bank by the wind. This is in reference to positive response to a winged ant imitation during periods of calm, which, incidentally, was quite frequent. At the time, however, observable numbers of winged ants were not adequate to sustain an interest in further examination of the subject. This began to change toward the end of the 1980s as the incidence and volume of winged ants on the water increased to levels never before witnessed on the Henry's Fork. In Montana, a short distance north, a similar phenomenon was taking place. River guides were among the first to notice the increased numbers of winged ants on the Madison, with which came a proportionate interest from the trout. Upstream on Hebgen Lake, winged ants joined *Callibaetis* and Trico mayflies as targets for cruising trout known as "gulpers" on the hot summer days leading into autumn.

While not consistent in this regard, there were times when the number of winged ants on these three distinctly different fisheries was as dense as many mayfly or caddis hatches, and the dry-fly action was even more intense. Undoubtedly, the most consistent and striking feature associated with trout response to winged ants is the uninhibited and sometimes vicious way they attack the fly. Of course, this applies to only the upper end of the scale where individuals as large as size 8 are found. Still, a size 14 is fully capable of evoking extremely aggressive reaction, and this size of winged ants became very common.

Neither Lempke nor I could recall anything remotely resembling the now commonly known attraction that winged ants had become. Progressively more reliable, they actually began to supersede the larger aquatic invertebrates in their ability to gain the attention of anglers seeking fast and easy fishing. Discussions with other thoughtful and experienced observers brought about a reasonable and fairly widespread theory pertaining to the relatively sudden surge in the population and significance of winged ants. Drought, with its hot and dry conditions, was a feature of that period. Quick and early withering of plant life so necessary to the welfare of many creatures could logically explain an elevation in the concentration of insects found close to waters where vegetation remains capable of sustaining life when more distant areas do not. Not eager to complicate my position in this matter, I willingly signed on to the reasoning of this hypothesis. Lempke, however, was not as easily convinced of its accuracy. Citing the single most noticeable contradiction to the normal behavior of winged ants as justification for questioning the soundness of an otherwise reasonable assumption, Bing pondered the possibility that something completely different might be happening.

Although limited in range without an assisting wind, winged ants possess aerial mobility that can carry them beyond common distance from preferred habitat, which could explain their presence at midstream during calm conditions. But there was one perplexing problem with this explanation. On the Henry's Fork, the arrival of often great quantities of winged ants on the surface was not preceded by a proportionate airborne migration from land. As if by magic, they would suddenly appear on the water, and trout response was instantaneous. Averaging a robust size 14, the light brown or honey-colored variety were of particular interest because they were seldom found anywhere but on the water, and Bing isolated his attention on this principal contributor to the mystery.

If Bonnie were asked to name her favorite dry fly, it would undoubtedly be a Black Winged Ant. Given a choice, she prefers to fish upstream, and the technique worked well on this Henry's Fork surface feeder. RENÉ HARROP PHOTO

Indifferent to the separation of winged ants and aquatic wasps, Brady Wheeler fishes a crossover pattern on this Idaho spring creek. Apparently this indifference was shared by his target, as this fine cast was rewarded by an enthusiastic acceptance of the fly. BONNIE HARROP PHOTO

While purely amateur in status, Bing Lempke possessed the inquiring mind of a schooled entomologist. Thorough and systematic in his methods, Bing had a library of reference books that included every entomological study performed on the Henry's Fork during his lifetime, and he was personally acquainted with many of the authors. Organized rows of labeled specimen vials lined the shelves of his fly-tying room, and a large microscope rested on the desk near his vise. Bing's flies were meticulously tied down to size 28, and each imitation was based upon actual reference from his extensive collection of preserved insects. The pride taken in knowing exactly what he was imitating was evident in his insistence on referring to the naturals by their scientific name.

Convinced he was on a path to significant discovery, Bing entered a period of near obsession with the intriguing winged ants of the Henry's Fork. For more than a year, Bing poured over volumes of reference material relating to winged-ant behavior with particular attention applied to their role in the diet of trout. Nothing he found in print provided any explanation for the phenomenon, which fueled his determination to an even higher level. Bing found it impossible to understand how the likes of Swisher and Richards, Caucci and Nastasi, and other insect investigators of the Henry's Fork had missed such a vital contributor to angling prosperity on the great river. A string of

Winged ant TOSHI KARITA PHOTO

letters and phone calls posing specific questions relating to experiences with winged ants produced little enlightenment from a host of known authorities of the time. Three years into the quest, Bing tracked me down along the river at Last Chance with some amazing news. A month earlier, he had sent winged-ant specimens to a professor of entomology at a Montana university with the hope that an expert outside the fly-fishing community could shed some light on the subject. Breathless from a near sprint along fifty yards of stream bank, Bing excitedly delivered the announcement that he believed would put the longstanding questions to rest. According to the professor, the specimens were not winged ants or any other terrestrial for that matter. Though the source provided little additional information beyond the revelation that the insects were actually aquatic wasps, Bing was ecstatic to see his efforts bear fruit. More than twenty years later, however, the subject remains somewhat vague and controversial. Bing passed away in

1991, leaving an explanation that has gained only minor subsequent expansion and less than unanimous acceptance among anglers of today.

A close relative of ants, wasps resemble ants in general appearance, which helps to explain why one can be mistaken for the other. All but a few varieties of wasps are terrestrial, and those that are not are very difficult to research. A single paragraph found in the 1936 edition of *An Introduction to Entomology* by John Henry Comstock contains information that supports what Bing was told a few years prior to his death, and nothing I have found has added substantially to my understanding of the subject. According to Comstock, the adults of certain parasitic wasps descend beneath the surface of the water in order to oviposit. One of these is a parasite of caddis larvae, while others are known to lay their eggs in the eggs of various aquatic insects. My internet searches provide nothing additional with respect to the behavior of aquatic wasps either above or beneath the water.

Clearly beneficial as an attractant to trout, aquatic wasps have only fairly recently become significant to the fly fisher. This is supported by the absence of documentation, both scientific and anecdotal, as it applies to the Henry's Fork or other nearby waters where the parasites are known to exist.

Nothing I have learned has led to imitating or fishing the wasps in any condition other than as a dry fly, and no acquaintance has indicated otherwise. Some reference has been made to the practicality of fishing a submerged ant pattern, but never in association with the diving behavior of aquatic wasps. It must also be remembered that Lempke was able to obtain verification of only one species, which was the sizable, honey-colored variety. On the Henry's Fork, it is common to see other examples of similar shape but differing size and color. Black, red, and deep maroon are familiar colors that are typically imitated without knowledge of the insect's true identity. There is little question that at least some if not most varieties are terrestrial, and it is logical to assume that many are indeed winged ants.

I have experienced days on the Henry's Fork and Madison Rivers when the volume of wasps on the water is as impressive as many mayfly or caddis hatches. The same can be said of Hebgen Lake, where Bonnie and I spend a sizable portion of the summer season. Due to excess competition from the naturals, these occasions do not provide the fast and easy action found when the appearance is somewhat sparse and trout are hunting for the insects.

The level of fishing pressure factors into the need for improved imitation of any trout food. While still referred to as winged or flying ants, most fly shops in the Yellowstone area recommend these imitations during the prime period of opportunity on local waters. Better imitation brings greater success when trout become conditioned to

the danger of careless decision in accepting or rejecting any food form. A high number of anglers fishing winged-ant imitations has created the need for greater accuracy than was required only a decade ago, but the right imitation continues to attract a very aggressive response. As is the case with many other insect subjects, many of my recent winged-ant patterns incorporate CDC in their construction, and I am especially pleased with a realistic aquatic wasp pattern using shaped turkey biots for the wings.

On the water, aquatic wasps do not display significant motion such as might be expected. When fishing aquatic wasps, a drag-free presentation is critical in duplicating the behavior of the natural, and a light tippet is often required. Breaking the tippet is common due to an undisciplined reaction to the enthusiasm trout frequently exhibit when accepting the fly.

The wasps seem to prefer the warmest time of the day to make their appearance. An hour or so either side of noon is most typical during July and August, but expect a later arrival as the days grow shorter. The freezing nighttime temperatures of early to mid-September put an annual end to aquatic wasps as a fishing factor, but this can be extended in years of unusually hot and dry weather. Remarkably, wind does not seem to play a negative role in the appearance of aquatic wasps if the air temperature is adequate for their comfort. Like other water-bound insects, a windy day can roll helpless wasps into defined drift lines along the edge. The similarity ends, however, with the urgent and observable riseforms that identify trout feeding on this obviously preferred prey. Flotation and visibility overshadow realism on choppy water, whether wind-related or otherwise, and it pays to carry flies created specifically for these conditions. Increase your fly's flotation and visibility by adding an extra few turns of hackle or increasing the fullness of the CDC wings. Calm conditions will find the wasps well-dispersed on the surface, and the appearance will usually last for an hour or less. However, the trout retain a fondness for these favorites, which makes fishing an imitation a practical choice at times when the naturals are not present on the water.

For locals and visitors alike, the time of the aquatic wasps has become a much anticipated period that carries as much excitement as other insect happenings on the Henry's Fork. Understandably, it is considered a positive factor in the current picture of this legendary trout stream. At this time, there is no scientific evidence supporting any negative impact associated with a noticeable increase in the numbers of the aquatic parasites. However, there may very well be a downside to the behavioral characteristics of organisms known to prey upon other aquatic invertebrates that add value to the health of a fishery.

Any observer of natural communities acknowledges cyclical patterns that inhibit absolute certainty in determining whether any change is short-term or permanent. Alterations or inconsistencies of habitat are the usual culprit in any downturn in populations of hatch-producing insects, which can in turn translate to a proportionate reduction in the creatures that depend upon them for subsistence. From the 1980s until now, drought in varying duration has been a significant weather feature of the Yellowstone region, which includes the Henry's Fork and other notable trout waters. Through this period, inadequate winter flows have received the majority of the blame for the diminishing ability of many of these waters to sustain life. But while the scientific accuracy of this assessment cannot be challenged, other recently discovered factors can also come into play. Whirling disease was virtually unknown as a major contributor to trout mortality little more than a decade ago, but it is now considered to be one of the most sinister of all threats to the fisheries of Yellowstone country. New Zealand mud snails possess the ability to completely replace all forms of aquatic invertebrates, and this potential alone forms a dark cloud over the future of fly fishing as it currently exists. There are other examples of known predatory activity within aquatic insect communities, but to this point, aquatic wasps have not been identified as a problem.

The story of aquatic wasps has been in my mind for several years, and I didn't begin writing about them with any intent of creating alarm. In fact, the thought of the winged parasites being anything other than a benign gift to fly fishers did not present itself until I was nearly halfway through the text. It was only when revisiting the scant information from *An Introduction to Entomology* while writing that a sobering sense of curious possibility entered my consciousness.

According to Comstock, caddis larvae and the eggs of other unspecified aquatic insects that act as hosts for aquatic wasps are consumed and therefore lost to their respective communities. Is it possible that mayflies are among the other aquatic insects that are being attacked by aquatic wasps? A larger question is whether a correlation exists between a perceived increase in aquatic wasp activity and a depression in key hatches of caddis and mayflies. And, if so, can parasitic depredation of aquatic food forms be connected to a corresponding decrease in trout population? My concerns in this regard only come from pondering a possibility; I don't have direct supporting evidence. Over many years, I have witnessed fluctuations in trout and insect populations on the Henry's Fork and other waters of the Yellowstone region. Peaks and valleys have always been temporary, and most can be scientifically explained. To my knowledge, parasitic wasps have not been proven guilty of over-consuming their aquatic prey base in any water close to Yellowstone. The danger of this occurrence would likely be associated with one or more additional factors that could limit the integrity of aquatic insects groups. Gulls, swallows, and other birds of opportunistic nature consume vast quantities of insects on the water and in the air, and trout cannot be forgotten as extremely efficient predators. Concern has also been expressed over the negative impact of wading anglers when their numbers reach levels of high concentration over a sustained period.

For better or worse, aquatic wasps now occupy an elevated position within a lengthy list of insects capable of enticing trout to the surface. And while clearly among the ranks of known predators of familiar trout foods, they retain value even to those anglers who may not be aware of their true identity. In this instance, ignorance is not to be condemned. A good winged ant pattern in the right size and color will work just fine when wasps are on the water, and I'm sure the trout will forgive the mistake. Personally, I believe that fly fishing needs its mysteries, and aquatic wasps are only one among many.

BONNIE HARROP PHOTO

Black Winged Ant

Hook:	TMC 100 BL size 12-20
Thread:	Black 8/0 UNI-Thread
Abdomen:	Black TroutHunter Pro dubbing
Stabilizer:	1 black moose hair on each side of abdomen
Wing:	Strip of mallard wing quill reinforced with flexible cement and trimmed to shape
Hackle:	Black Whiting
Thorax:	Black TroutHunter Pro dubbing

BONNIE HARROP PHOTO

Red and Black CDC Winged Ant

Hook:	TMC 206 BL size 12-20
Thread:	Black 8/0 UNI-Thread
Abdomen:	Red TroutHunter Pro dubbing
Stabilizer:	1 black moose hair on each side of abdomen
Wing:	Paired medium dun TroutHunter CDC feathers
Hackle:	Black Whiting
Thorax:	Black TroutHunter Pro dubbing

BONNIE HARROP PHOTO

Amber Duxback Winged Ant

Hook:	TMC 206 BL size 12-20
Thread:	Tan 8/0 UNI-Thread
Abdomen:	2 amber (golden-brown) TroutHunter CDC feathers cupped over light honey TroutHunter Pro dubbing
Wings:	2 natural tan TroutHunter CDC feathers mounted flat over abdomen
Hackle:	Brown grizzly Whiting
Thorax:	Brown TroutHunter Pro dubbing

BONNIE HARROP PHOTO

Dark Honey Water Wasp

Hook:	TMC 100 BL size 12-20
Thread:	Tan 8/0 UNI-Thread
Abdomen:	Dark honey TroutHunter Pro dubbing
Stabilizer:	1 black moose hair on each side of abdomen
Wings:	Brown right and left TroutHunter turkey biots trimmed to shape over natural brown CDC
Hackle:	Brown Whiting
Thorax:	Trico TroutHunter Pro dubbing

Flav
carbon pencil with watercolor tint
11 x 14 inches

Flavs

The Little Drakes of Summer

In the copper glow of twilight it appears only as an indistinct bump, but a wriggling on shiny water is an indication that life accompanies the drifting form. The sudden protrusion of a single dark wing enlarges the form as an urgent struggle for freedom begins. Within seconds the shapeless mass is transformed into a figure familiar to all who seek the riches of great dry-fly water. Viewed only in silhouette, it is still recognizable as an emerging mayfly, not truly large but certainly substantial and robust. Liberated from the anchor of its former self, the freshly emerged dun tests new wings in a clumsy fluttering that yields considerable disturbance but no lift from the liquid world it is trying to escape. A subsequent effort is somewhat stronger, but full function in a foreign realm does not come quickly. Resting now, it glides motionlessly on the current for a foot or so, perhaps waiting for muscles to warm and wings to dry. Again, unsteady wings tap vigorously on the water in a signal of imminent departure, but there will be no third attempt at flight. Instead, there is a glint of silver, and the mayfly vanishes in a vicious swirl. It is the way of the wild where life feeds life, and on a trout stream it is the beginning of the hatch.

For nearly two hours, until evening fades to black, there will be countless repetitions of the act, and with it one of angling's supreme pleasures. Tempted from the depths by a floating feast, big aggressive trout put aside customary shyness in a feeding binge that borders on gluttony. There is little that is subtle in the surging riseforms, or the sometimes frantic flailing of those fortunate enough to partake in this unique gift of opportunity. Indeed there is magic in the moment, and it happens far more frequently than one might imagine.

Summer in mountain country can seem a mere blip on the seasonal screen if sunny warmth is the sole description. Still, despite its briefness, it has rewards not offered at other points on the calendar, not the least of which are the oversized mayflies known as Drakes. While the benefits of a hatch size 12 and even larger are obvious, Brown, Gray, and Green Drakes can be a fickle lot. Unpredictable in timing, duration, and quantity, they can be difficult if not impossible to plan for, and frequently must be considered a bonus by those fortunate enough to hit action of any significance. However, anglers should be encouraged that there is a slightly smaller mayfly that hatches with a lot more reliability. It has failed to gain the glamour status of its larger cousins, but there is little to lament when it appears each year. In most hatch charts or angling publications, it is known as the Small Western Drake, but on the Henry's Fork, we simply call them Flavs. Short for *Drunella flavilinea*, the Flav is no giant in physical size, but it looms large in the arena of western fly fishing. A solid size 14, it can lure the largest fish to the surface while providing welcome relief

Fishing Flavs at sunset can be a daily exercise from early June through early August on several rivers in Yellowstone country. The presence of mule's ear wildflowers along the Henry's Fork coincides with the Little Drakes of summer. BONNIE HARROP PHOTO

from the squint flies that typically dominate hatching activity. Combine this with certain unique characteristics that make Flavs especially appealing to trout, and you have what some would consider to be the ultimate hatch.

Although my own relationship with the Little Drakes of summer is centered in Yellowstone and the three states that surround it, friends and other sources tell me that good hatches also occur in Oregon, California, and Colorado. Ideal Flav habitat appears to be medium to fast water, but I can cite numerous examples where slow currents flowing over clean gravel have delivered outstanding Flav fishing. Meadow stretches of the Yellowstone, Firehole, and Madison in the park all hold vivid memories of dry-fly glory and excitement. On the catch-and-release water of the Henry's Fork, Flavs are among the longest and most anticipated hatches of the year. Exact hatch dates vary from stream to stream, being influenced by such factors as water level, elevation, or thermal activity, as is the case with some Yellowstone waters. There is one constant, however, which can be counted on—they always come during the longest days of the year. June, July, and even August are prime months to find Flav fishing in the Rocky Mountain West.

When Flavs hatch, nymphs, spinners, and duns often combine to produce a dozen or more hours of almost constant activity. Granted, this is not always the case, but Flav time is a lengthy period of opportunity and a heavy hatch

or spinnerfall is not required to attract the attention of trout, once they have a taste of these tempting morsels.

Flavs are closely related to the legendary Western Green Drakes, and their appearance reflects this connection. They are compact, muscular insects, which can make the tall, slate gray wings appear quite long in relationship to the body. Distinctly smaller, Flav duns resemble the size 10 or 12 Green Drakes in basic silhouette, but not color. Freshly hatched Green Drakes are, as the name implies, a deep jade green with vibrant, almost chartreuse markings on the abdomen, thorax, and legs. Contrarily, Flavs are a muted olive and brown, which means that effectively matching the insect is more than simply tying a smaller version of its more famous counterpart.

It is likely that size and numbers alone do not fully explain the pronounced fondness displayed by trout when Flavs make their annual appearance. Many of the most familiar hatching insects emerge high enough in the water column to produce what appear to be riseforms. But in reality the disturbance is created by fish feeding near but not actually on the surface. Flavs, on the other hand, get the business done right on top, so a floating imitation will be in the right zone throughout the hatch. It is quite possible that this extremely thin collection area simplifies the act of feeding. Add to this the fact that Flavs seem to experience unusual difficulty in freeing themselves from the nymphal skin, and again in gaining flight once they have left the cumbersome shuck behind. Often they flutter and tumble awkwardly about on the surface in a period of helpless and tantalizing vulnerability before leaving the water. These tendencies translate to pronounced availability, which is undoubtedly difficult for most trout to resist. It also helps to explain why a high-floating imitation of a fully developed dun works better at Flav time than during most other hatches.

It is common to expect an early evening emergence on bright warm days, with activity peaking just before dark. However, cool, wet weather will accelerate the hatch clock, with a strong arrival of duns beginning around midday and stretching for as long as four or five hours. It is also not surprising to encounter emerging Flavs in the late morning or early afternoon. This seems to occur most frequently on dry days that are not too hot but can be quite windy, and is usually a rather low-key preliminary to the main event, which fires up around dusk. Although typically sporadic and somewhat sparse, these brief matinee events seldom fail to attract the attention of trout, although the water is frequently devoid of fishermen at these times.

Taken as a whole, any mayfly above size 18 is larger than average on western trout waters. To be relieved of the eyestrain of trying to track tiny flies on a long line is not among the most trivial benefits of a Flav hatch. Neither are the 4 and 5X tippets these chunky mayflies permit. Big trout on pressured waters are never suicidal, but there is something truly uncommon in the way they respond to Flavs. Although peak activity commonly occurs before heavy weed growth complicates the currents, this is not the only reason that presentation is easier. A modest amount of drag may actually enhance the realism of the artificial by suggesting the squirming struggle of an emerging or freshly hatched dun. Occasionally an intentionally induced twitching of the fly will divert attention away from a competing natural—if it is well timed and not too aggressive.

The tendency of trout to hunt drifting Flavs reduces the need for pinpoint accuracy, especially when the number of available insects is on the light side. Trout looking up will see a tall, winged imitation and sometimes move a foot or more to reach it, which is unlike their response to smaller insects. This wider window of visibility is especially helpful in minimizing the need to cast directly over the trout when fishing upstream. A delivery made six inches to the right or left is far less alarming, yet the drifting fly will be seen by the wary trout.

A local favorite for dun-hunting trout is a high-floating thorax style developed by Henry's Fork regular Don Laughlin. Its most prominent feature is the upright wing of dark CDC, which conforms to its natural counterpart. A biot body and sparse collar of hackle clipped in a wide V on the bottom complete the deception. A high-winged cripple or

It took a careful stalk of nearly ten minutes before Rich Paini was within casting range of this impressive surface feeder. It was one of several taken on various Flav patterns during a memorable day on the Ranch water of the Henry's Fork.
RENÉ HARROP PHOTO

a hairwing style similar to Craig Matthews's great Sparkle Dun gives superior visibility while preserving the illusion of vulnerability associated with a partially emerged Flav dun.

Occasionally a wily old veteran will feed exclusively on Flavs in the earliest phase of emergence. In such instances it is best to show a lower profile in the presentation, one which emphasizes more nymph than dun in its configuration. The CDC Biot Cripple and Captive Dun are two variations of the same concept. The former features short CDC wings angled back over the body, while the latter incorporates a bubble-like loop of CDC over the thorax to imply fresh wings not yet free of the nymphal skin. Both are low-floating imitations that ride flush in the film. They are most likely to be required during an especially heavy hatch when fish have greater opportunity for elevated selectivity. Constructed with soft, lively components that flex naturally with the currents, they can be particularly tempting when manipulated delicately with the rod tip. Expect the rises to be more subtle than when the naturals are more mobile a little later in the emergence process. Rises on placid water are subtle—as for a much smaller fly—and on quicker currents can be almost indiscernible.

When Flavs hatch with other insects, they often outcompete larger food forms for the trout's attention. On the Henry's Fork, for example, Flavs frequently are the item of choice even when mixed with the giant Brown Drakes, which emerge in the evening and are roughly double the Flavs in size. A morning hatch of Pale Morning Duns is often interspersed with flush-floating Flav spinners, which can go unnoticed by an angler who is not paying close attention. It would be embarrassing to admit the number of times I have fallen victim to complacency while fishing an

A Flav spinnerfall can keep you on the water until nearly dark. It was after 10 p.m. when I hooked the last fish of the day on a lower Henry's Fork float in late June. RICH PAINI PHOTO

While certainly no giant, this hefty rainbow was a real handful in heavy current. She took a Flav CDC Thorax while feeding tightly against a shaded bank on the lower Henry's Fork. Gareth Jones provided welcome assistance in landing the muscular fish. RICH PAINI PHOTO

obvious hatch that masked the actual objective of a feeding fish.

Flav spinners are similar to those of other mayflies in the waning hours of their existence. Mating and laying eggs are the final living acts, but their service as a food source does not necessarily end with death. Fallen spinners with outstretched wings and motionless bodies are a target incapable of escape. As a rule, mayfly spinners will not return to the water unless weather conditions are ideal. This eliminates periods of wind, precipitation, or intense heat. In summer, there are occasions when a variety of mayfly spinners will occupy the water at the same time. Perfect conditions typically occur in early to midmorning or just before dark. Although requirements of approach and presentation can be basically equal, it is important to acknowledge that trout, as individuals, will not necessarily key on the same food type when a varied menu is available. In the case of a complex spinnerfall, when it is impossible to see the flush-floating naturals at casting distance, the pace of the rise is often the best clue as to which type is being taken. By comparing the rhythm of a feeding fish to a breakdown of individual spinners observed closeby, you can sometimes coordinate fly selection with the most likely natural objective. The time span between rises to smaller but more numerous spinners is typically shorter than with a more sparse scattering of larger insects. Side-to-side feeding movement is an indication

that a larger quarry is the target of the hunt. A blend of Flavs and PMDs is a common occurrence that demonstrates the individualistic nature of trout as it applies to selectivity. Despite the insects' minor variance in color and sometimes only a few millimeters' difference in size, large trout often choose to ignore one in favor of the other. And nearly countless are the times I have found myself alternating between two different sizes of the same spinner pattern in order to satisfy the exacting selectivity from one trout to another. Overall, however, Flav spinners will hold their own even when outnumbered by as many as four or five to one. The same can be said when the plump spentwings are in competition with major Drake spinners, which are larger but usually fewer in number.

Despite their above average size, Flavs share the same negative common to all mayflies during the spinner stage. Gone is the sail-wing profile, which is fairly easy to spot even at a distance. The problem is compounded on broad shallow flats, or big water where greater depth inhibits access other than by floating. Big cruisers in thin water are notoriously difficult to approach as they skim hapless drifting spinners from the surface. Attempting to creep up from behind in order to shorten the distance is futile when the fish is feeding away more quickly than you can effectively wade. The best alternative is to make a long, gentle presentation, usually across and slightly downstream. Although accurate in both appearance and the way they ride the water, closely

A Flav emergence is often an evening event that can fall on the heels of or even overlap a different summer hatch. The appearance of Flavs on this particular day in early July brought welcome relief from a demanding PMD hatch. Trout display a fondness for Flavs that few mayflies can equal. MASA KATSUMATA PHOTO

imitative spent-wing images like the CDC Biot Spinner can be lost among the naturals, which, at times, carpet the water. A viable solution to this inherent problem is a Rusty or Olive Paraspinner. Despite minimal height and volume, the white CDC wing post shows up as a prominent indicator of fly location at a rather remarkable distance.

Like all mayflies, Flavs possess transparent wings in the spinner stage. But dark, heavy vein patterns spread across the surface account for some flexibility in adjusting wing shade to accommodate light conditions, which are less than ideal. Observing this characteristic led to the development of a versatile pattern that serves double duty during the evening period when sunlight begins to fade and a Flav spinnerfall overlaps an emergence. The fly is tied with an olive or rusty brown biot abdomen and matching dubbing for the thorax. Paired, dark gray CDC feathers tied three-quarters spent comprise the wing, and there is no hackle. The silhouette spinner gives the appearance of either a drowned or developing dun not yet fully stable and erect on the water. Both are attractive in terms of vulnerability, as is a freshly arrived spinner not yet completely expired. Even though the elevation on the water is somewhat minor, the contrast of a dark wing against a bright surface is substantially beneficial in tracking the fly when more conventional designs become lost in the glare.

In the right conditions, sight nymphing can provide visual drama nearly equal to an emergence or spinnerfall.

This becomes especially true during Flav time when a high sun irradiates the stream bottom, revealing subsurface enthusiasm similar to what is frequently observed on top. Slipping up from behind to feed a fraudulent imitation to an aggressively nymphing trout is about as much excitement as I need when the surface is quiet and the alternative is a long nap in the grass.

Adverse conditions of light, weather, or water do not necessarily deny access to subsurface feeding activity. The key is to avoid empty water by methodically probing the most likely holding areas where concentrated numbers of nymphing trout improve the odds of success. Quick riffles or defined pools of increased depth conceal the location and activity of trout from predatory eyes. Large rocks, logs, or other sheltering objects are favored lies for large individual fish. Dead drifting a good nymphal imitation of the Flav in these areas, during the appropriate season, is a productive way to fill hatchless periods. Because the size of the insect is not minor, it is not unusual for a hungry trout to charge several feet to intercept a passing nymph. This wider acceptance zone serves to minimize the number of casts required to cover a likely holding area, an important factor when blind casting with nymphs.

Although originally intended to be a rather general nymphal representation, the Turkey Tail is a dead ringer for a Flav in its underwater stage. Similar in construction to the classic Pheasant Tail, it makes functional use of the

Male Flav spinner TOSHI KARITA PHOTO

large and beautifully marked plumage from the tail fan of a wild turkey.

The season of the Little Drakes is a diverse period of climatic extremes. I have shivered through a June snowstorm on the Firehole, where geyser-warmed water produced conditions ideal for a strong emergence of Flavs. Two months later I was sweating beneath an August sun while fishing Flavs to big, lake-run cutthroats on the Yellowstone only an hour's drive away. In between was a remarkable day spent with pal and fishing photographer Tom Montgomery on a prolific and somewhat remote tailwater section of the Henry's Fork. No experience in recent memory better illustrates the amazing fishing potential Flavs can offer.

As usual when fishing with Tom, we were running late when our young but extremely knowledgeable guide Eli Blackburn launched the drift boat at the end of an obscure brush-choked road where a deeper and stronger Henry's Fork separates steep canyon walls. We had struggled for nearly a week with equally uncooperative fish and weather while working together on a project in and around Yellowstone Park. A float trip several thousand feet lower in elevation was an impulsive decision that we hoped would allow us to recoup some time lost to a cold, wet storm, which had shut down virtually everything in the high country. Just the warmth from a long missing sun alone was reward enough, but the flash of rising trout brought feelings of expectation to the beginning of the ten-mile float.

Tom is as handy with a fly rod as he is with a camera, and within fifteen minutes he was solidly connected to an

Emerging Flav TOSHI KARITA PHOTO

acrobatic 17-inch rainbow. It was just the beginning of two action-charged hours spent firing 60-foot and longer casts to big greedy trout that slashed ravenously at a stupendous number of Flav spinners. While several days of chilling temperatures and near constant rain had not disrupted the strong daily emergence, the effect on spinner activity was profound. Intolerable weather conditions had consolidated three or four broods of Flavs into a single spinnerfall of massive proportions. The result was some of the fastest and most exciting dry-fly fishing either of us had ever experienced. Many of the browns and rainbows were large, and despite the exclusive use of 4X tippets, we had both expended our supply of size 14 Rusty Paraspinners before the action finally subsided around noon.

Following a leisurely streamside lunch and a short rest to revive tired, aging muscles, we entertained ourselves well into the afternoon fishing Flav nymphs along the edge and around any fishy-looking structure away from the banks. At around 4:30 p.m., with little more than a mile remaining before the takeout, we began to observe rising trout. Again it was Flavs that triggered the renewed surface activity, but this time they were duns rather than their flush-floating counterparts. From then until nearly dark we enjoyed the luxury of fishing high-floating hackled patterns, although the larger fish continued to require a fairly long cast.

Later, beneath a blazing sunset that ignited the opposing horizon, a second wave of spinners began to appear. With the jagged Tetons lifting like frozen flames against the skyline, we continued to find acceptance of duns and cripples. But as the emergence began to fade with the light, the attention shifted progressively more toward the spent form. We switched to a Silhouette Spinner, and for a time were able to maintain visual contact with the crossover pattern. Eventually, however, we were casting to the sound as much as the sight of the rise as darkness enveloped the tranquil scene. Conversation ceased, and the only sounds were the soft creaking of the oars and the whisper of the line. Suddenly a sharp crack as startling as a rifle shot shattered the stillness only a dozen yards from the boat. Clearly irritated by the nocturnal invasion of its usual privacy, a large beaver had sounded its displeasure with a resounding smack of its powerful tail against the darkened water. At 11:00 p.m.,

Flav nymph TOSHI KARITA PHOTO

there was really no reason to argue. After twelve hours of almost constant action, we were as nearly spent as the fallen mayflies that had kept us out until this late hour. A waxing moon contributed weakly to faint starlight as Eli pushed the final few yards to our waiting vehicle and we loaded the boat amid the eerie sounds of night.

It had been a remarkable day in terms of the number and size of trout both landed and lost. But in retrospect, I think back most fondly on shared pleasure and the little drakes that made it possible. Like the longest days of summer, they are special.

BONNIE HARROP PHOTO

Don's Drake

Hook:	TMC 100BL size 14-16
Thread:	Olive 8/0 UNI-Thread
Tail:	4-5 moose hairs
Abdomen:	BWO TroutHunter goose or turkey biot
Thorax:	BWO TroutHunter Pro dubbing
Wing:	Paired dark gray TroutHunter CDC feathers
Hackle:	Whiting grizzly dyed dun clipped on bottom

CDC Flav Biot Standard

Hook:	TMC 100BL size 14-16
Thread:	Olive 8/0 UNI-Thread
Tail:	Dun hackle fibers or Whiting Coq de Leon
Abdomen:	BWO TroutHunter goose or turkey biot
Thorax:	BWO TroutHunter dubbing
Wing:	Paired dark gray TroutHunter CDC feathers
Hackle:	Whiting grizzly dyed dun

Flav Biot Sparkle Dun

Hook:	TMC 100BL size 14-16
Thread:	Olive 8/0 UNI-Thread
Shuck:	Sparse brown Antron dubbing blend
Abdomen:	BWO TroutHunter goose or turkey biot
Thorax:	BWO TroutHunter Pro dubbing
Wing:	Coastal deer hair

CDC Flav Last Chance Cripple

Hook:	TMC 100BL size 14-16
Thread:	Olive 8/0 UNI-Thread
Shuck:	Sparse brown TroutHunter CEN dubbing over 3 wood duck fibers
Abdomen:	Brown TroutHunter goose or turkey biot
Thorax:	BWO TroutHunter Pro dubbing
Wing:	Paired TroutHunter natural dark dun CDC feathers angled over hook eye
Hackle:	Whiting grizzly dyed dun

CDC Flav Silhouette Spinner

Hook:	TMC 100BL size 14-16
Thread:	Olive 8/0 UNI-Thread
Tail:	Whiting Coq de Leon
Abdomen:	BWO TroutHunter goose or turkey biot
Thorax:	BWO TroutHunter Pro dubbing
Wing:	Paired dark gray CDC feathers tied 3/4 spent

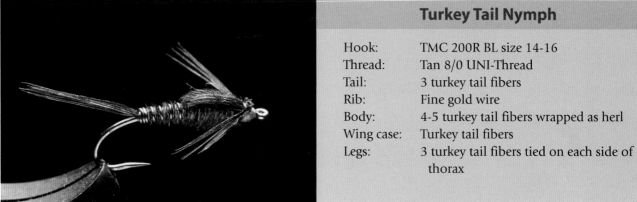

Turkey Tail Nymph

Hook:	TMC 200R BL size 14-16
Thread:	Tan 8/0 UNI-Thread
Tail:	3 turkey tail fibers
Rib:	Fine gold wire
Body:	4-5 turkey tail fibers wrapped as herl
Wing case:	Turkey tail fibers
Legs:	3 turkey tail fibers tied on each side of thorax

BONNIE HARROP PHOTO

Flav CDC Biot Cripple

Hook:	TMC 100 BL size 14-16
Thread:	Olive 8/0 UNI-Thread
Shuck:	Sparse brown Antron dubbing blend over 3 wood duck fibers
Abdomen:	Brown TroutHunter goose or turkey biot
Thorax:	BWO TroutHunter Pro dubbing
Wing:	Paired TroutHunter natural dark dun CDC feathers tied short and angled back over body
Legs:	Brown Hungarian partridge

BONNIE HARROP PHOTO

Flav CDC Captive Dun

Hook:	TMC 100BL size 14-16
Thread:	Olive 8/0 UNI-Thread
Shuck:	Sparse brown TroutHunter CEN dubbing blend over 3 wood duck fibers
Abdomen:	Brown TroutHunter goose or turkey biot
Thorax:	BWO TroutHunter Pro dubbing
Wing:	Paired TroutHunter natural dark dun CDC feathers folded over back of thorax to form a bubble
Legs:	4-6 olive CDC fibers tied on each side of thorax, clipped to 3/4 body length

BONNIE HARROP PHOTO

CDC Rusty Paraspinner

Hook:	TMC 100BL size 14-16
Thread:	Rust 8/0 UNI-Thread
Tail:	Whiting Coq de Leon
Abdomen:	Rusty spinner TroutHunter goose or turkey biot
Thorax:	Rusty spinner TroutHunter Pro dubbing
Wing post:	Paired white TroutHunter CDC feathers, clipped to 1/3 body length
Wing:	Whiting grizzly hackle tied parachute style, clipped over hook eye in a wide V

Callibaetis
carbon pencil with watercolor tint
11 x 14 inches

Callibaetis

The Speckled Mayfly of Quiet Water

Although it is two hours past dawn, a heavy mist rests on the surface of the lake, where the only sound is the lapping of water on the sides of the small boat and the creaking of oars. Morning arrives coolly in the high country of southwest Montana, and though it is mid-July, I can see a slight shivering of the small, dark-haired figure a few feet in front of me. There is a distinct chill in the air, but I know my wife trembles as much from anticipation as from any temperature-related discomfort. We are there for the trout, and if all goes according to plan, the action will begin within an hour.

Gradually, the visibility improves and the agitating sound of the oars is replaced by the soft humming of the electric motor as we reach deeper water. Signs of a mostly submerged weed bed appear in the distance, and within minutes we are anchored in a relatively open channel that separates heavy growth of aquatic weed. It is now a waiting game as a slowly climbing sun burns away remnant tendrils of rising mist that linger among the cool pines that line the shore, and formerly chilled fingers are now free to fuss with leaders and flies as we pass time in the quiet serenity. Several other boats bearing like-minded anglers are scattered randomly within view but out of earshot. Like us, they wait in patient anticipation for the first appearance of the speckled-wing mayflies that will convert the shiny flawless surface to a busy gaming field of rising trout.

It is nearly nine a.m. before Bonnie spots the first dark head that appears almost magically from the liquid mirror. Although only a single rise, it signals the beginning of some of the most intriguing feeding behavior of the entire year. Several minutes tick by with no repeat appearance of the trout, but on my left sleeve is perched a single delicate mayfly, its distinctly veined transparent wings glistening over a tannish colored body. About a size sixteen, it is the *Callibaetis* of quiet water and an item of high interest to the trout that reside there.

The sound of line being stripped from Bonnie's reel brings my attention back to the water, where her focus is riveted upon a widening ring about eighty feet from our position. Seconds later, and ten feet closer, another rise pierces the surface. Feeding progressively toward the boat, the lone trout is methodically picking off individual insects from the sparse scattering of *Callibaetis* spinners that have begun to appear on the water. Although its path is not clearly defined, the general direction of travel will bring the fish within a forty-foot cast as it feeds along the edge of the weed bed. Clearly, there will be opportunity for but one shot before the cruising trout passes by and out of range.

Laying enough line on the water to load the rod with a single false cast, my wife tenses as the objective draws closer with each appearance. By now, each rise is accompanied by an audible gulp, which lends even more excitement to the

Bonnie and I use this ten-foot johnboat, affectionately known as "The Tub," to prowl the edges of Hebgen Lake in pursuit of the famous gulpers. The low profile and quiet electric motor allow a close approach to these big surface feeders. BONNIE HARROP PHOTO

situation, and at fifty feet it is time to take action. Proportionate to an increasing volume of insects on the water, the riseforms are now about six feet apart and only two feet from the distinct edge of the weed bed. The timing of the cast is perfect, and the little spinner gently arrives at just the right location to intercept the deliberate surface feeder. The slow wink of a cotton-white mouth engulfs the fraudulent offering and then smoothly disappears from view. A second later, Bonnie's rod bows against the furious weight of an 18-inch rainbow that thrashes violently on the surface before plunging down into the twenty-foot depths. With a strong 5X tippet, Bonnie has the upper hand as long as the heavy-bodied fish remains in open water. It will be a different story, however, if her opponent decides to bore into the dense submerged weed growth. For nearly five minutes the defiant fish wages a deep-water battle, but gradually the relentless pressure of the rod begins to take its toll. Closer to the surface, it seems to panic, and the diminutive grandmother is twice forced to turn back an effort that would send her prize into the tangled vegetation and certain freedom. With the rod held high overhead, she lifts the tiring trout to the surface and expertly guides it into the waiting mesh of the long-handled landing net.

Salt-and-pepper wings fill the air and litter the water as my wife checks the fly and tippet knot before turning her gaze back toward the water. Within less than ten minutes from the time she had hooked the first fish of the day, the placid lake seems alive with audibly feeding trout as they gorge themselves on helpless *Callibaetis* spinners. It will be nearly four hours and countless casts before the predictable breeze will abruptly erase all signs of insect and trout activity, thus ending another day of some of the most remarkable fishing of the entire season. Compelled to the point of near addiction, we will return to the lake many times before the frost of autumn and the calls of bugling elk puts an end to this annual event.

Known primarily to lake fishermen, *Callibaetis* mayflies are well distributed across the country, but nowhere are they more important than in the quiet waters of the Mountain West. Easily identified by distinctly specked wings, they inhabit lakes, ponds, and some slow-moving streams that are generally characterized by a silted bottom and substantial aquatic vegetation. In the Yellowstone region, their emergence usually coincides with the arrival and departure of summer, and once underway, the hatch is as reliable as any in the waters they occupy. Ranging from size 14 to size

Callibaetis *spinner* TOSHI KARITA PHOTO

18, they provide visual relief from the tiny Tricos that often share the same habitat and have a similar time frame for emergence. Inherently suited to pleasant weather conditions, *Callibaetis* above elevations of five thousand feet make their appearance as both spinners and duns during the most comfortable periods of a summer day, which makes them a unique and valuable hatch during the hottest time of year when other hatches begin to thin and midday dry-fly fishing becomes less available.

As important as, if not more important than, the other stages, *Callibaetis* spinners appear as morning begins to warm, usually from eight to nine a.m. Less frequent but not uncommon on some waters is an evening spinnerfall that arrives just before dusk. In ideal conditions, a morning spinnerfall can last for more than three hours, but an evening spinnerfall is somewhat shorter. Wind or extreme temperatures can alter the timing of any spinnerfall.

In their final stage, *Callibaetis* differ in a number of ways from other mayfly spinners. Graceful and delicately marked, they are strong fliers that remain active in the air and on the water for a longer time than most of their ephemerid counterparts that fly only short distances before falling inert on the surface and remaining that way until death.

It is common to see *Callibaetis* spinners dip to the surface and then rest there for a time before regaining flight. With wings held upright, they can easily be mistaken for duns, which can inspire a faulty pattern selection since

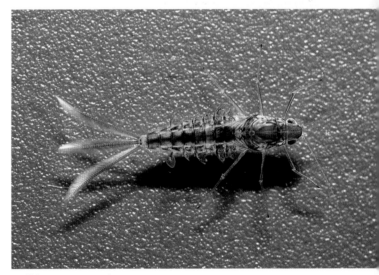

Callibaetis *nymph* TOSHI KARITA PHOTO

there is considerable physical difference between the two stages. Although distinctly marked as in the dun stage, the wings of the spinner are transparent, rather than opaque, and the body is considerably lighter in color. Once the dying insect has arrived on the water for the final time, it often flutters its wings for a long time. Although some say this attracts fish, I know of no way to duplicate this unique behavior with an artificial fly.

The broad, shallow flats of the Harriman Ranch on the Henry's Fork are prime *Callibaetis* habitat. Here, timing a *Callibaetis* spinnerfall depends on rising early and making

Rich Paini and a hefty Kamloops rainbow from Sheridan Lake in Idaho. A Callibaetis nymph twitched just beneath the surface was just too tempting for the big cruiser to resist. RENÉ HARROP PHOTO

Bonnie took this Hebgen Lake gulper on a CDC Callibaetis Paraspinner. Schools of sizable rainbows and browns cruise this extremely fertile lake on calm summer mornings. The *Callibaetis* hatches generally last from late June through early September. RENÉ HARROP PHOTO

an hourlong hike to the interior. Although relatively low in population, the trout are large and seldom disturbed by more than a few ambitious anglers. In quiet water little more than knee deep, cruising trout of often massive proportions can be spotted at a distance of more than a hundred yards. At times they may appear as a small group, but the largest are usually solitary feeders that spurn the company of lesser individuals.

Although very slow, a distinct current keeps the fish feeding uniformly in the same general direction, but the path is never a straight line. Here, it is a game of stalking to a predetermined point of interception that will hopefully put the cruising target into casting range. With enough spent insects on the water, the trout will assume a rhythmic feeding pace that does not entail as much lateral movement as when the food is more sparsely scattered. Timing in this situation is as critical as accuracy, and both can be equally difficult to perfect. With enough spinners on the water, a foraging trout can spend as much time with its nose above the surface as beneath. This makes tracking the fish easier and improves your chances of making an accurate cast and presenting the fly in the correct line of travel. However, the cast must be timed to coincide with the natural pace of each rise, which can be daunting when the distance gets much beyond fifty feet.

Correct imitation can be complicated by the presence of more than one insect form on the water at the same time. The trout's feeding behavior will offer clues about which fly to select. Trout are especially fond of expired spinners because of their vulnerability. The density of the insects on the surface will dictate the distance between rises and the path of travel when the trout is cruising. Unhurried rises separated by only a foot or so combined with minimal side-to-side movement indicate that the trout are feeding on fully spent spinners because they are usually in greater numbers due to their inability to leave the water. The most effective imitations in this situation are low in profile and difficult to see when a longer cast is required. As in other instances when you cannot clearly see the fly, gently tighten the line when the rise appears close to where you think the fly is located. Luck plays a part in this tactic, but it is often the only choice for selective trout in clear, slow-moving water.

The emergence of *Callibaetis* duns commonly takes place around noon and sometimes between dusk and dark. In either instance, it is not unusual for the beginning of the emergence to overlap the end of a spinnerfall. It is unlikely, however, that feeding trout will shift their attention away from the spinners until they are considerably outnumbered by the upright stage of the insect. Because of their mobility, *Callibaetis* duns will evoke more urgent rises compared to the more relaxed responses to the down-wing stage. The ability to take flight makes any mayfly dun a more elusive target, which can help to explain why emergers are often a more enticing *Callibaetis* imitation than a fully winged pattern. Insects injured or substantially delayed in the process of gaining freedom from the nymphal shuck might have a higher profile on the surface and therefore be effectively imitated by highly visible patterns known as cripples that are more attractive to opportunistic trout seeking an easy catch.

In calm conditions, trout can be found cruising in open water as they hunt down fully or partially emerged *Callibaetis* duns. However, emergence typically provides a lower concentration of available food than a spinnerfall, which dictates a somewhat random feeding pattern and rises that create considerably more disturbance. Unhindered by a modest wind, *Callibaetis* duns continue to be an available food source into early afternoon during many days of their emergence. Look for isolated feeding activity along downwind shorelines or against exposed weed beds where *Callibaetis* can collect in a concentrated mass. Weak-willed anglers who depart the water at the slightest hint of a breeze often deprive themselves of some of the most voracious feeding binges to be found all summer long when trout are drawn to a windblown feast. Short of gale force, wind is a manageable inconvenience that can work for rather than against you.

Because of the length of their seasonal availability, *Callibaetis* nymphs become a familiar food source where they hatch. Fishing a Callibaetis nymph in shallow moving water makes good sense an hour or so before an expected hatch. Submerged aquatic weed growth is prime habitat for the underwater stage, and although sometimes difficult to spot in these conditions, trout seem to sense a feeding opportunity long before actual emergence begins. Slender and graceful swimmers, the nymphs seem to become somewhat energized as they prepare to enter a new dimension of their existence. Twitching a weighted imitation in the proximity of a nymphing trout can be an action-packed prelude to the time when a floating pattern becomes appropriate. Because *Callibaetis* nymphs are not helpless in the current at this time, the imitation can be fished on a tight line from nearly any angle. Being able to see the trout is an advantage, although you may find yourself fishing to a disturbance that may or may not break the surface.

By both preference and convenience, Bonnie and I devote the large majority of our fishing hours to wadable moving water. And although *Callibaetis* occupy the river that flows not far from our doorstep, there is a time when the call of a forty-mile distant lake will not be denied. No longer a closely guarded secret, Hebgen Lake rests just across the border separating Montana and Idaho. This fer-

Small watercraft can be transported in the back of a pickup. This allows access to waters that are not easily reached with larger boats, which require a developed launching site.
BONNIE HARROP PHOTO

tile manmade impoundment hosts a remarkable population of brown and rainbow trout that grow quickly to impressive size. Like most stillwaters, Hebgen is limited in its production of diverse aquatic insect life, but its hatches of *Callibaetis* mayflies have become legendary. And though it is completely dependent upon perfect weather conditions, I am aware of no natural insect event that is more compelling to an aging couple who love the dry fly, and a 10-foot, flat-bottom skiff fitted with a small electric trolling motor becomes a familiar occupant of the bed of my '79 Chevy pickup from mid-June until early September.

Callibaetis time in the high Rockies is a precarious mixture of weather extremes that can range from a stifling ninety-degree calm to a raging blizzard. Between these opposites are the ideal summer mornings that arrive with temperatures in the high thirties and progress to a midday peak of about seventy-eight degrees. Predicting such conditions borders on the impossible when the fishing destination lies at the foot of the Continental Divide, where weather patterns can collide with nearly all the force that nature allows. A conservative guess is that one in three trips to Hebgen will end before the boat is ever launched due to a pesky morning wind that will eliminate any chance of a productive day. But when all elements of *Callibaetis* comfort are in place, we will join numerous others who scatter about the placid water in an assortment of watercraft ranging from sophisticated, high-horsepower outboards to small personal flotation craft.

Whether in moving or stillwater, a morning spinnerfall is the typical beginning of *Callibaetis* activity, with emergence following closely behind. And while cruising trout are also a shared similarity, it is a difficult game on water with no current to induce a consistent directional feeding pattern. Casting to a trout that is constantly changing course is one of the most frustrating dry-fly experiences, but this challenge is also what makes a successful connection something special. An added complication is the need to select and stay with one of what is frequently many surface feeders that come into casting range. This is a game of intense mental and physical discipline. An otherwise proficient angler can be reduced to a humiliated wreck when the action gets hot and heavy. It is common to be tempted away from an identified target by a larger trout or one that is easier to reach, but succumbing to this weakness can quickly result in a frantic loss of timing and critical execution. Changing casting direction in mid-stroke inevitably results in a time-consuming tangle and the loss of precious fishing opportunity.

In addition to humans, winged predators such as osprey, bald eagles, pelicans, and great blue herons recognize the ability of *Callibaetis* to bring trout from the depths. For this reason, trout in stillwater rise to the surface from a deeper level than on rivers where underwater structure and the stream bottom serve as concealment from overhead danger. The reluctance to remain near the surface means that the distance between rises is nearly always greater than on moving water. Rises separated by five to ten or more feet are not easy to pattern, especially when the direction of travel can change at any moment. Close observation of a single fish is beneficial to determining the path of travel from one rise to the next. The deliberate rise of a trout feeding on spinners will reveal a turning motion when a change of direction is imminent.

A deep-holding trout can see a single fly on the surface from a remarkable distance, which you can use to your advantage when the artificial has minimal competition from the naturals. Trout are much easier to fool when they are hunting for individual insects early in the spinnerfall, and a fly cast within five or six feet of a surface feeder is quite likely to receive some attention if it lies in the line of travel. It is a different story, however, when the volume of spent mayflies intensifies and the trout can feed at their leisure. Although timing the rise can become somewhat simpler, the artificial may be lost amid a host of naturals, and a perfect cast is often ignored. To some extent, this can be countered by fishing a pattern that is slightly higher in profile than the real thing but still retains the key features of the spinner. The logic is that a taller image appears more quickly in a trout's window of vision than one that lies flush on the surface. A CDC Paraspinner was designed to address this need with the added advantage of superior visibility on the water when compared to a conventional spinner pattern. A slender, segmented abdomen of dyed goose biot with a matching dubbed thorax is supported by long, splayed tails and oversize grizzly hackle, which does a superb job of imitating the mottled wings of the natural when tied parachute-style with the forward fibers trimmed over the hook eye. A white CDC post trimmed to one-third the normal length provides both flotation and visibility without excessive deviation from the natural.

Although usually different on moving water, even a modest riffling of a stillwater surface will often discourage trout from rising to *Callibaetis*. It is typical for the wind to arrive shortly after noon on any given day in the western Rockies, but exceptions do exist. *Callibaetis* duns emerging toward the end of the spinnerfall can extend the fishing for several hours if the lake surface remains calm. A relatively high-floating CDC Last Chance Cripple is a deceptive representation of a freshly emerged dun that cannot escape the attention of a foraging fish. Similar in coloration to the spinner, with the exception of a darker wing, this pattern is easy to see and will support a nymph dropper suspended about a foot beneath the surface. A CDC Biot Thorax is also effective when the cruising trout are looking for *Callibaetis* duns. The grizzly hackle on both patterns mimics the distinctive mottling of the natural. A *Callibaetis* nymph fished independently of an indicator fly can be effective during emergence when retrieved with quick, short strips of the line hand.

Although strictly a fair-weather mayfly, *Callibaetis* occupy an important position in the diet of trout and also in the hearts of those who become attached to the excitement they can provide. With a dedication to fly fishing that equals my own, Bonnie seldom speaks more fondly of any experience than a day spent with the gulpers of Hebgen Lake. So named because of the audible expulsion of air at the end of a rise, gulpers have come to symbolize the *Callibaetis* experience of which she is so fond. It is not a game of numbers but rather a time in the season when every trout comes with a price of humility and many fruitless casts. With a half dozen fish hooked over three or four hours of almost nonstop casting as a very respectable average for anyone, each is special and extremely appreciated. And her smile is more than adequate payment for a proud husband who spends more time at the oars than casting.

Whether on still or moving water, *Callibaetis* time is a period when simply being there is a joy in itself. In the comfort of summer that is far too short in the high country, all distractions of a responsible and civilized life are obscured by the sights and sounds of the natural world. Other seasons have their own unique charm and some hatches provide faster action, but the speckled mayflies and the time when they are present signify the more gentle aspects of fly fishing. And fortunate are those who understand these things.

BONNIE HARROP PHOTO

Callibaetis Nymph

Hook:	TMC 200R BL size 14-18
Thread:	Gray 8/0 UNI-Thread
Tail:	Barred wood duck
Rib:	Fine gold wire
Abdomen:	Gray/olive TroutHunter CEN dubbing tied slender
Wing case:	Dark brown marabou
Thorax:	Gray/olive TroutHunter CEN dubbing over double wraps of ribbing wire

Note: This is a moderately weighted pattern to be fished just prior to and during emergence.

BONNIE HARROP PHOTO

Callibaetis CDC Last Chance Cripple

Hook:	TMC 100BL size 14-18
Thread:	Tan 8/0 UNI-Thread
Tail:	Sparse tuft of gray/olive TroutHunter CEN dubbing over barred wood duck
Abdomen:	Gray/olive TroutHunter goose biot reversed to create a fuzzy effect
Thorax:	Callibaetis TroutHunter Pro dubbing
Wings:	Paired medium dun TroutHunter CDC feathers angled 45 degrees over hook eye
Hackle:	Whiting grizzly

Note: This high-profile cripple pattern mimics a freshly emerged dun that cannot escape the nymphal shuck.

BONNIE HARROP PHOTO

Callibaetis CDC Biot Emerger

Hook:	TMC 100BL size 14-18
Thread:	Tan 8/0 UNI-Thread
Tail:	Barred wood duck
Abdomen:	Callibaetis TroutHunter goose biot
Thorax:	Callibaetis TroutHunter Pro dubbing
Legs:	Brown Hungarian partridge
Wings:	Paired medium dun TroutHunter CDC feathers tied ³/₄ body length

Note: This fly imitates a fully hatched Callibaetis before its wings have fully lifted into an upright position.

BONNIE HARROP PHOTO

Callibaetis CDC Biot Thorax

Hook: TMC 100BL size 14-18
Thread: Tan 8/0 UNI-Thread
Tail: Ginger Whiting Coq de Leon
Abdomen: Callibaetis TroutHunter goose biot
Thorax: Callibaetis TroutHunter Pro dubbing
Wings: Paired medium dun TroutHunter CDC
            feathers
Hackle: Whiting grizzly trimmed on bottom

Note: This is a high-floating and realistic dun pattern.

BONNIE HARROP PHOTO

Callibaetis Biot Partridge Spinner

Hook: TMC 100BL size 14-18
Thread: Tan 8/0 UNI-Thread
Tail: Ginger Whiting Coq de Leon
Abdomen: Callibaetis TroutHunter goose biot
Thorax: Callibaetis TroutHunter Pro dubbing
Wings: Paired gray partridge feathers tied spent

Note: Use this flush-floating pattern when extra realism is required.

BONNIE HARROP PHOTO

Callibaetis CDC Biot Paraspinner

Hook: TMC 100BL size 14-18
Thread: Tan 8/0 UNI-Thread
Tail: Ginger Whiting Coq de Leon
Abdomen: Callibaetis TroutHunter goose biot
Thorax: Callibaetis TroutHunter Pro dubbing
Wing post: Paired white TroutHunter CDC feathers
            trimmed to ⅓ usual length
Hackle: Whiting grizzly two sizes larger than
            usual, tied parachute style and trimmed
            over eye to form a wide V

Note: This spinner pattern has higher visibility than most.

BONNIE HARROP PHOTO

Callibaetis CDC Captive Dun

Hook:	TMC 100BL size 14-18
Thread:	Tan 8/0 UNI-Thread
Tail:	Sparse tuft of gray/olive TroutHunter CEN dubbing over barred wood duck
Abdomen:	Gray/olive TroutHunter goose biot reversed to create a fuzzy effect
Thorax:	Callibaetis TroutHunter Pro dubbing
Legs:	Natural light tan TroutHunter CDC fibers divided on both sides of thorax and trimmed to ½ body length
Wing case:	Medium dun TroutHunter CDC feathers cupped over thorax to create a bubble effect

Note: This low-floating emerging pattern is fished in the film either alone or trailing a higher profile cripple or dun pattern.

Trico
carbon pencil with watercolor tint
9 x 11 inches

Tricos

A Lesson in Thinking Small

Not long ago, while cleaning a long neglected corner of my garage, I came across a remarkably well-preserved fly tackle catalog from the mid-1960s. The cover was torn and the printing was faded, but I could read enough to interrupt my early winter task with the revival of memories from a long-gone era. More isolated than now, my home in eastern Idaho lay many miles away from any source of sophisticated tackle or fly-fishing information during the first twenty or so years of my life. During that time, illustrated catalogs from a handful of mail-order companies provided the most revealing link to the world of serious fly fishermen, and I devoured their contents with the hungry mind of youth.

Revisiting the old catalog was a mental journey back to a time when fishing was purely for sport with no professional ambitions to complicate my learning process. Dog-eared pages marked the location of commercially tied flies that I used as a basis for improving the rather crude imitations I was tying at the time, and I smiled at the thought of how far we have come since then. But outdated fly design was not the most striking evidence of the weaker understanding of hatch-producing insects that existed in the not-too-distant past. With nearly a hundred different patterns displayed in full color, not a single fly smaller than size 18 was offered for sale.

Reflecting back on forty years of professional fly tying, it is sobering to remember that the size 20 and smaller flies, which now represent nearly half of my annual production, did not have a place in the general fly-fishing market when I began in the trade. But as I continued to ponder the subject of small flies, my mind returned to the early days on the Henry's Fork when midsummer brought an end to most of the hatches of larger mayflies, leaving me with challenges I could not understand or handle. As with most when they are new to the sport, catching fish was more important to me than learning, and for several years I would usually move to easier water when things got tough. Retreating to the South Fork of the Snake or the Teton brought a small sense of redemption for my failures farther north, but the compliant cutthroat of those waters were only a temporary substitute for the thrill and satisfaction of the defiant rainbows of the Henry's Fork. Gradually, I learned and matured, and solutions to former mysteries began to reveal themselves.

Acute observation of the water is a learned skill that must be accomplished to truly advance as an angler. In nature, secrecy is a tool of survival. For the human predator, understanding is the measuring stick of growth, and its progress does not necessarily end. For more than a decade, my fishing success was dependent upon flies no smaller

Clouds of glistening wings over streamside vegetation announce the arrival of a Trico spinnerfall. This sheltered side channel of the Henry's Fork is ideal habitat for one of the most important mayfly hatches of the season. BONNIE HARROP PHOTO

than size 16. Insects smaller than that were deemed too insignificant to be a viable temptation to big trout, and truly small flies went completely unnoticed. Abandonment of this mistaken notion happened rather abruptly one memorable day in mid-July nearly five decades ago.

It was nearing ten a.m. on a morning that promised little more than a sparse scattering of medium-size mayflies or a few small terrestrials before wind and the summer midday heat would end the limited opportunity in the area of the Harriman Ranch known as Millionaire's Pool. Resting in the tall grass of a small island, I watched four departing anglers with whom I had shared the water earlier as they made their way upstream and out of sight. Like them, I had labored fruitlessly over rising trout that fed at a pace far more accelerated than could be justified by what I was seeing on the water. While it was easy to empathize with the humbled quartet, the bitter pill of defeat was not made less difficult to swallow by the single remaining angler whose fortunes differed radically from my own.

Clearly a man of experience and superior skill, the stranger had taken at least three very respectable trout in little more than an hour, while the others who shared the wide, shallow flat went fishless. From a distance of more than a hundred yards, I admired the graceful delivery of the fly as he worked the long bamboo over the shallow weeded current. His delicate accuracy with casts approaching fifty feet in length demonstrated clear separation between our respective abilities, but this provided only partial explanation for results that put my own to shame.

Despite my limited casting range, I had earlier managed to move into position to get several good shots at rising fish that were not put off by my comparatively clumsy presentations. A modest sprinkling of size 14 mayflies I would later learn were *Callibaetis* was all I could see on the water, and I had selected my pattern accordingly. That the trout were far busier than one might expect with such meager incentive to rise did not register as a clue that my choice of flies might be incorrect. While every cast was not perfect, there were numerous times when the drift seemed right, and I tensed in anticipation of a take, which never came. Disappointment gradually turned to frustration as the sight and sounds of another's success began to point a humiliating finger at my ineptitude. Despite my best effort, it was impossible to ignore the periodic indications of a trout being hooked and played. From the corner of my eye, I could see the bowed rod, and the sound of a singing reel was not music to the ears of an unwilling spectator.

Clear, shallow water and extremely wary trout dictate a long, delicate cast with a fine leader. At size 20 or smaller, Tricos present an even greater challenge on this placid section of the Henry's Fork. BONNIE HARROP PHOTO

That is probably the only day that I have welcomed the end of feeding activity on one of the most beautiful pieces of water I have ever fished. But as the typical wind of late morning erased all signs of rising trout, I moved forward in hopes of intercepting the prosperous angler as he made his way toward the near bank. Pride among anglers normally discourages a concession of inferiority to another, but the brashness of youth can supersede this questionable protocol. An undignified charge across fifty yards of knee-deep water is not the most impressive way of gaining introduction, but it was an act I will never regret. With patience beyond what I deserved, the man bent low to the water and then motioned me to join him for a closer look. Trapped on the edge among bits of floating weed and other windblown debris were remnant specimens of tiny dark mayflies that had eluded my attention until that moment. Lying flush on the water with wings outstretched, they were nearly invisible from a distance greater than two feet. "Trico spinners," was the answer to my unspoken question, and he finished the conversation by clipping the bedraggled fly from his tippet and placing it in the palm of my hand. For more than a minute, I marveled at the smallest dry fly I had ever seen, and he was gone before my mumbled words of thanks could reach his ears.

There was much to ponder on the long walk back to my car, and I arrived at the parking area just in time to see my benefactor pull away in a dusty vehicle bearing Pennsylvania plates. The stranger had not given his name, and I never saw him again. But the revelation bestowed upon a rash young angler remains a compelling influence to this day.

A fitting follow-up to my chance meeting with the eastern stranger might describe how I immediately began to capitalize on the hidden opportunities presented by Tricos and other insects that can require a size 22 or smaller imitation, but it did not go that way. Dependent upon personal tying for all my flies, it would be more than a year before my skills were refined to the level needed to construct a viable representation of such minute organisms, and the problems did not end there. Finding a source for the miniature hooks and ultrafine tying thread was not an easy task, and hackle smaller than size 18 was nearly impossible to secure. My tackle throughout most of the 1960s could only be described as crude at best. A cumbersome fiberglass rod and 7-weight line would not perform the delicate presentation displayed by the gentleman from Pennsylvania nor would they cushion the resistance of a heavy trout, and my standard 4X tippet would barely fit through the eye of a size 22 hook. Adding to the cost of

These anglers await a Trico spinnerfall on the calm water of Millionaire's Pool on the Henry's Fork. Trico-feeding rainbows of surprising size cruise the flat surface from early summer through early autumn on many western waters. BONNIE HARROP PHOTO

replacing these outdated items was the expense of a smooth running reel capable of protecting a precarious hook hold and fragile tippet through a battle of long runs and acrobatic leaps. Eventually, however, improved skill and equipment came together, and my venture into the realm of small flies and big trout began to unfold.

Much of the process of growth is dependent upon a willingness to accept and pursue things not easily accomplished. Understanding extremely small insects and fishing their imitations effectively came with a long list of requirements that differed from the rudimentary approach that carried me through my first dozen years as a fly fisherman. Learning to see and think small when it came to matching hatches was a tough road through the first several years of exploring this evasive dimension as it applies to the pursuit of large trout. With Tricos as a starting point, I would learn that maximizing my productive time on the water required a near complete revision of the way I perceived the behavior of mature trout and their feeding tendencies. And the lessons learned while focusing upon a single type of mayfly would extend through a host of other insects that, because of their small size, were similarly difficult to observe and understand. Today, flies size 20 and

smaller are as common in my vest as those that are larger, and their role is no less vital to my overall fishing success.

Tricos' availability in great quantity during the spinner stage helps to explain why even large trout will isolate their feeding attention on Trico spinners. Lying flush on the water with wings in the spent position, the spinners can create the impression that trout are feeding on an invisible hatch, but close scrutiny can reveal thousands of immobile food items that often go unnoticed by the casual angler. Trout can justify feeding on the surface when capture of one or more insects is assured with each rise, and a Trico spinnerfall can fill that order. Continuous feeding over the course of an hour or more would not occur if the effort did not provide a significant reward.

For a decade or more, I focused on the reliable appearance of Trico spinners without regard for the other stages, which remained obscure to me throughout that period. Developing the ability to execute a long-line presentation was enhanced by specialized tackle that matched the need for gentle accuracy when fishing small flies over large and wary trout. Results came slowly when it came to hooking and landing the red-flanked bruisers, but eventually my competence with the lighter gear improved to the point where a trout of 18 or more inches was no longer the great intimidator of days past. The visual challenge of following the drift of a tiny fly amid hordes of naturals brought a new level of concentration that would elevate my efficiency in all aspects of fly fishing, and I credit Tricos for helping in the development of this vital component of success.

Like other mayflies, Tricos consolidate on the water during a spinnerfall that follows emergence and mating. A major difference, however, is that this generally happens within an hour or so of emergence. The transparent wings of mating Tricos form sparkling clouds along the banks of prime Trico habitat directly prior to a spinnerfall. A spinnerfall will occur in ideal conditions through most of summer and into early autumn, which means the timing of the insects' arrival on the water will vary as the season progresses. Adverse to direct sun rays and wind, a Trico spinnerfall can occur as early as 7 a.m. on the hottest days of summer, when the chill of evening has left the water. As the days grow shorter, the timing grows progressively later, and it is not especially rare to encounter Tricos in early evening in the later months of their presence.

Such was the case on an early October day on the Snake River just south of Yellowstone. It was nearing sunset when my photographer friend Dan Callaghan stopped his van near an old stock bridge that crosses a wide, slow-moving stretch of the big river. Silhouetted in the distance, the Tetons formed a towering backdrop for the scenic shots that kept Dan occupied for nearly an hour. In water too

deep for wading, dozens of cutthroat lazily sipped Trico spinners from the placid surface as I hastily rigged my rod and began casting from shore. With the water at a level typical of the season, nearly a hundred feet of exposed river rock separated my position from any obstruction to the backcast while I fished at a distance that was often as far as I could throw. Characteristically cooperative, the cutts took the little black spinner like it was candy until darkness forced an end to both photography and fishing.

Four days and two hundred miles later, I was fishing Tricos in early afternoon on the Bighorn in central Montana while Dan again shot photos. As the Bighorn is nearly three thousand feet lower in elevation than the Snake, temperatures there were nearly twenty degrees warmer, and the Tricos responded accordingly. My friend passed away about twenty years later, but his memory, like the Tricos, continues on the waters we so often shared.

My intimacy with the Tricos extended from the Green in southern Wyoming to the Missouri in western Montana, with several dozen notable spring creeks and tailwaters between the two. But I learned rather abruptly that the significance of these rather diminutive mayflies is not limited to the Rocky Mountain West.

By the early 1970s, Bonnie and I were struggling to establish ourselves as full-time professional fly tiers. Our accounts were mostly local, small, and subject to seasonal limitations that prevented any breakthrough to this ambition. This changed, however, when we were introduced to

Trico *spinner* TOSHI KARITA PHOTO

Colorado angler Frank Smethurst stalks a nymphing rainbow along the bank of the Henry's Fork. It is a mistake to ignore the potential of fishing the nymphal stage of Tricos and other diminutive mayflies. RENÉ HARROP PHOTO

the Orvis company, which was providing full-time employment to several dozen fly tiers at that time. Although seldom produced for resale, we had learned to tie very small flies for our personal use, and they fell directly in line with what Orvis was looking for. It was only a short time after providing samples of our work that we received an order for more than 36,000 flies. Nearly 30 percent of the order was comprised of Tricos size 20 and smaller, and the number grew over the seventeen years that we supplied flies to that company. Through that experience, I learned that Orvis had been selling large quantities of Trico patterns to anglers in nearly every geographical region of the United States far in advance of our association. It is now common knowledge that few if any mayfly species is more widely distributed in this country, but it was certainly an awakening to me as a younger man.

The growth of my understanding of mayflies in general did not parallel the progression of my knowledge of Tricos. As angling attention began to fall heavily on the Henry's Fork and other fisheries in the Yellowstone region, the behavior of the trout began to change. Problem solving

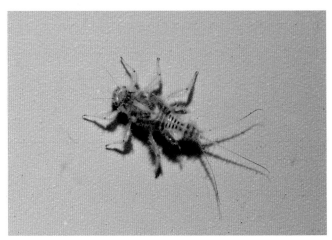

Trico nymph TOSHI KARITA PHOTO

through fly tying came as the result of a greater need for improved representation of the full range of stages in the life cycle as the practice of catch-and-release created more formidable adversaries. Specifically, it was the complexity of emergence both on and beneath the surface that dominated my creative effort at the vise, and it resulted in a radical change in my perception of matching the hatch.

While not actually a true stage of existence, emergers targeted the elusive progression of change from nymph to dun, and it was in this confined area of mayfly behavior that answers to many perplexing puzzles were found. While hatches of larger mayflies such as PMDs, Flavs, *Callibaetis*, and even Drakes received substantial attention in the emerging stage, it was several years before Trico emergers and duns became a noticeable factor in my personal fishing picture. This is understandable because a Trico spinnerfall continued to be a reliable exception to the increased difficulty that other mayflies had begun to present.

Uncompelled by necessity, there was little reason to alter the way I imitated and fished Trico spinners. The patterns seemed to be working fine, and I was usually satisfied with their productivity. Significant changes in fly design and construction did occur over time, but they were mainly due to increased availability and quality of fly-tying materials, with better flotation and visibility being the primary benefit. CDC and Whiting hackle are among the prominent improvements I have made in my Trico imitations, but of course, this applies to many other flies as well.

There is also a rather embarrassing explanation for allowing my understanding of Tricos to lag behind other mayflies that I considered to be more complex. A casual examination of Trico duns can reveal a reasonable similarity to *Baetis* mayflies in both size and color, and it was a pure case of mistaken identity that hindered an earlier appreciation for the value of the Trico's other winged stage. In stark contrast to the clear wings and blackish brown body of the spinner, Trico duns exhibit pale gray wings and an abdomen that can be light olive or a cream color. A consistently dark thorax and three tails rather than two separate this insect from a *Baetis* dun, which is also more slender throughout its length. Armed with a corrected perspective, I proceeded to incorporate what I had learned from other mayflies into a full range of Trico dun and emerger patterns.

A Trico emergence transpires over an hour or more prior to the spinnerfall, and although the density of upright duns is not typically equal to that of the spent-wing stage, the availability of Tricos in the process of hatching is frequently adequate to gain the interest of hungry trout.

Compared to the complexity of emergence, dealing with a spinnerfall is a relatively simple procedure of presenting an artificial that imitates the singular inanimate image of a dying or dead insect. Acceptance of the fly is made more difficult when the imitation joins a crowd of naturals, which is what usually happens during a Trico spinnerfall. Correctly duplicating the small size and low profile of the spinner means fishing a fly that is not easy to see on the water. Accuracy and timing are added to the constant requirement of a drag-free presentation, but these elements are certainly not unique to this situation.

During emergence, feeding activity that disturbs the surface does not necessarily mean that the fish has taken a dun. Intact nymphs are often targets that can produce what appears to be a rise simply because they are very close to the surface at the point of capture. Also, changes in both shape and color are taking place as the underwater form converts to the winged air-breathing stage. This process begins beneath the surface and is completed when the newly hatched dun has penetrated the film. Between those two points are a variety of possible positions and configurations that can influence fly choice. Emerging patterns that display characteristics of a partially emerged or undeveloped dun can vary in appearance and the way they are fished with respect to the surface. Therefore, finding the correct image and presenting it at the proper level can be a chore, especially when you consider the fact that not all trout will respond favorably to the same setup.

Patterns referred to as cripples are higher floating imitations of a fully winged dun that is trapped on the surface by the failure to gain full release from the nymphal shuck. The theory that trout recognize this encumbrance and the associated vulnerability seems to be correct. A Trico cripple fished during emergence has the advantage of being quite effective and easy to see as well.

Trico duns in perfect condition are not immune to trout attention. Parachute or no-hackle patterns in the appropriate size and color are both personal favorites for trout that are clearly taking from the surface. While always subtle, the rise to a Trico dun is never without the prominent display of the trout's nose, which can frequently be surprisingly impressive.

Reflecting on a relationship with Tricos that now spans nearly five decades is a mental journey back to an innocent time when the deeper mysteries of water and trout began to open for an inquiring young mind. And while secrets continue and puzzles remain unsolved, I credit these miniature mayflies with providing a challenge that must be answered by all who seek growth and maturity in the limited segment of fly fishing where hatches rule and an imperfect cast is worthless. The countless days of pleasure mixed with frustration are indeed memorable, but they do not describe the ultimate personal value of fishing Tricos. The significance of learning to think and see beyond the obvious extends to many mayfly species and through other aquatic and terrestrial insects as well. Tying and fishing extremely small flies is not any easy undertaking, and it takes time to reach a level of confidence and competence that allows both to become standard practice. But tiny organisms do comprise a sizable portion of the diet of even large trout in many waters, and the angling opportunity that accompanies this behavior cannot be overstated. Accepting this reality and the challenge that goes with it is a large step forward, and Tricos are only the beginning.

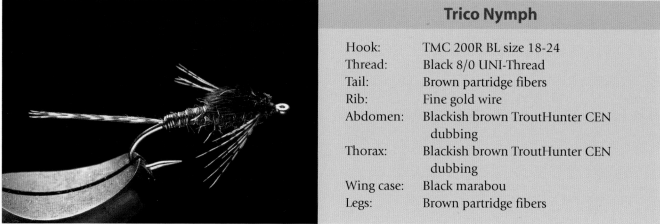

BONNIE HARROP PHOTO

Trico Nymph

Hook:	TMC 200R BL size 18-24
Thread:	Black 8/0 UNI-Thread
Tail:	Brown partridge fibers
Rib:	Fine gold wire
Abdomen:	Blackish brown TroutHunter CEN dubbing
Thorax:	Blackish brown TroutHunter CEN dubbing
Wing case:	Black marabou
Legs:	Brown partridge fibers

BONNIE HARROP PHOTO

Trico CDC Biot Emerger

Hook:	TMC 100BL size 18-24
Thread:	Black 8/0 UNI-Thread
Tail:	Dark brown partridge fibers
Abdomen:	Olive TroutHunter goose biot
Thorax:	Trico TroutHunter Pro dubbing
Legs:	Dark brown partridge fibers
Wings:	Paired white TroutHunter CDC feathers

BONNIE HARROP PHOTO

Trico CDC Biot Parachute

Hook:	TMC 100BL size 18-24
Thread:	Black 8/0 UNI-Thread
Tail:	Whiting Coq de Leon
Abdomen:	Olive goose biot
Thorax:	Trico TroutHunter Pro dubbing
Post:	Paired white CDC feathers trimmed to length
Hackle:	Whiting grizzly

Trico No Hackle

Hook: TMC 100 BL size 18-24
Thread: Black 8/0 UNI-Thread
Tail: Whiting Coq de Leon
Abdomen: Olive TroutHunter Pro dubbing
Thorax: Trico TroutHunter Pro dubbing
Wings: White duck quill wing segments

BONNIE HARROP PHOTO

Trico CDC Biot Spinner

Hook: TMC 100 BL size 18-24
Thread: Black 8/0 UNI-Thread
Tail: Whiting Coq de Leon
Abdomen: Trico TroutHunter goose biot
Thorax: Trico TroutHunter Pro dubbing
Wings: Paired white CDC feathers tied spent

BONNIE HARROP PHOTO

Trico CDC Hackled Biot Spinner

Hook: TMC 100 BL size 18-24
Thread: Black 8/0 UNI-Thread
Tail: Whiting Coq de Leon
Abdomen: Trico TroutHunter goose biot
Thorax: Trico TroutHunter Pro dubbing
Wings: Paired white CDC feathers tied spent
Hackle: Whiting grizzly dyed dun

BONNIE HARROP PHOTO

Pale Morning Dun
carbon pencil with watercolor tint
11 x 14 inches

Pale Morning Duns

The Defiant Hatch

As an older man who has spent the majority of his life entangled in the mysteries of water, it might seem difficult to select one subject that rises above all else in terms of sustaining its original interest. While nothing in fly fishing can be taken for granted, there are aspects in which time can bring a degree of comfort when it comes to the business of handling situations involving a large trout and a single insect type. And one might assume that age would bring an attraction to those insect events that provide maximum simplicity to the mental and physical demands of prevailing over a worthy adversary. But it is not the appearance of large food forms and their inherent ability to make trout more vulnerable that I most look forward to in any season. Certainly, there is appreciation for the giant Salmonflies and big Drakes that can drive trout to a near frenzy, but these are often fleeting incidents that seldom last more than a week or so.

Smaller insects of interest like Tricos, *Baetis*, or midges are more reliable in their annual appearance, which, combined with a substantial length of availability, makes them significant factors in the diet of some surprisingly large trout. Due to their extremely small size, these hatches create unique problems, but in my experience their ability to defy common technique in presentation and imitation fades in comparison to a familiar mayfly that is not even particularly small. From tiny spring creeks to mighty tail-waters, they are found throughout the Rocky Mountain West wherever waters flow clean and clear. Beginning as early as May and continuing sometimes until November, their appearance will always attract the attention of trout. They are commonly known as Pale Morning Duns, and in my life they are special.

Like many who enter fly fishing at an early age, I began fly tying as a concession to economic limitations, and continued in that way for the first dozen or so years of my involvement. Gradually, however, the naiveté of youth gave way to an awareness that my progress as an angler depended on not simply having flies but on having the right imitation for the varying situations that must be confronted on my home water. As personal angling ambitions evolved, I left that uncomplicated period when random success with any trout was a satisfactory reward for my effort on the water. Because they were there, the big rainbows of the Henry's Fork became the primary focus of my attention. And because they were elusive, my fly tying took on a different emphasis that connected the images that spilled from my vise to the problems associated with a quarry that seemed to become more sophisticated with each passing year.

While only a part of the trout's diet, mayflies seemed to command the most attention when it came to creating situational patterns that relate to very specific behavioral

Wind is not always a fly fisherman's enemy. A brisk breeze was preventing PMD duns from leaving the water when I hooked this acrobatic tail-walker. A CDC PMD Biot Cripple duplicated the partially emerged duns that littered the choppy surface.
BONNIE HARROP PHOTO

characteristics on the part of trout and a preferred food source. With multiple variations, each mayfly hatch posed individual requirements that must be met if a pattern were to be deemed viable. Advancement in pattern design was usually driven by some failure during the heat of conflict with an especially alluring and resistant trout. This, of course, presumes that a faulty presentation was not the culprit leading to defeat. Over time, many of the questions pertaining to mayfly imitation have been answered, and the contents of my fly boxes tell the story of a journey toward greater understanding of these complex organisms and their relationship to my standing as a fly fisherman. And while there is always room for improvement, I am generally confident in the ability of my flies to cover the essential requirements of nearly any mayfly hatch that might be encountered in the Yellowstone region.

This is not to say that I prevail in every engagement with a sizable fish, for there are far more explanations for failure than a faulty fly. Like anyone else, I endure the proverbial butt kicking from more fish than I care to admit. But over time I have systematically developed a certain comfort in my relationship with familiar hatches that routinely appear over the course of a season. And while new ideas in fly tying are ongoing, I am not usually pressured

to redeem wounded honor by creating a new fly. An exception, however, applies to a welcome yet perplexing category of mayflies that persist in their ability to defy my best ambitions with a rod or at the vise. Within a few weeks of their first sighting on the Henry's Fork, the Pale Morning Duns and the trout they attract will offer an almost daily opportunity to be humbled, and this will typically last from late spring well into September.

Known commonly as PMDs, Pale Morning Duns are nearly synonymous with the western fly-fishing experience. They exist where water of the right chemistry and temperature combine to create the ideal balance of clean stream bottom and aquatic vegetation. This includes nearly every state from Colorado westward, and the number of streams where PMDs are present is nearly countless. Most notable for hosting impressive hatches of PMDs are waters within or flowing relatively close to Yellowstone National Park in Idaho, Montana, and Wyoming. Here they are among the most reliable mayflies to appear each season, but when the hatch extends over several months, they can also be the most frustrating to solve.

As indicated by name, PMDs were originally designated by a pale olive yellow body and light gray wings. But since the early 1970s, it has been learned that significant color variations exist within a group of mayflies that in most other facets of appearance and behavior are nearly identical. In the dun stage, wings can be a very pale gray to almost slate in color, and body coloration can range even more widely. A bright yellow body is not uncommon on some spring creeks, and the naturals on some tailwaters have a definite orange cast. On the Henry's Fork, what would be considered normal coloration can be joined by distinctly pink or olive variations, and I have seen some that are a medium shade of brown on the back of the abdomen. A visual characteristic that identifies these mayflies as belonging to an associated group is the pronounced yellow coloration in the forward veins of the wings and the joints of the legs.

As might be expected, the colors of PMDs can also vary in the nymph and spinner stages, which can add further complication when it comes to precise visual duplication. However, most hatch-oriented anglers rate size and shape ahead of color in order of imitative importance. But while this may provide some cushion against certain failure, color accuracy should be a consideration in selecting the right fly. My own experience has shown that an especially selective trout can show a marked preference for one color variation over another when multiple choices are present.

In relatively bright conditions, floating duns and spinners are seen more in silhouette when viewed from below, which helps to reduce color as an identifiable characteristic. In evening or overcast days, however, it can be a different story, as backlighting diminishes and color becomes more relevant.

Nymphal or emerging patterns fished either fully or partially submerged are subject to full scrutiny with regard to color in any light condition during daytime hours. While keen attention is usually given to the details of an emerging pattern, a degree of carelessness frequently accompanies the tying or selection of a PMD nymph. Because they are available over a much longer period, nymphs become considerably more familiar to foraging trout that can learn a painful lesson when a mistake is made. In clear water with moderate current, big, hook-savvy trout are no less repulsed by a faulty nymph than any other phase of mayfly imitation.

Although weed beds are not their exclusive habitat, PMDs seem to flourish in lush weed beds where undulating currents serve to complicate the drift of a fly. Drag will invariably negate the appeal of even the most accurate artificial, and no factor has stronger influence in gaining success during a hatch of PMDs. Whether through instinct or conditioning, trout that survive to advanced age seem especially dependent upon the ability to recognize flawed presentation as a means of avoiding a dreadful encounter with a human enemy.

The average caster does not necessarily have the precise control needed during an emergence of PMDs, and a common tackle setup can be deficient as well. While a wide and deeper tailwater can require a cast longer than forty feet, it

Female Pale Morning Dun spinner TOSHI KARITA PHOTO

One of Japan's most accomplished anglers, Masa Katsumata has become a Henry's Fork regular. Masa took this robust hen on a CDC Rusty Biot Spinner during a PMD spinnerfall.

RENÉ HARROP PHOTO

is always advantageous to keep the range between the target trout and yourself below that distance. This will allow you to use a lighter, more delicate line, which is less likely to cause disturbance to the trout both on the water and in the air. A leader of less than twelve feet in length can be problematic in situations where overhead movement or shadow can be instantly detected as a warning of danger. A light tippet of 5X or lighter will do the best job of flexing with tricky currents, thus allowing the fly to drift in the most natural manner possible.

Developing confidence in an upstream presentation will enable a close approach from behind the fish, thereby helping to minimize the casting distance. With a gentle delivery from this position, it is usually possible to sustain a PMD fishing situation that may require numerous fly changes and dozens of casts. Short-range accuracy with a long leader is a casting skill unto itself, and plenty who can smoothly execute a cast of sixty feet or more experience difficulty managing situations that emphasize close-up control rather than distance. Subtle rod manipulations that deliver the fly to the correct location while providing adequate leader slack for an unhindered drift require a trained hand and a sensitive tip. One must also realize that while the name implies morning activity, Pale Morning Duns can easily appear on a breezy afternoon on many waters. While

pleasant to fish with during calm conditions, a slow action rod can be a handicap when wind complicates an already demanding set of presentation problems. A medium-fast rod works best for me when cutting through a stiff breeze. A line developed specifically for this type of fishing performs better in the wind while providing the energy needed to turn over a long leader. I currently use an Airflo Ridgeline Tactical in DT4 for the majority of my fishing.

As an attractant to big trout, PMDs place an added burden of performance on the reel. On broad water like the Henry's Fork, reel-scorching runs of more than one hundred yards must frequently be weathered once the opponent has succumbed to the fly. A good large arbor reel has adequate capacity for the line and plenty of backing, with a smooth and reliable drag system as an additional feature. Combined with concentration and practiced techniques of playing and landing, this setup makes netting a 20-inch or better fish on a light tippet and relatively small fly more than just a slight possibility.

While sometimes double the amount of time, an average four-hour hatch of PMD duns can become consolidated into an hourlong, or slightly longer, spinnerfall. This can occur in the calm and cool of either morning or evening with the result often being an intense feeding binge that brings nearly every trout to the surface. While this certainly could not be described as opportunity for easy fishing, the challenges of a PMD spinnerfall are not nearly as extensive as those that accompany emergence. Dead and dying spinners arriving on the water from above remain consistent in both physical appearance and position on the water throughout the time they are available to trout. A spent-wing pattern in the correct size and color makes fly selection a relatively simple component in the process of dealing with a spinnerfall.

Matching the feeding pace of a sometimes moving target can be a chore when there are countless naturals competing with your fly for attention. But trout feeding on floating spinners are only looking upward to the surface and are without the distraction of insects rising from beneath as is the case during emergence. A perfect presentation timed to match the rhythm and location of a feeding fish is all that is needed when combined with the right imitation, but there have been times when I have spent the entire span of a spinnerfall trying to make this happen with a single large trout. I rely primarily on an olive-yellow or rust-colored pattern for most PMD spinner activity on the Henry's Fork, with the lighter shade usually being more applicable on some other regional waters.

Fishing a high-floating dun makes perfect sense early in the hatch and then later toward the end when PMD numbers are relatively sparse. Obeying the urge to feed, even large trout will find acceptability in a prey that is likely to thwart capture by leaving the water when options for a less mobile source are not easily available. During emergence, PMD duns can also drift away from ideal habitat where concentrated numbers and assorted emerging forms are not a strong factor in causing the trout to avoid a high-floating pattern. On breezy days, it is not unusual to find a big trout tucked close against the bank where wind collects PMD duns well outside the main flow of hatching activity. While always a testy casting situation, a big bank feeder usually provides a stationary target, thereby eliminating some of the problems associated with a trout that is fully involved with the complexity of emergence.

In my experience, a big surface-feeding trout will nearly always prefer an undeveloped form that is not yet able to fly over one that can leave the water at any instant following emergence from the underwater stage. This applies to nearly any aquatic insect, but it is particularly apparent during a hatch of PMDs. In fact, I have put more observation, thought, and experimentation into this feature of fishing PMDs than any other insect subject. While failures far outnumber successes in my attempt to find efficient answers to multiple questions pertaining to specific imitation of emerging PMDs, there is little question that my abilities as both fly tier and angler have benefited from this decades-long endeavor. Pursuing top-feeding trout is the sport I most enjoy, and PMDs provide as much opportunity for this kind of fishing as any hatch in the season.

A low-floating emerging pattern is nearly always my first choice when I am certain that the trout is taking from the surface during the peak of a PMD hatch. The CDC Captive Dun is a flush-floating pattern that resembles a nymph but incorporates key color features that imitate a dun that is only partially emerged from the nymphal shuck. In its current form, this go-to pattern is a derivative of dozens of modifications to the original concept, and I am not certain that further change does not lie in store. Even the most realistic patterns are woeful counterfeits of lively emerging PMDs, which are very difficult to imitate. Building motion into the visual image of an artificial is especially problematic when the fly must be fished without movement counter to the current.

While a smaller factor in the early weeks of its seasonal emergence cycle, the struggling motion of freeing itself from the nymphal shuck seems to allow trout to separate a living PMD form from an imitation. Also, when full emergence into the dun stage is delayed in the film, a period of enhanced availability, while usually quite short, is enough to bring a greater certainty of capture. On waters where PMDs hatch daily over a period of months, older trout can become brutally efficient in avoiding an artificial that does not manifest both the appearance and behavior of the transitioning insects. Since movement of hatching PMDs is against the restraint of the nymphal shuck rather than the current, it is extremely difficult to duplicate while

Pale Morning Dun nymph TOSHI KARITA PHOTO

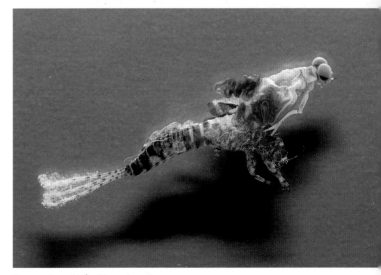

Emerging Pale Morning Dun TOSHI KARITA PHOTO

allowing the artificial to drift without drag. Occasionally, it is possible to tempt an unsuspecting trout into a mistake by applying a very subtle twitch with the rod tip, which can activate the extremities of the artificial in a way that suggests the struggling motion of the natural. Remember, however, that the drag accompanying this maneuver poses considerable risk in alarming a contented trout unless the technique is executed to perfection.

While one of CDC's most valuable characteristics is its ability to float well, it is the inherent softness that allows CDC to flex with the current, or a rod-imparted twitch, that makes it particularly suited for imitating emerging PMDs. When incorporated into the wings, legs, and tails of the patterns, CDC allows the fly to float without adding unwanted bulk and while providing maximum response to any motion-producing influence. Higher floating cripples and dun patterns also benefit from these features, and nothing in my experience works better than CDC for spinner wings.

A careful approach from downstream took Bonnie to within twenty-five feet of this busy surface feeder. The big rainbow took a CDC PMD Captive Dun, which is one of the most reliable patterns for this complex hatch. RENÉ HARROP PHOTO

In general, nymph fishing is not associated with a high degree of finesse or complexity. In clear water of modest depth, however, PMD nymphs can provide challenges that are quite similar to those of fishing the above-water stages. With daily appearance over a sustained period of time, PMD nymphs are an anticipated food source that becomes clearly recognizable to trout. And in this regard, appearance and behavior of the natural must be considered equally with the other stages if one expects to take full advantage of this often overlooked opportunity.

Locating and then fishing to a special trout in a one-on-one encounter is a personal thrill regardless of whether it transpires above or beneath the surface. Sight nymphing, either alone or with the help of a spotter who calls out instruction, can have its own unique rewards and satisfaction when distinct factors of stealthy approach, correct fly selection, and precise presentation come together. PMD nymphs typically possess adequate individual size and occur in enough volume to attract the most serious players of the underwater world, where the most enticing trout will seldom feed on top. Some of the largest fish I have ever hooked have taken a PMD nymph at the exclusion of numerous other offerings. The requirements of effectively fishing PMD nymphs are fundamental when there is no hatch, but the game can change quite dramatically during the peak of emergence.

Areas of especially heavy aquatic weed growth are known to host great quantities of PMD nymphs. When concentrated in such isolation, a PMD emergence offers numerous choices to trout in terms of image, behavior, and location in the water column. Emerging nymphs in a variety of configurations join cripples and fully emerged duns, drawing a trout's attention to the surface. While offering significant opportunity, conventional subsurface nymphing is commonly put aside in favor of rising fish that reveal their size and location with distinct clarity.

For decades it was common belief that trout rising to the surface selected their prospective victim by concentrating their attention upon what was happening overhead. Understandably, much has been made of the trout's window of vision as it applies to a floating food source, and in many instances it is very important. However, there is a phase in PMD emergence in which a riseform does not signify the interception of something drifting overhead. While I cannot state with full certainty that the following behavior quirk is peculiar to this hatch, there is no doubt that a surface disturbance during a PMD emergence does not necessarily indicate the acceptance of a floating insect.

Because of great abundance during emergence, nymphs lifting toward the surface are routinely targeted by trout looking forward rather than upward. In the case of PMDs, the process of change from nymphs to duns begins at significant depth with the splitting of the wing case as the first indication of this transition. Almost at once, an intense struggle for escape creates motion that, when added to the fresh new color of the emerging dun in the thorax area of the nymph, serves as a trigger in attracting the attention of some trout.

Why a trout would be selective to this stage of emergence is unclear, but sampling stomach contents can show instances when transitioning nymphs comprise 100 percent of a trout's food intake. With only large trout seeming to exhibit this behavior, it appears at least possible that nymphs in this condition may represent an opportunity to avoid succumbing to a cleverly disguised hook. Even the most deceptive artificial is not capable of change once it is presented to the trout, but the change in an actual nymph is constant and very obvious once the process of emergence begins. Neither can a submerged fly rise toward the surface without the angler applying tension that is counter to the speed of the current. Feeble swimmers at best, PMD nymphs lose all subsurface mobility during transition to the dun stage. This means that they are drifting without significant resistance to the current as they rise toward the surface. With emerging nymphs as the exclusive objective, trout move aggressively about as they hunt down the preferred insects. Frequently, the consumption point occurs close enough to the surface to create the impression of a rise when actually the insect has been targeted well underwater and then followed to the top.

Duplicating the appearance and behavior of a hatching PMD nymph involves using soft material that will create the illusion of a natural as it vigorously works to escape the nymphal shuck. Soft fibers of partridge, grouse, or CDC do the best job, and the fly must be slightly weighted to penetrate the surface. Present the fly from a quartering upstream position, and drop it well above the trout. Allow the fly to sink as it drifts toward the target, and then stop the process by removing slack line with a lift of the rod tip. This will cause the fly to swing upward toward the surface, with a pulsing motion coming from gentle twitches of the rod tip. This technique relies upon luck to a considerable extent, but it is the only way I know of to approximate the elusive natural rise to the surface of a hatching PMD nymph. Of course any large trout has made an amazing blunder when it mistakes an artificial for an actual living creature. But some blunders are more easily enticed than

Notorious for inducing extremely selective feeding behavior, a PMD hatch can create marathon sessions with individual trout. This Henry's Fork rainbow finally accepted a PMD Hatching Nymph during an engagement lasting nearly an hour. BONNIE HARROP PHOTO

others, and this aspect of fishing PMDs ranks right at the top of the difficulty scale.

Reflecting upon the many years in which PMDs have asserted themselves against my will to overcome their complexity, I find myself stimulated rather than discouraged by an ongoing feud that appears to be without end. PMDs have been the source of some of my most humbling failures, both at the vise and with a rod, but I also owe many of my most invigorating victories on the water to the existence of this special hatch. Over time, some facets of fly fishing have lost some ability to invade my thoughts and spur effort toward a higher degree of accomplishment. But if concern for losing interest in a sport I have loved for so many years should ever creep into my consciousness, I need only remember the Pale Morning Duns and the unfinished business they continue to represent.

BONNIE HARROP PHOTO

PMD Nymph

Hook:	TMC 200 R BL size 14-20
Thread:	Tan 8/0 UNI-Thread
Tail:	Wood duck fibers
Rib:	Fine gold wire
Body:	Rusty olive TroutHunter CEN dubbing
Wing case:	Brown marabou
Legs:	Brown Hungarian partridge fibers

BONNIE HARROP PHOTO

PMD Hatching Nymph

Hook:	TMC 200 R BL size 14-20
Thread:	Tan 8/0 UNI-Thread
Tail:	Wood duck fibers
Rib:	Fine gold wire
Body:	Rusty olive TroutHunter CEN dubbing
Wing case:	Ball of yellow TroutHunter CEN dubbing secured to top of thorax
Legs:	Mixed yellow CDC and light brown Hungarian partridge fibers

BONNIE HARROP PHOTO

PMD CDC Captive Dun

Hook:	TMC 100 BL size 14-20
Thread:	Tan 8/0 UNI-Thread
Tail (shuck):	Sparse tuft of rusty TroutHunter CEN dubbing over wood duck fibers
Abdomen:	Rusty spinner TroutHunter goose biot
Thorax:	PMD TroutHunter Pro dubbing
Wing case:	TroutHunter light dun CDC
Legs:	Yellow CDC fibers

PMD CDC Biot Dun (Pink Phase)

Hook:	TMC 100BL size 14-20
Thread:	Tan 8/0 UNI-Thread
Tail:	Sparse CDC fibers over Whiting Coq de Leon
Abdomen:	Pink cahill TroutHunter goose biot
Thorax:	Pink cahill TroutHunter Pro dubbing
Wings:	Paired light dun CDC TroutHunter feathers
Legs:	Butts of CDC wings tied back and trimmed

PMD CDC Biot Cripple (Yellow Phase)

Hook:	TMC 100 BL size 14-20
Thread:	Yellow 8/0 UNI-Thread
Tail:	Sparse tuft TroutHunter CEN dubbing over wood duck fibers
Abdomen:	Rusty spinner TroutHunter goose biot
Thorax:	PMD TroutHunter Pro dubbing
Wings:	Paired light dun TroutHunter CDC feathers
Legs:	Light brown Hungarian partridge fibers

PMD CDC Biot Spinner (Yellow Phase)

Hook:	TMC 100 BL size 14-20
Thread:	Yellow 8/0 UNI-Thread
Tail:	Whiting Coq de Leon
Abdomen:	PMD TroutHunter goose biot
Thorax:	PMD TroutHunter Pro dubbing
Wings:	Paired light dun TroutHunter CDC feathers tied spent

Baetis
carbon pencil with watercolor tint
9 x 12 inches

Baetis

Last Chance

Heavy, wet snow encrusts the felt soles of my waders as I ease gingerly onto a thin apron of ice at the river's edge. Luckily, I do not fall as the ice cracks beneath my weight and I stumble into six inches of water. Dime-size white flakes melt quickly into my wool gloves and obscure the far bank a hundred yards away. But the October storm does not hide three big rainbows that feed in unison sixty feet upstream. Relieved that my undignified entry has not disturbed the thoroughly occupied trio, I regain my footing and begin to cautiously make my way up toward them over a coarse rock-strewn bottom. The going is slow, and I inch my way to within thirty feet before stopping to examine the situation more closely.

The fish are feeding in eighteen inches of water on the inside edge of a deep slot that serves as instant security should anything threatening come into play. One careless move on my part and they will vanish at once into the icy depths. The downstream player is not the largest of the three, but it is nearest to my position. A cast to a bigger target would mean throwing over the closer fish, and the result would be predictable. The water appears nearly black against the ashen sky, and the small mayflies that pepper the surface are indistinct through my snow-spattered glasses. Wiping them on the collar of my fleece jacket helps to some degree, but close inspection is not necessary. It is *Baetis* time, and in these conditions, the likelihood of any other mayfly appearing on the water is highly remote. I have been here before on many occasions over the years, and the size 22 Emerger was knotted to the 7X tippet before I ever left my truck.

A narrow drift line where quick and slow water meet collects scores of the tiny olive insects, and the target fish pushes eagerly against the food-laden seam. A perfect cast will place the fly six inches above the rise, and a perfect drift will match the feeding rhythm. Two inches right or left will take it off line and out of the zone of acceptance. If I see the fly, it will be only because drag has pushed it across the surface at a speed completely unlike that of the naturals. Only the absence of wind makes the situation seem even remotely possible, and even then it will take more than a little luck. You cast more by feel at times like this, but somehow you instinctively know when the presentation is right. And that is how it goes when the third cast just feels good, and the trout rises exactly when I sense the fly is where it should be. I tighten to solid unyielding weight and then a desperate plunge into heavy water.

Beyond the channel lies more than a hundred feet of open water, but in this season it is less than a foot deep. Reluctant to leave the safety of a deeper flow, the big rainbow thrashes briefly on the surface against the sting of the tiny hook before diving toward the bottom to slug it out. With a weight in obvious excess of the $2\frac{1}{2}$-pound breaking

As October snow signals the end of another season, fall *Baetis* provide the final opportunity to fish a mayfly hatch on the Henry's Fork and many other waters. BONNIE HARROP PHOTO

point of the tippet, the fish is in total command. Only its refusal to charge recklessly across the shallows gives hope of any chance of prevailing. But in the chilled water of winter-like conditions, the rainbow does not exhibit the violent resistance so typically associated with its species. Turning its head with lateral pressure, I force the fish to fight the current more than the rod, and it begins to tire fairly quickly. Rather than attempting to lift its considerable weight, I lead it slowly toward the near bank by keeping the rod low and parallel to the shoreline. Gentle but constant pressure brings the fish into thin water, where all advantage of current or depth is lost. Still, a forceful shake of the head or a quick surge against the rod would easily fracture the precarious connection. With depth inadequate to maneuver a net, I cradle the broad body against my lower leg and slide the rod onto the ice at the water's edge. Keeping the muscular rainbow mostly submerged, I pluck the little olive from the upper jaw and then guide the pulsing body into deeper water. For half a minute I admire the magnificence of an autumn rainbow, then watch it disappear effortlessly into the darkened water.

The common mental image of fall is like a calendar photo replete with colors symbolic of the season and bathed in warmth by a low-angled sun. At lower eleva-

tions, fall brings welcome relief from incessant heat while preserving a period of relatively comfortable weather for as long as several months. Autumn in the high country, however, is a different story. Morning frost in late August marks the beginning of a season that a mountain-dwelling hermit who has since passed on once described to me as a collision between summer and winter. The wisdom of those words rings loud and clear when temperatures plunge below zero in mid-September or when an October day brings near eighty degrees. Snow can come at any time, and a heavy rain can change the character of a river in a matter of hours. One might think that such varying and unpredictable extremes would discourage the pursuit of mayfly hatches and rising trout, but such is not the case. Fall, for all its vagaries, has become the favored season for a relatively rare breed of angler who is willing to put sensibility and physical comfort aside for one last chance to feed an addiction to the dry fly. Although it would be a misrepresentation to portray autumn in the Rocky Mountain West as a tumultuous period of climatic extremes, it is important to recognize the unpredictability of the final days before true winter sets in, which can be as early as late October in some years. Typically, fall begins and ends early above six thousand feet elevation, and within that brief

Baetis *male dun* TOSHI KARITA PHOTO

window of late-season opportunity lie golden days of such perfection as to be almost indescribable. Remarkably, however, some of the best fishing happens on the days that seem least hospitable.

Known commonly as Blue-Winged Olives or BWOs, *Baetis* are among the most unusual mayflies in existence. Their vast geographic distribution and a propensity for cold weather make them uniquely suited to the committed angler who seeks quality dry-fly fishing at almost any cost of discomfort or frustration. Although their typically small size and the low water conditions of the late season serve to complicate the picture, *Baetis*, with their surprising size and numbers, are a reliable attraction to trout. It is a time for delicacy in all facets of tackle, approach, and presentation. A *Baetis* hatch will demand your best, but in return you will become a more enlightened fly fisher.

There is a special intimacy with the water when flows are low and a summer's growth of aquatic weed concentrates the fish into distinct and accessible holding areas. Things only imagined during late spring and summer are suddenly revealed in the clear and gentle currents of autumn. There is no better time to observe the life that dwells within a river, and no greater way to learn the ways of trout and the life forms they depend upon for existence.

My wife Bonnie is small in stature and a non-swimmer. She is also, however, one of the most enthusiastic and determined anglers I know. The Henry's Fork, our home river, is quite wide but relatively shallow in the areas we prefer

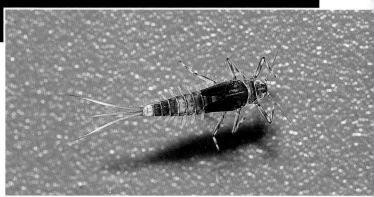

Baetis *nymph* TOSHI KARITA PHOTO

most. Although only slightly above average in size, I am able to roam at will about most of the water we fish together. It is a different story for Bonnie. Water that reaches my waist crowds the top of her waders, which makes it a perilous venture at times. To her credit, Bonnie does good business while being limited to fishing the shallow flats or along the edges of deeper water. But in the fall when wading ceases to be such a risky undertaking, my wife becomes a free-ranging predator. With the confines of deep, heavy currents gone, virtually no trout in view is immune from her purposeful attention. Bonnie prefers an upstream presentation and stalking trout from behind. Once in position, she is relentless, and I have seen her put more than an hour into an especially resistant fish. Fall is Bonnie's favorite season, and *Baetis* is her favorite hatch. It is this time of complete freedom on the water that she almost always lands her best fish of the year. Her crowning achievement as an angler occurred in mid-October when she stalked, fooled, and landed a 23-inch hen on 6X and a size 22 *Baetis* dry

With several feet of snow on the peaks of the Centennial Range as witness, the author fishes the final day of the season on the upper Henry's Fork. While synonymous with the coming of winter, *Baetis* are also the first mayflies to appear when spring arrives in the high country and everything begins again. BONNIE HARROP PHOTO

fly. Equally impressive was that she got the job done with a half dozen spectators coaching from the observation deck at the upper boundary of the Harriman State Park. Although visibly marked by years of surviving in the wild, the great fish was strong, healthy, and close to 6 pounds.

In general, western *Baetis* range from size 18 to 24. They exist in most waters and are a factor on the surface for much of the year. However, in the cooler months they begin to dominate the action, and eventually they become the main game. With midges as the lone exception, *Baetis* represent the only hatching activity when the days become short and low temperatures prohibit the emergence of other aquatic insects. With little or no competition for attention, *Baetis* attract the interest of trout grown urgently aggressive in advance of the lean days of winter.

Fish migrate to winter habitat when water levels begin to recede. These are usually areas where greater depth provides comfort and security. Feeding areas are frequently different, but always close by. Larger trout have a tendency to feed in surprisingly shallow water. Venturing into such hazardous territory carries high risk, and the fish have little tolerance for careless wading or an errant cast.

On bright days, an autumn *Baetis* hatch will usually begin in late morning and continue sporadically well into the afternoon. Peak activity can occur just before dark during warmer weather. During periods when the hatch is relatively sparse, a breeze that collects the little mayflies against the bank or along the edges of exposed weed beds is an advantage. The largest trout seek such areas where a concentration of insects serves to justify the effort of rising to such a small food source.

A question that may never be answered is why the best fishing so often occurs in some of the most raw weather that fall can deliver. Ideal hatching weather seems to be heavily overcast with temperatures at or only a few degrees above freezing. And light rain or wet snow seems to help rather than hinder the action. For whatever reason, chill, gray, and even damp days bring intensified hatching activity that can keep the fish up and eating steadily for as long as four or five hours. Such days are awaited with great anticipation by hardy souls who understand the peculiarity of *Baetis*. The sight of half an acre of rising trout may seem unbelievable to some, but I have experienced it many times on big rivers like the Snake, Yellowstone, Bighorn, Missouri,

Baetis *spinner* TOSHI KARITA PHOTO

and the Henry's Fork. Smaller waters like the Madison and Firehole also get their share of *Baetis* activity, as do many spring creeks throughout the Rocky Mountain West.

Emergence is undoubtedly most important, but a *Baetis* spinnerfall should not be overlooked. Sight nymphing is a productive way to fill the quiet times, and a small *Baetis* nymph twitched close to the surface can work when a rising fish resists a floating imitation. A medium olive seems the dominant body color of *Baetis*, and the wings are smoky gray. In general, *Baetis* conform to the coloring the term Blue-Winged Olive suggests, but some range in color from tan to gray. The body color of *Baetis* spinners does not seem to vary much from the duns, although the wings become transparent during this stage.

Casting to trout in thin water is a different game than many are accustomed to playing. A presentation made quartering downstream has the advantage of placing the fly in the trout's view ahead of the leader. The downside to this strategy is the likelihood of bringing yourself, or the motion of casting, into the trout's window of vision. Working from behind the fish with an upstream presentation shortens the necessary casting distance by keeping you out of view, but there are limitations. Even at close range, delivering pinpoint accuracy with a slack leader is not child's play. With no opportunity to manipulate the drift with mending techniques or rod tip maneuvers, the cast must be perfect. The advantage of fooling the fish with the least number of casts possible cannot be overstated. A light, flex-

Baetis *nymph* TOSHI KARITA PHOTO

ible tippet of 6 or 7X will aid the fly in following subtle currents and prevent drag. A happy fish is one that feeds without knowing it is being fished to. Drag is recognizable to a savvy trout and must be absolutely avoided.

Having a fish take the fly often depends on determining which stage of the mayfly is being targeted. This can vary from fish to fish especially when the hatch is heavy. Carrying an assortment of nymphs, emergers, duns, and spinners can help you deal with the individual feeding preferences that can occur when fish have several choices from which to pick. Hitting on just the right fly can sometimes take more than a little time. Patience and determination will usually prevail, although you should make certain that the fish is of a size sufficient to justify the time and effort. Changing flies or adjusting the tippet can be excruciatingly difficult when you are shivering and your hands are numbed by the cold. Fortunately, crowds are seldom a problem at *Baetis* time, which means you can often move to a different fish when the one you are casting to proves to be simply too difficult.

Even the very big rivers like the South Fork of the Snake are host to substantial fall *Baetis* hatches. It is unlikely that any mayfly species enjoys broader distribution in the Rocky Mountain states than *Baetis*. BONNIE HARROP PHOTO

Although I have enjoyed many amazingly successful days of *Baetis* fishing, it has never really been easy. Trout in most western waters have spent six months or more trying to avoid artificial flies. By fall, they have become keenly adept at identifying fraudulent food and are quick to shy at the slightest disturbance of their territory. Shallow water flowing over dense weed creates brutally complex currents that can instantly corrupt the drift of the most carefully presented fly. Thankfully, most of us are also at our best during this time. With nearly a full season of casting, wading, and observing under our belt, we are as well prepared for this kind of fishing as we will ever be.

There is a social aspect to autumn fishing that contrasts the long days of the earlier season when twelve or more hours on the water are not uncommon. It is a different pace when mornings become frosty and darkness arrives early. Gone are the crowds of summer, leaving only those of uncommon sensitivity to the rhythms of a season both hostile and hospitable. "Impressive" is the best way to describe those who hunt the water at *Baetis* time. As a group they are knowledgeable and accomplished anglers who relish a challenge. Many are river guides who devote their

Morning frost often precedes a fall *Baetis* hatch. However, air temperatures usually must rise above the freezing point before the insects will appear in significant numbers.
BONNIE HARROP PHOTO

knowledge and skill to the enjoyment of others for much of the season. Others live in far-off places but are drawn here each year by forces they understand but cannot explain. It is a season when time in the fly shops and saloons often exceeds that spent on the water. Conversation in the hours between hatches is never more stimulating as old friendships are renewed and new ones are begun. There is always much to share and even more to learn when the last hatch of the season brings such dedicated and hopelessly obsessed anglers together. And it is the memory of these special days that gets us through the long winter to the time when it all begins again.

BONNIE HARROP PHOTO

Baetis Nymph

Hook:	TMC 200R BL Size 18-22
Thread:	Olive 8/0 UNI-Thread
Tail:	Wood duck flank
Rib:	Fine copper wire
Body:	Rusty olive TroutHunter CEN dubbing
Wing case:	Black marabou
Legs:	Brown Hungarian partridge

BONNIE HARROP PHOTO

CDC Floating Nymph (Baetis)

Hook:	TMC 206 BL size 18-22
Thread:	Olive 8/0 UNI-Thread
Tail:	Whiting Coq de Leon or wood duck
Abdomen:	Olive BWO TroutHunter Pro goose biot
Thorax:	Olive BWO TroutHunter Pro dubbing
Wing case:	Dark dun TroutHunter CDC cupped over thorax
Legs:	Olive CDC fibers

BONNIE HARROP PHOTO

CDC Hackled Dun (Baetis)

Hook:	TMC 100 BL size 18-22
Thread:	Olive 8/0 UNI-Thread
Tail:	Whiting Coq de Leon or medium dun hackle fibers
Abdomen:	Olive BWO TroutHunter Pro goose biot
Thorax:	Olive BWO TroutHunter Pro dubbing
Wing:	Paired medium dun TroutHunter CDC tied upright and divided
Hackle:	Whiting grizzly dyed medium dun

BONNIE HARROP PHOTO

CDC Biot Spinner (Baetis)

Hook:	TMC 100 BL size 18-22
Thread:	Olive 8/0 UNI-Thread
Tail:	Whiting Coq de Leon or light dun hackle fibers
Abdomen:	Olive BWO TroutHunter Pro goose biot
Thorax:	Olive BWO TroutHunter Pro dubbing
Wing:	Paired light dun TroutHunter CDC feathers tied spent

Index

Page numbers in italics indicate illustrations.

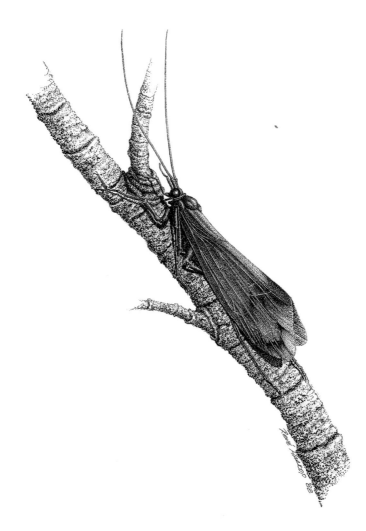